Chapter 1 **SHINING SEED**

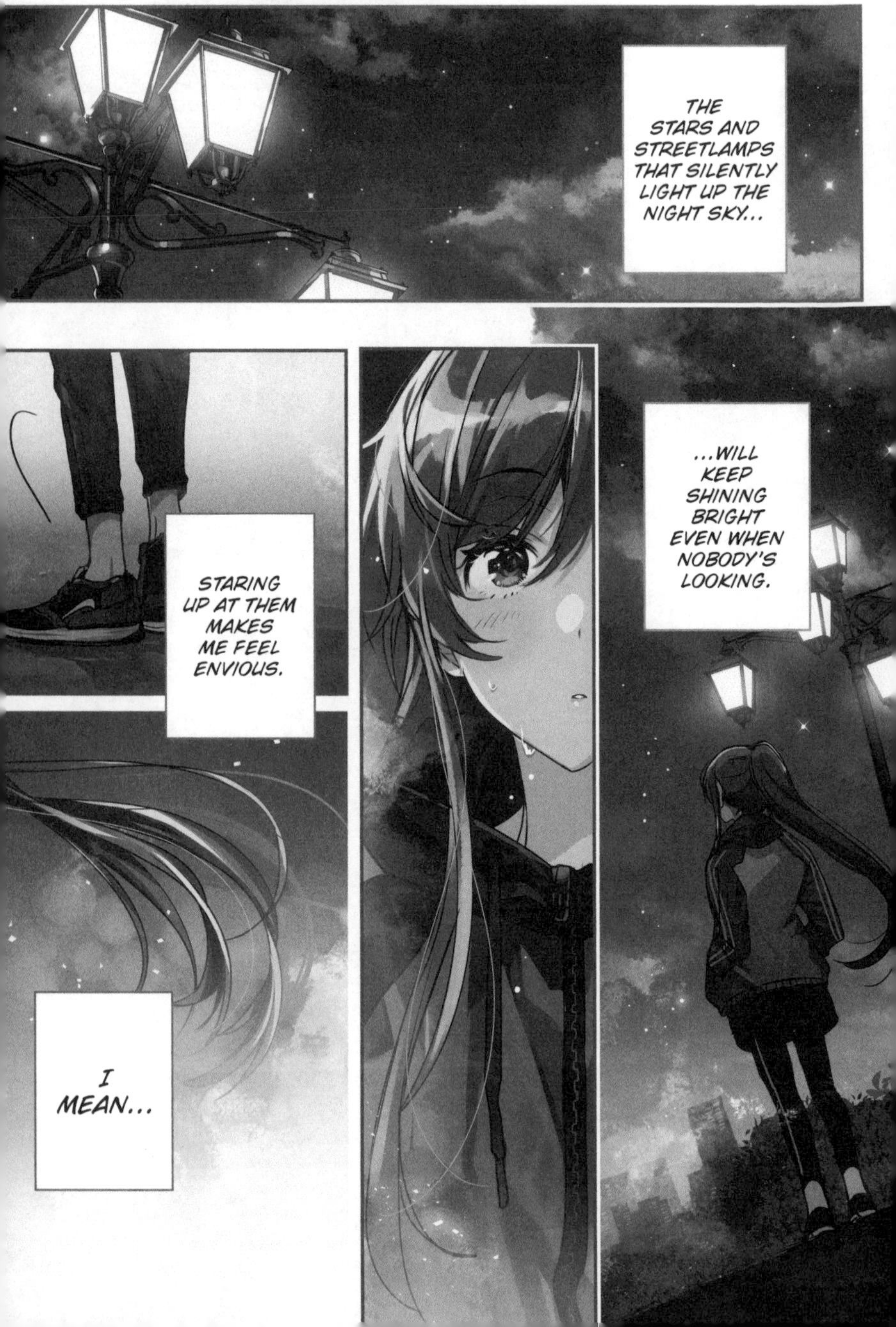
THE STARS AND STREETLAMPS THAT SILENTLY LIGHT UP THE NIGHT SKY...
...WILL KEEP SHINING BRIGHT EVEN WHEN NOBODY'S LOOKING.
STARING UP AT THEM MAKES ME FEEL ENVIOUS.
I MEAN...

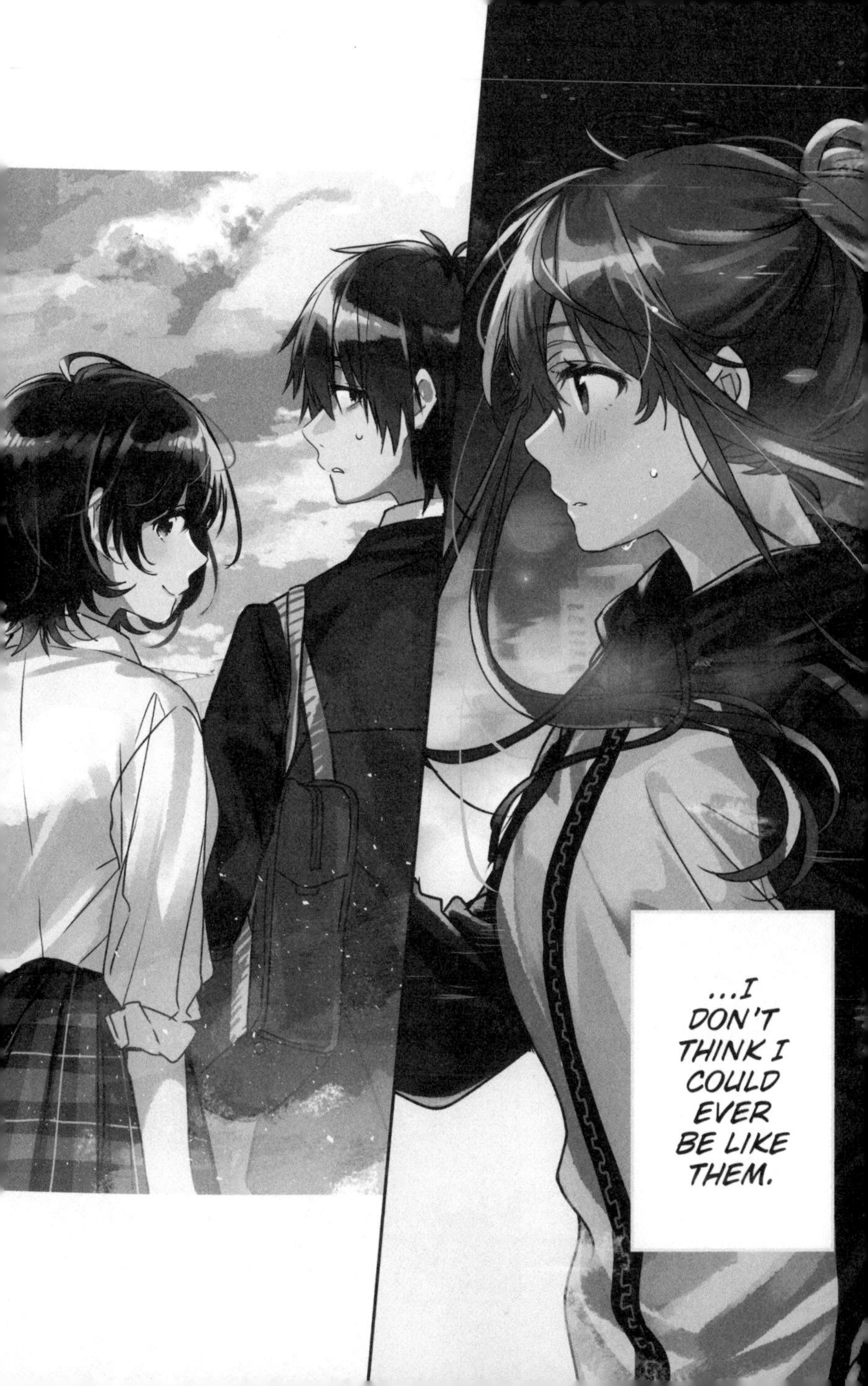
...I DON'T THINK I COULD EVER BE LIKE THEM.

Chapter 1
SHINING SEED

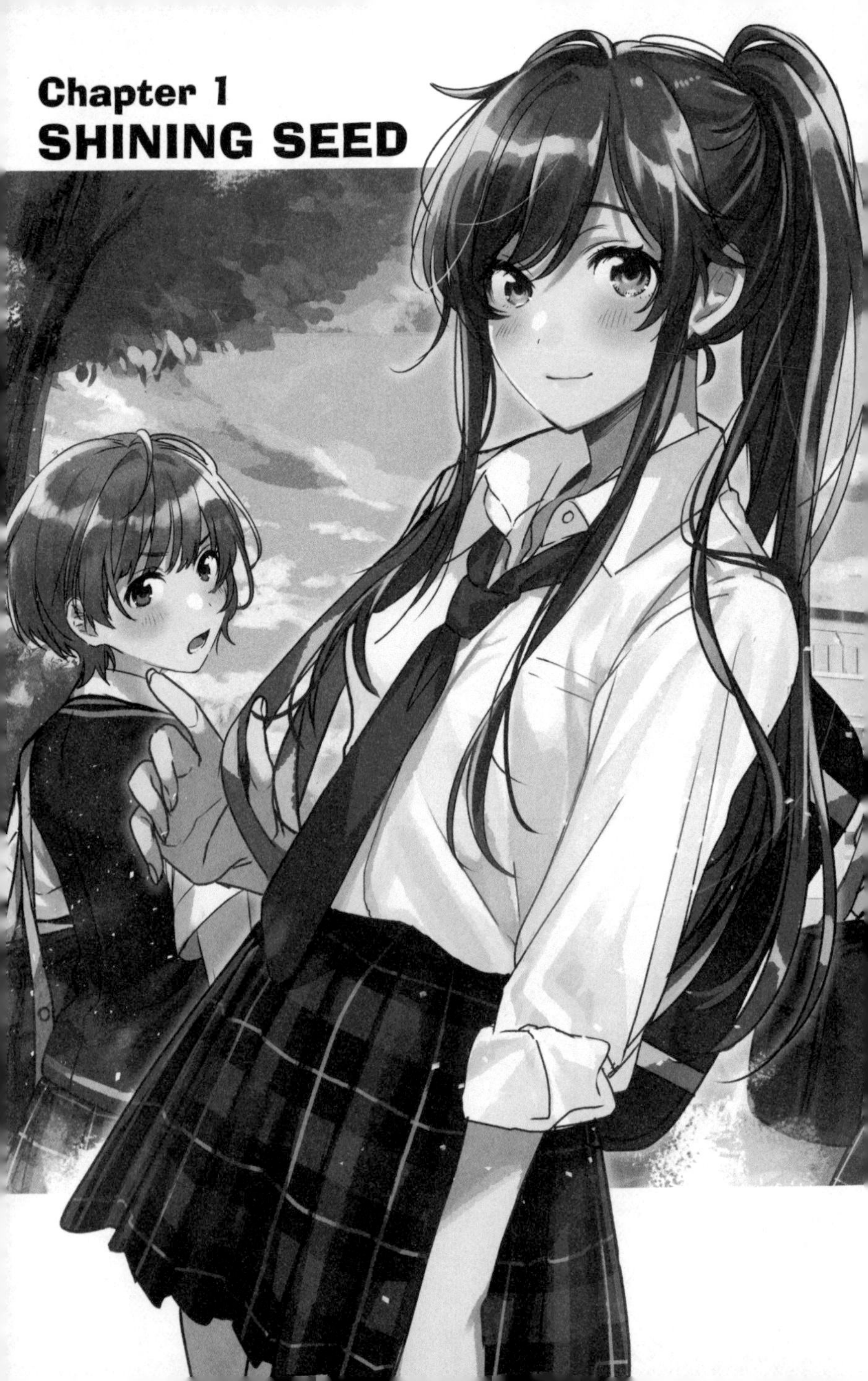

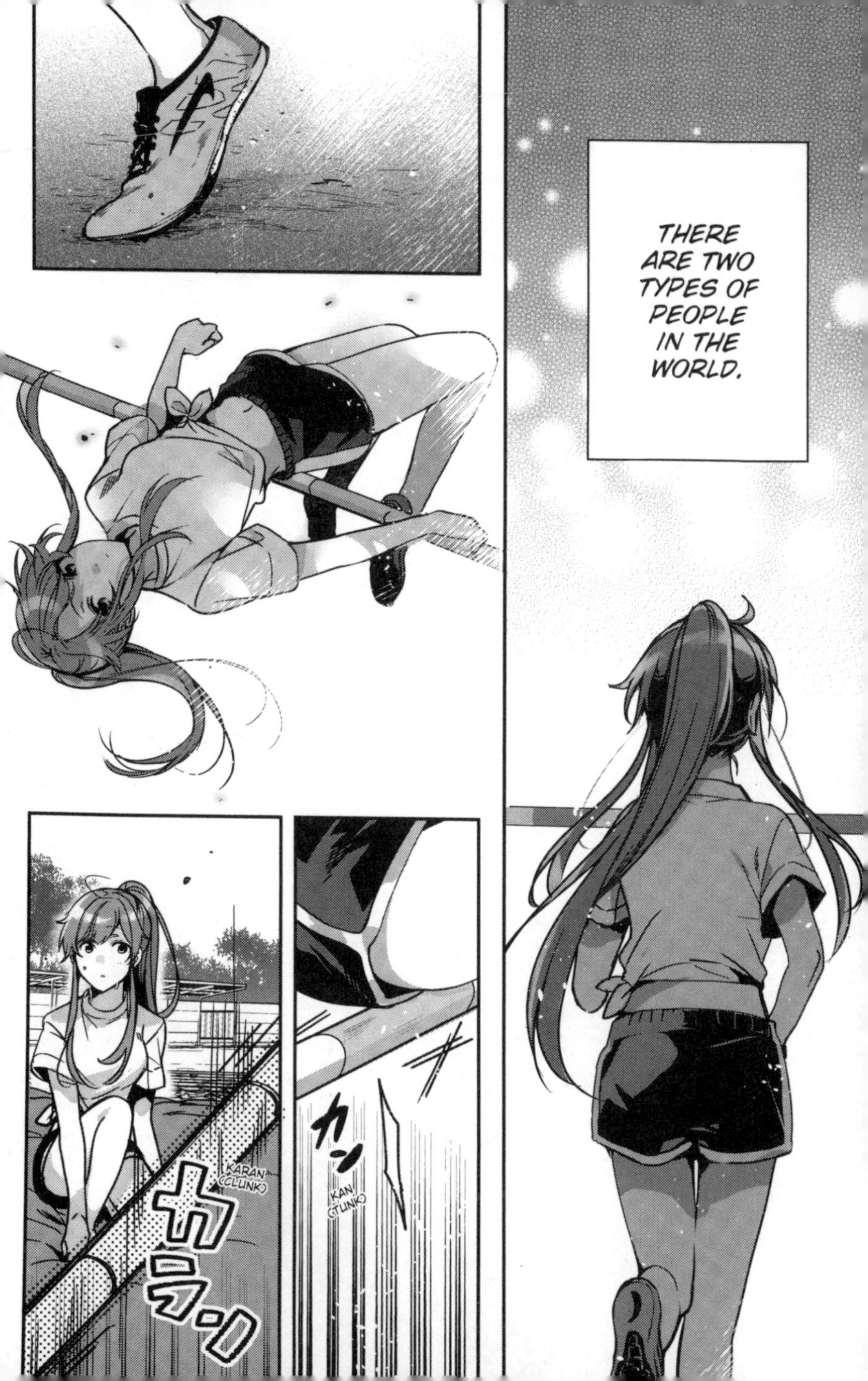
THERE ARE TWO TYPES OF PEOPLE IN THE WORLD.
カン
KAN (TUNK)
カラン
KARAN (CLUNK)

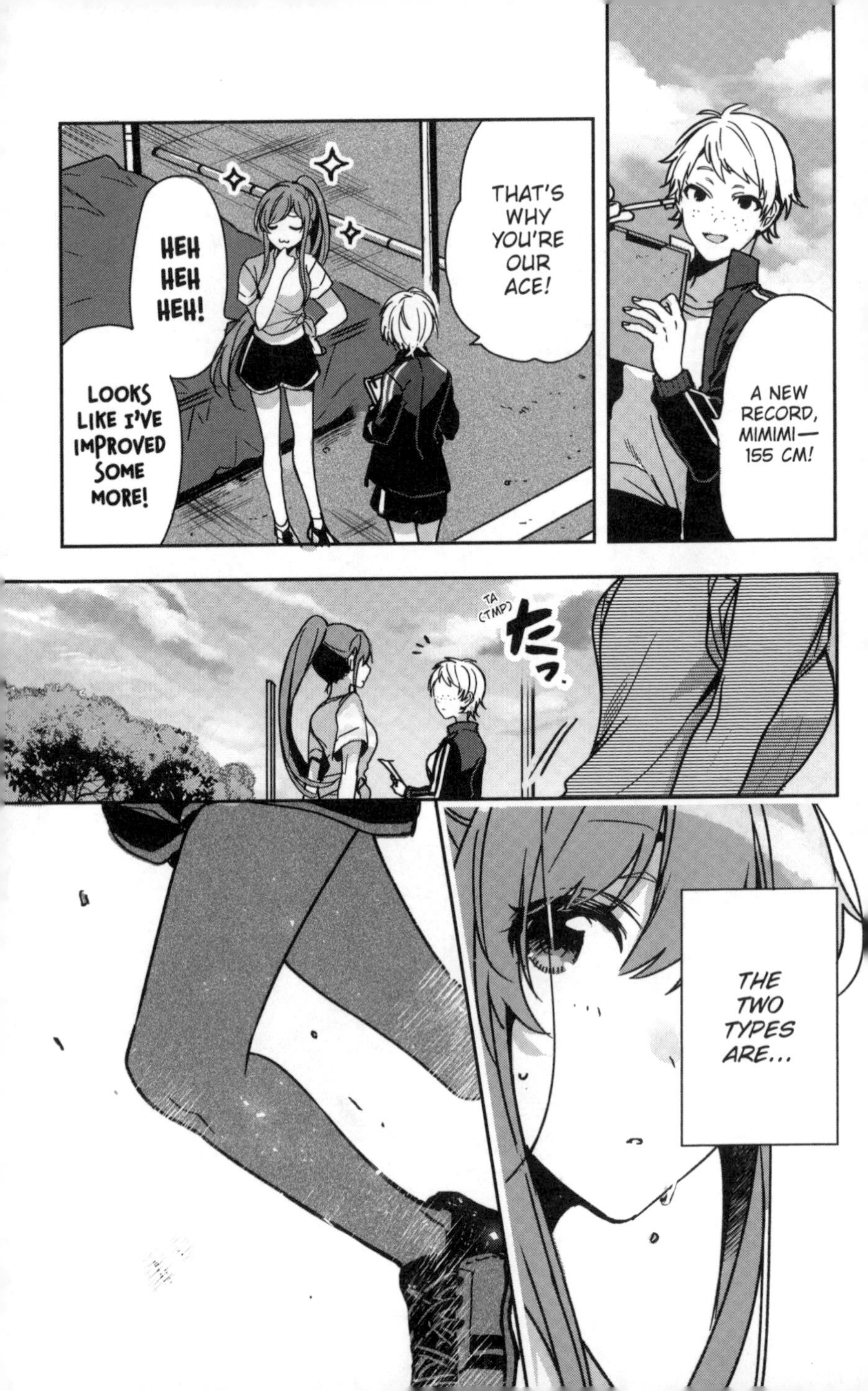
A NEW RECORD, MIMIMI—155 CM!
THAT'S WHY YOU'RE OUR ACE!
HEH HEH HEH!
LOOKS LIKE I'VE IMPROVED SOME MORE!
TA (TMP)
THE TWO TYPES ARE...

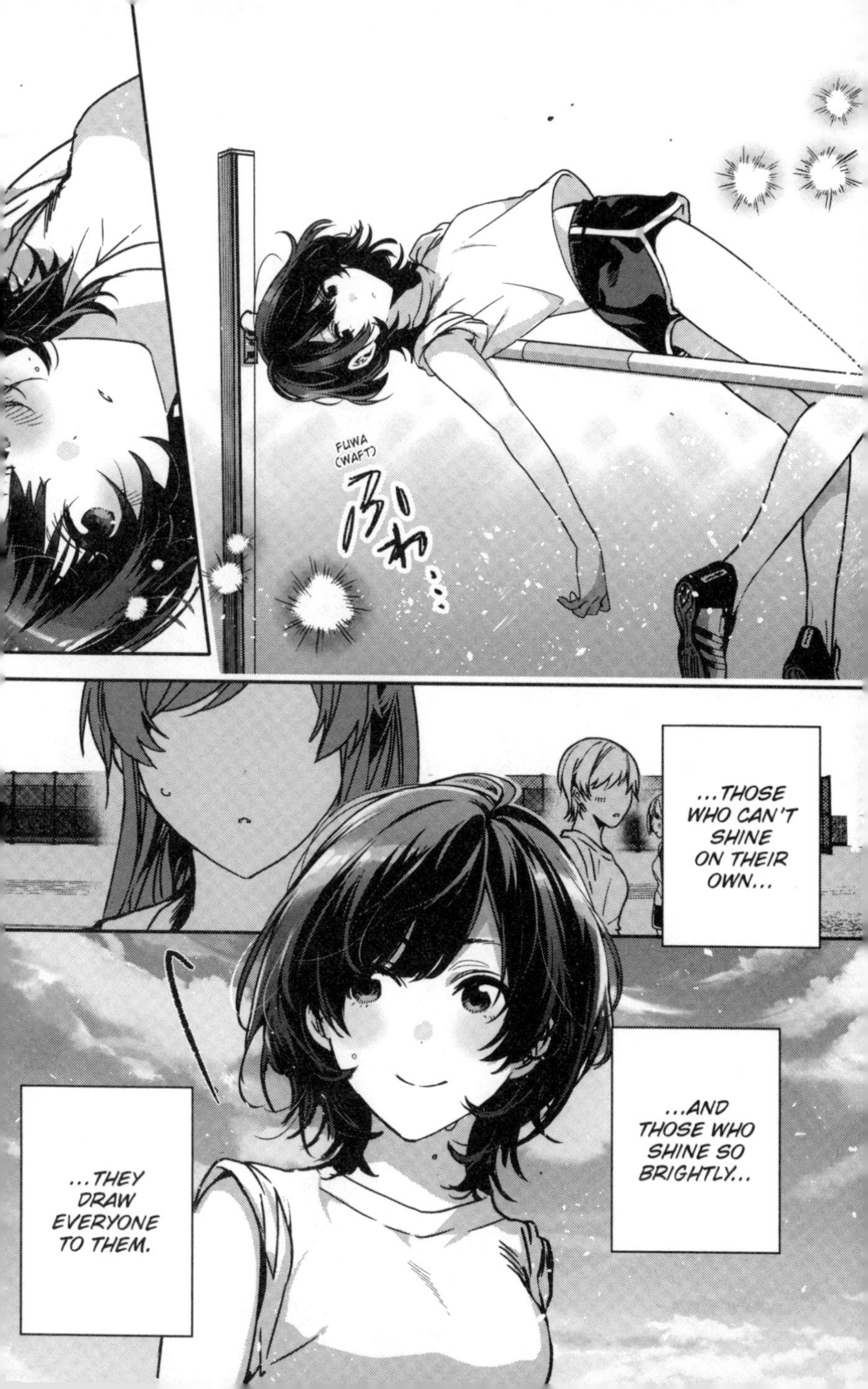
FUWA (WAFT)
ふわ…
…THOSE WHO CAN'T SHINE ON THEIR OWN…
…AND THOSE WHO SHINE SO BRIGHTLY…
…THEY DRAW EVERYONE TO THEM.

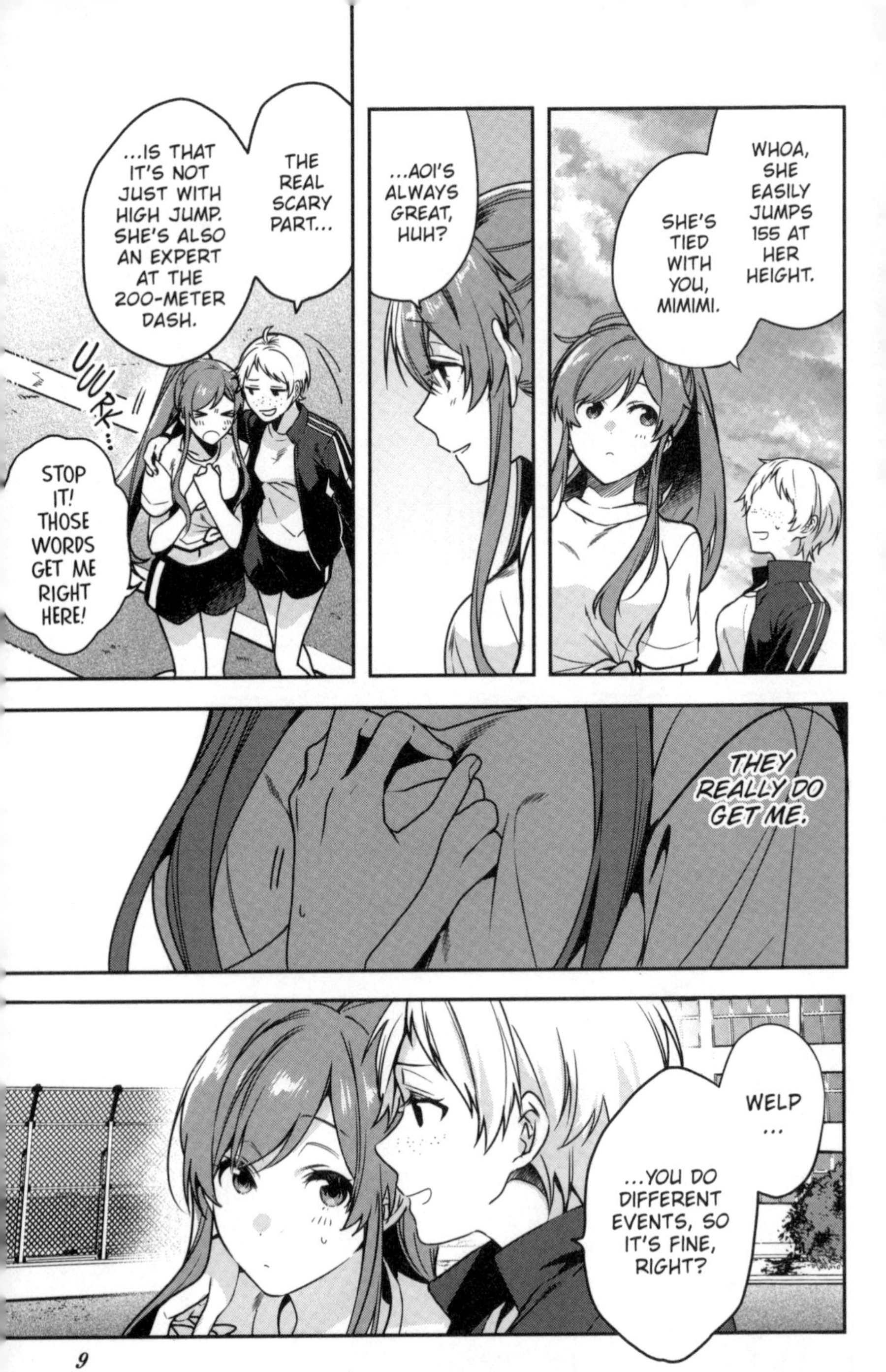
WHOA, SHE EASILY JUMPS 155 AT HER HEIGHT.
SHE'S TIED WITH YOU, MIMIMI.
...AOI'S ALWAYS GREAT, HUH?
THE REAL SCARY PART...
...IS THAT IT'S NOT JUST WITH HIGH JUMP. SHE'S ALSO AN EXPERT AT THE 200-METER DASH.
UUURK...
STOP IT! THOSE WORDS GET ME RIGHT HERE!
THEY REALLY DO GET ME.
WELP...
...YOU DO DIFFERENT EVENTS, SO IT'S FINE, RIGHT?

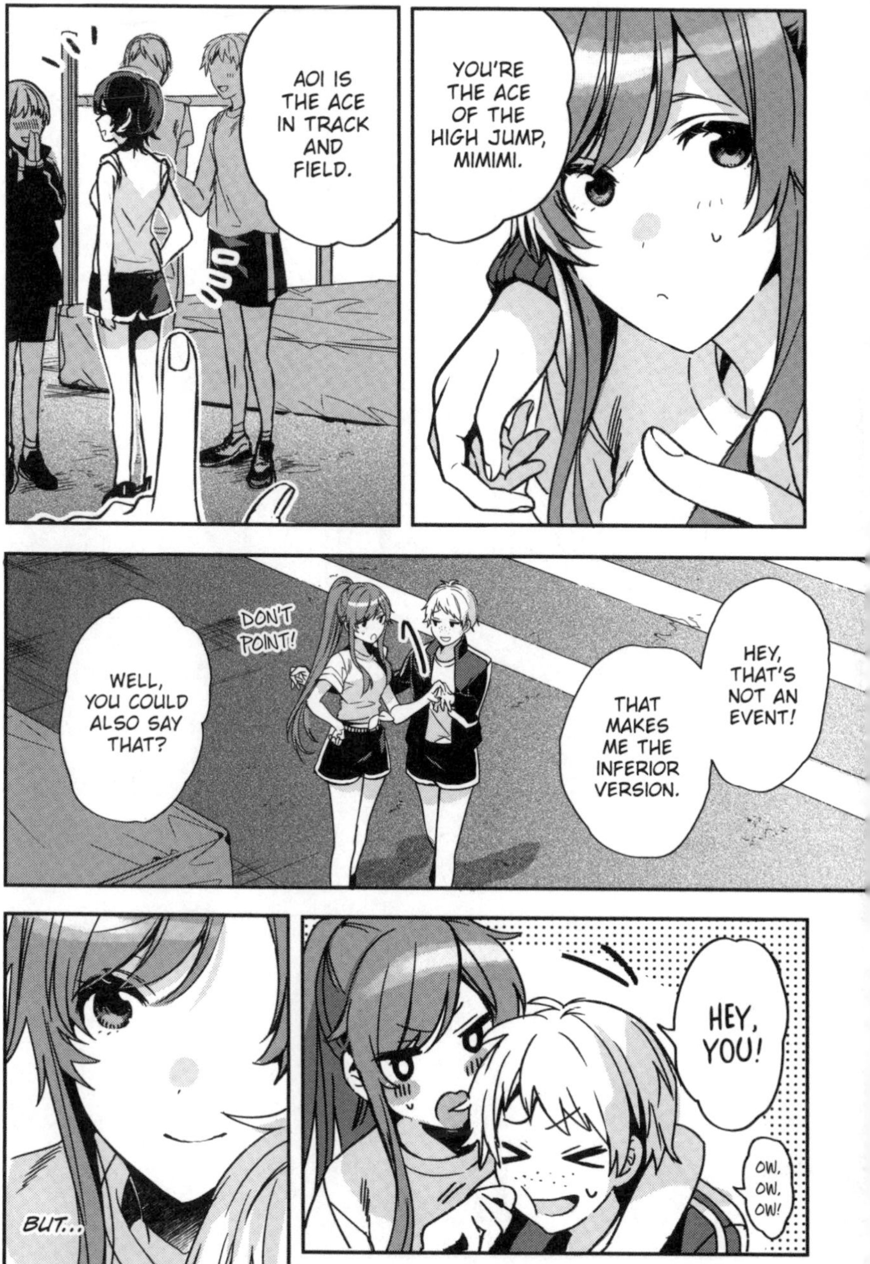
YOU'RE THE ACE OF THE HIGH JUMP, MIMIMI.
AOI IS THE ACE IN TRACK AND FIELD.
HEY, THAT'S NOT AN EVENT!
THAT MAKES ME THE INFERIOR VERSION.
DON'T POINT!
WELL, YOU COULD ALSO SAY THAT?
HEY, YOU!
OW, OW, OW!
BUT...

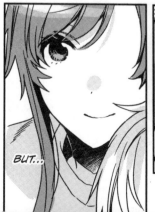

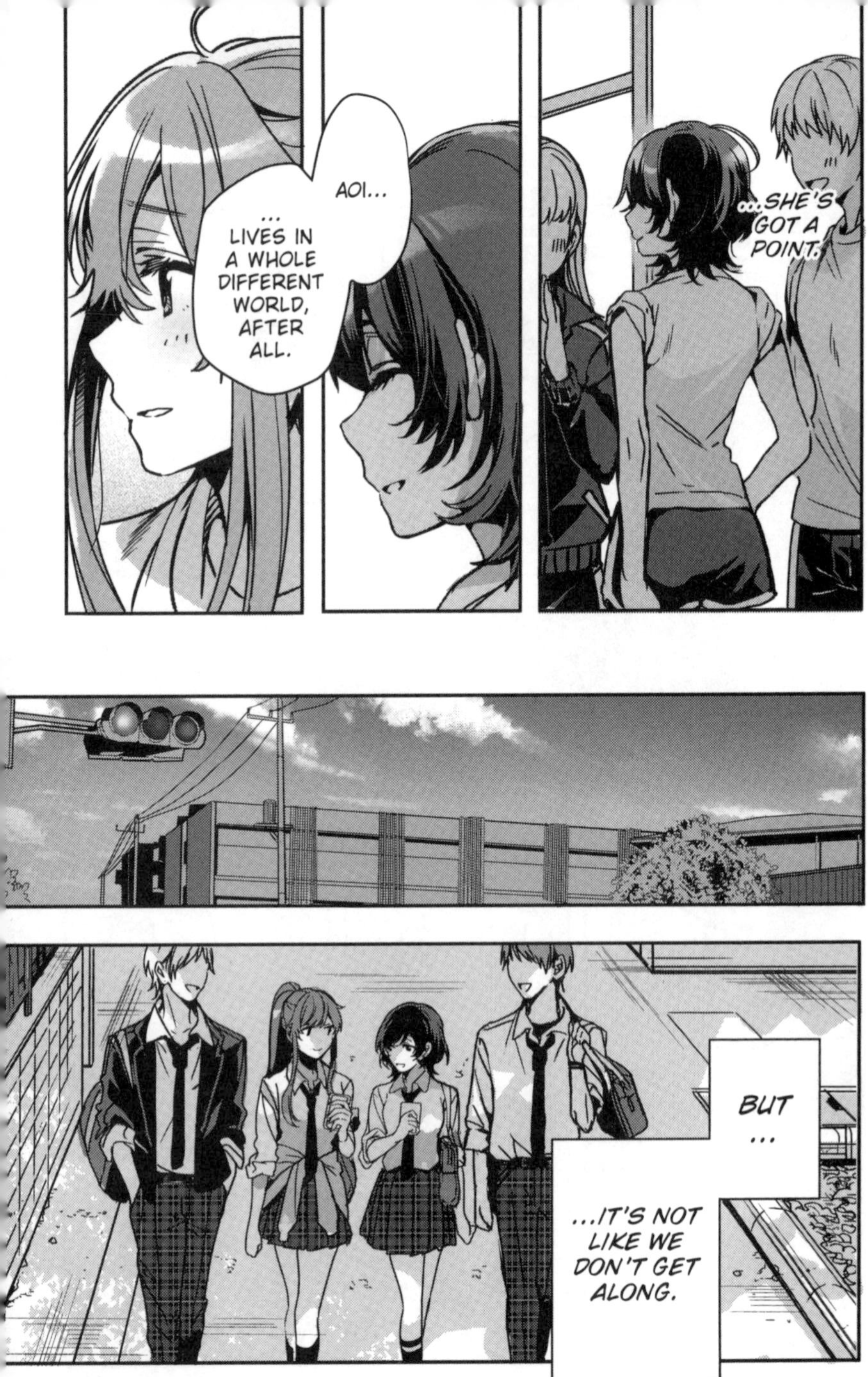
...SHE'S GOT A POINT.
AOI...
... LIVES IN A WHOLE DIFFERENT WORLD, AFTER ALL.
BUT ...
...IT'S NOT LIKE WE DON'T GET ALONG.

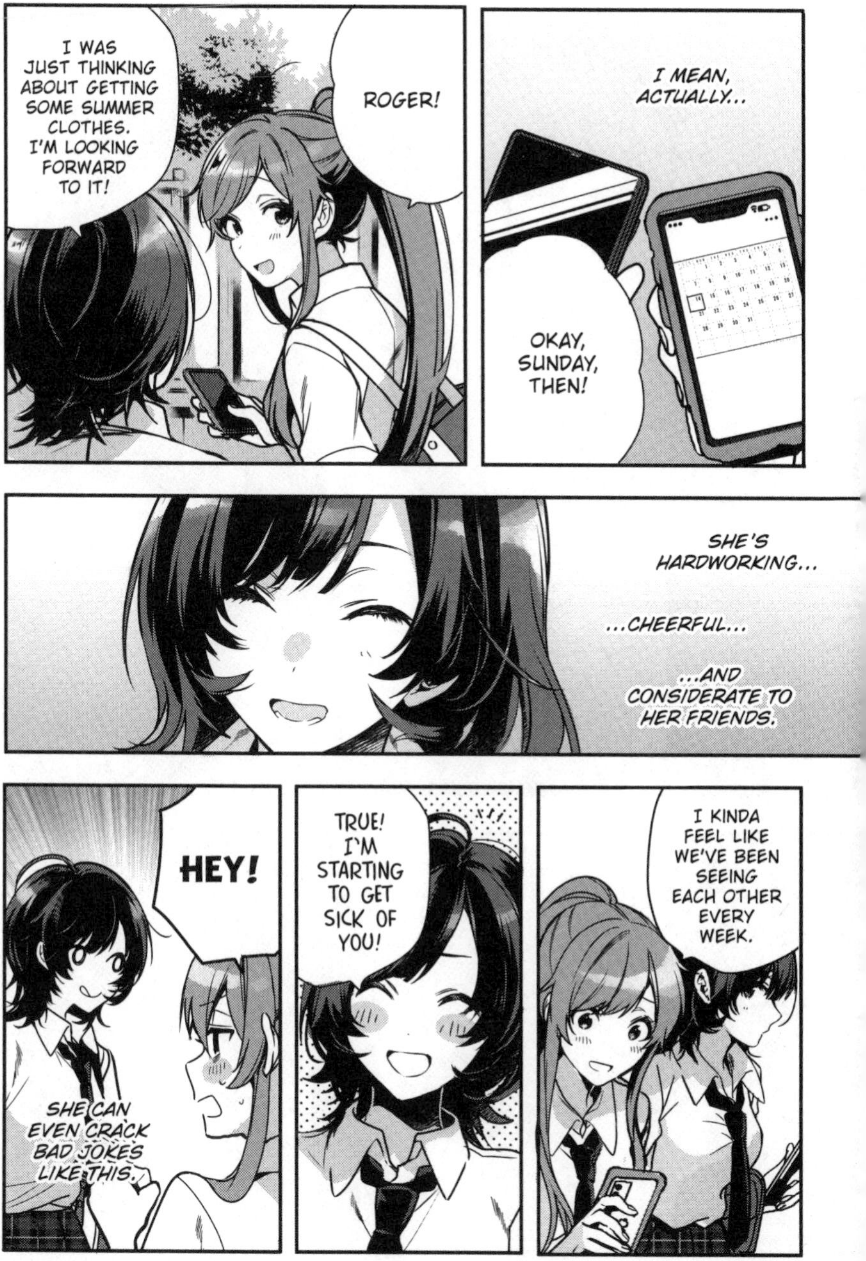
I MEAN, ACTUALLY...
OKAY, SUNDAY, THEN!
ROGER!
I WAS JUST THINKING ABOUT GETTING SOME SUMMER CLOTHES. I'M LOOKING FORWARD TO IT!
SHE'S HARDWORKING...
...CHEERFUL...
...AND CONSIDERATE TO HER FRIENDS.
I KINDA FEEL LIKE WE'VE BEEN SEEING EACH OTHER EVERY WEEK.
TRUE! I'M STARTING TO GET SICK OF YOU!
HEY!
SHE CAN EVEN CRACK BAD JOKES LIKE THIS.

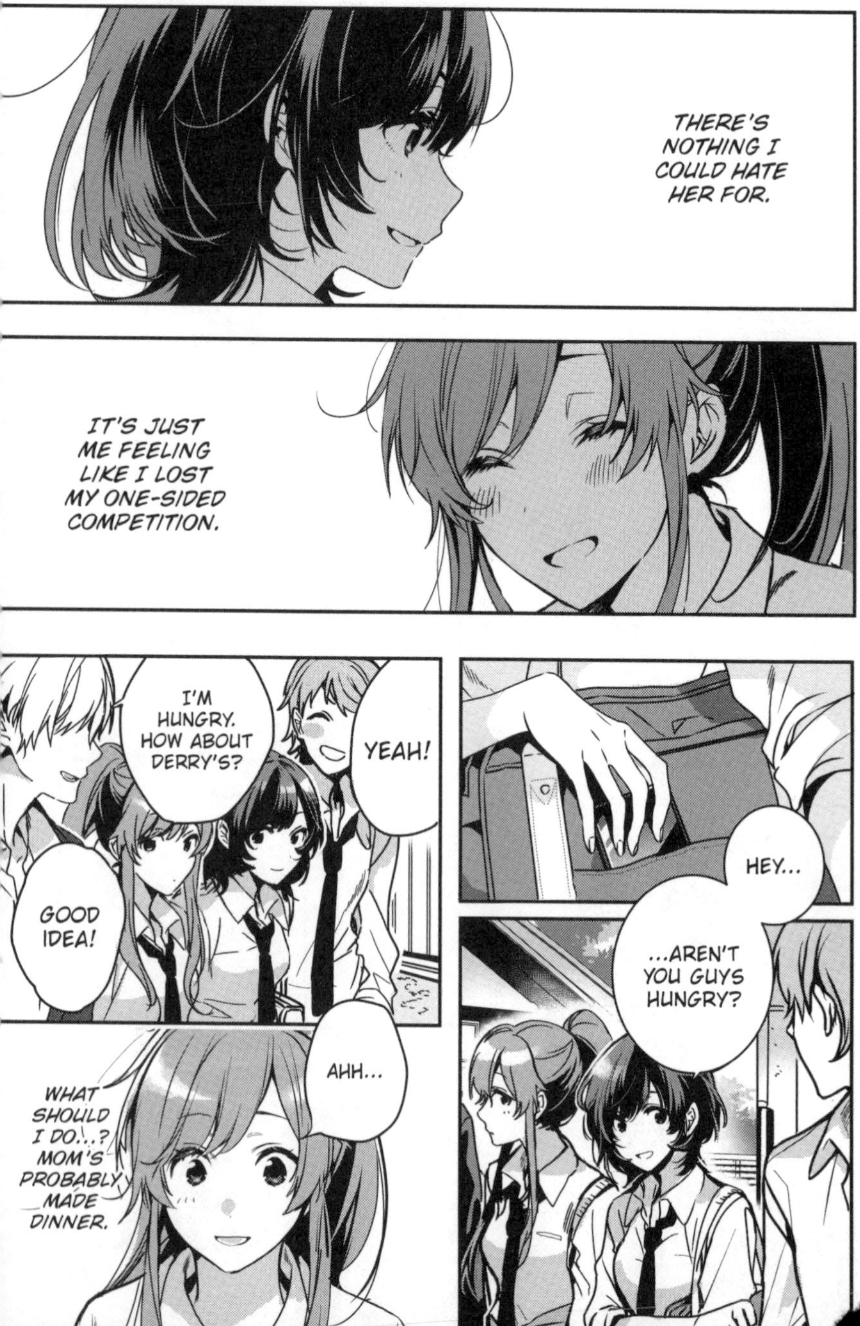
THERE'S NOTHING I COULD HATE HER FOR.
IT'S JUST ME FEELING LIKE I LOST MY ONE-SIDED COMPETITION.
HEY...
...AREN'T YOU GUYS HUNGRY?
I'M HUNGRY. HOW ABOUT DERRY'S?
YEAH!
GOOD IDEA!
AHH...
WHAT SHOULD I DO...? MOM'S PROBABLY MADE DINNER.

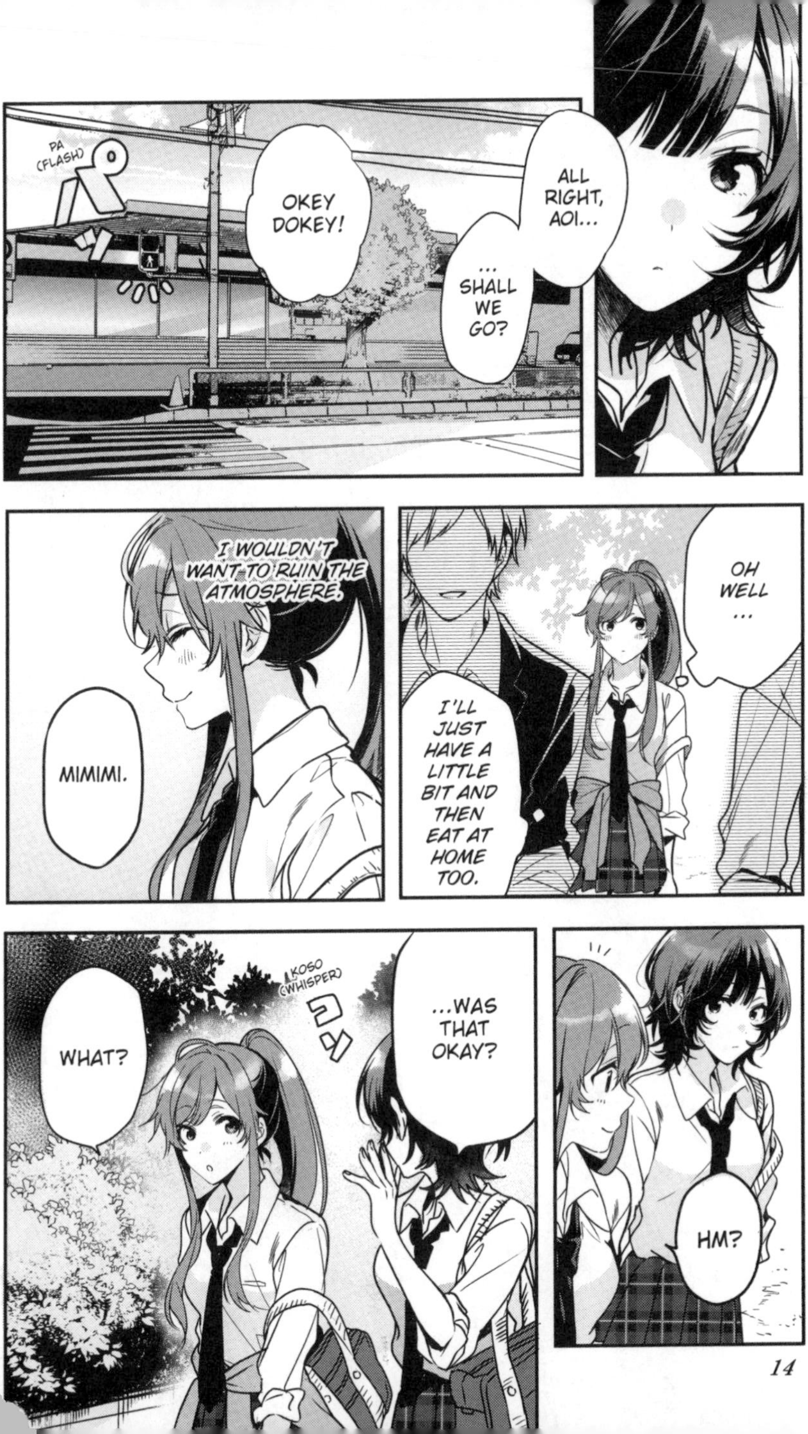
ALL RIGHT, AOI...
...SHALL WE GO?
OKEY DOKEY!
PA (FLASH)
OH WELL...
I'LL JUST HAVE A LITTLE BIT AND THEN EAT AT HOME TOO.
I WOULDN'T WANT TO RUIN THE ATMOSPHERE.
MIMIMI.
HM?
...WAS THAT OKAY?
KOSO (WHISPER)
WHAT?

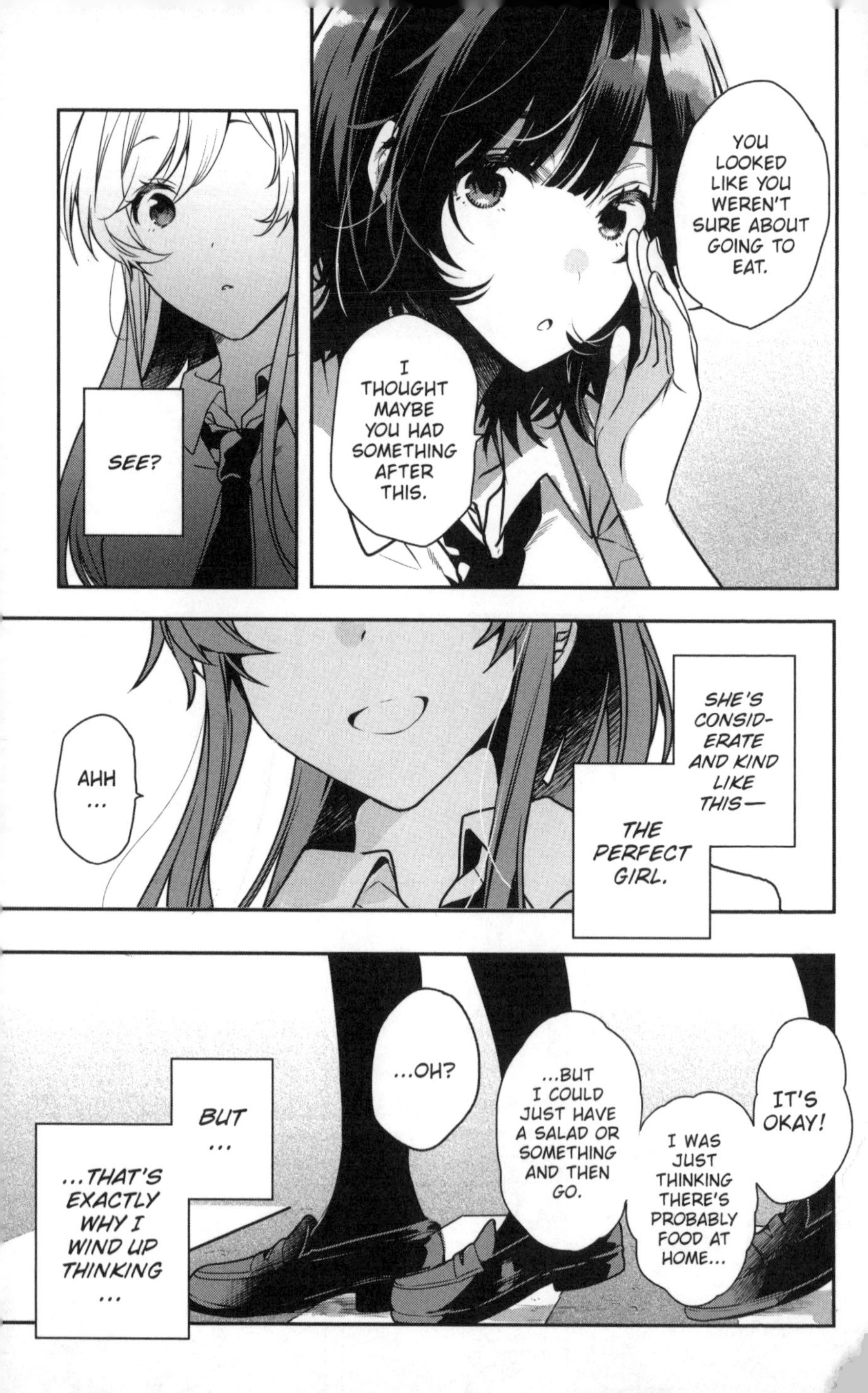
YOU LOOKED LIKE YOU WEREN'T SURE ABOUT GOING TO EAT.
I THOUGHT MAYBE YOU HAD SOMETHING AFTER THIS.
SEE?
SHE'S CONSID-ERATE AND KIND LIKE THIS—
THE PERFECT GIRL.
AHH ...
IT'S OKAY!
I WAS JUST THINKING THERE'S PROBABLY FOOD AT HOME...
...BUT I COULD JUST HAVE A SALAD OR SOMETHING AND THEN GO.
...OH?
BUT ...
...THAT'S EXACTLY WHY I WIND UP THINKING ...

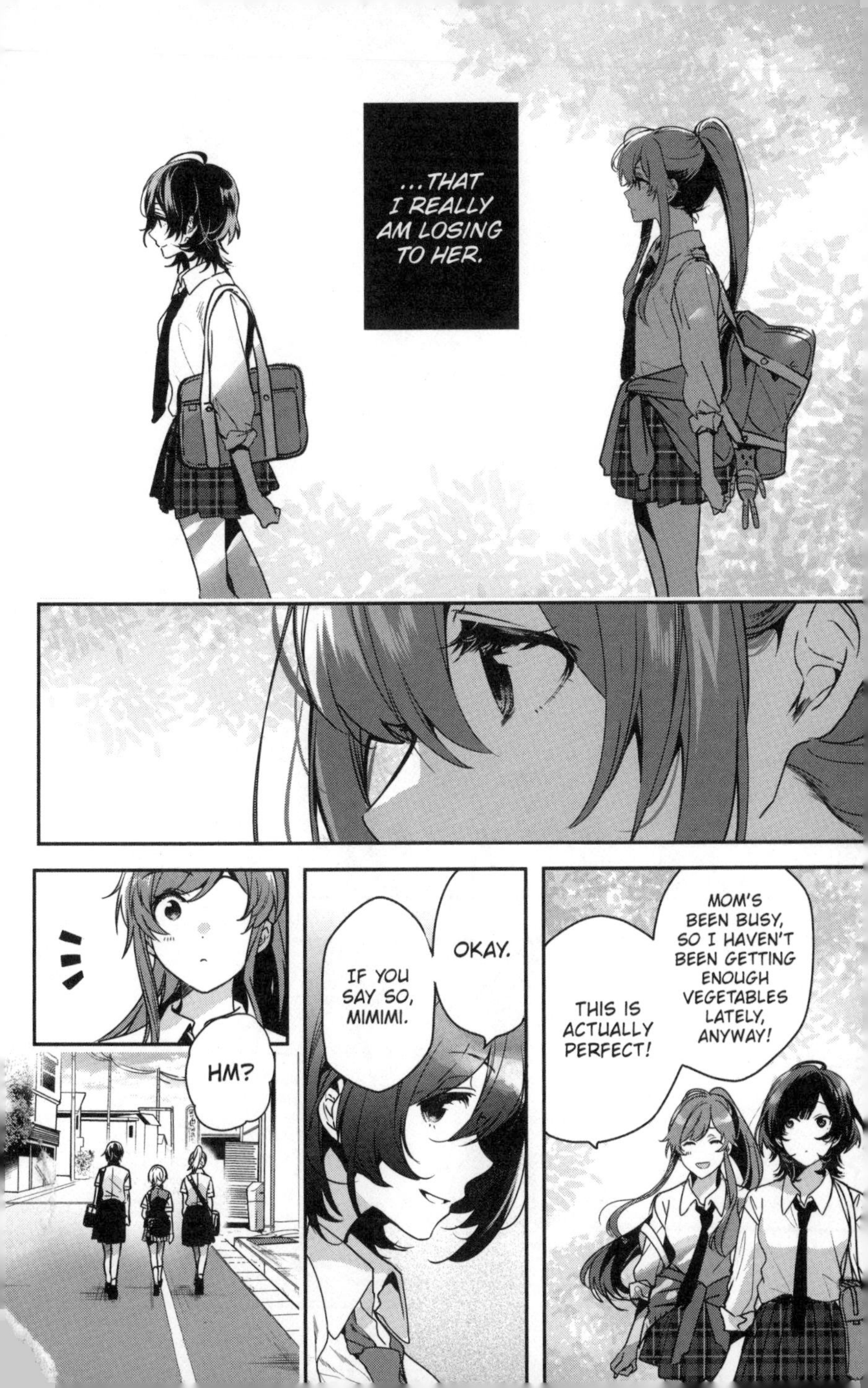
...THAT I REALLY AM LOSING TO HER.
MOM'S BEEN BUSY, SO I HAVEN'T BEEN GETTING ENOUGH VEGETABLES LATELY, ANYWAY!
THIS IS ACTUALLY PERFECT!
OKAY.
IF YOU SAY SO, MIMIMI.
HM?

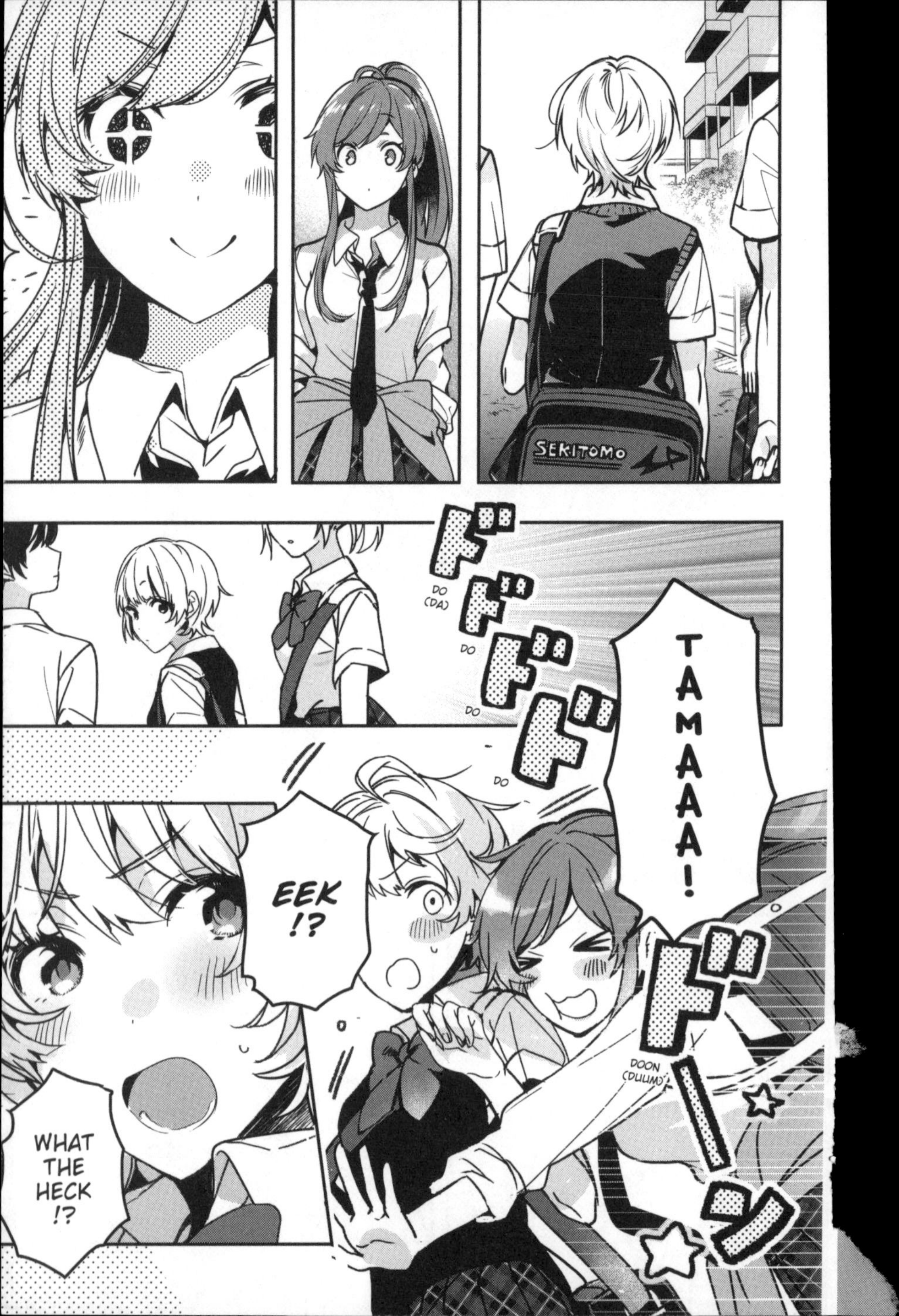
SEKITOMO
DO (DA)
DO
DO
DO
TAMAAAA!
DOON (DUUM)
EEK!?
WHAT THE HECK!?

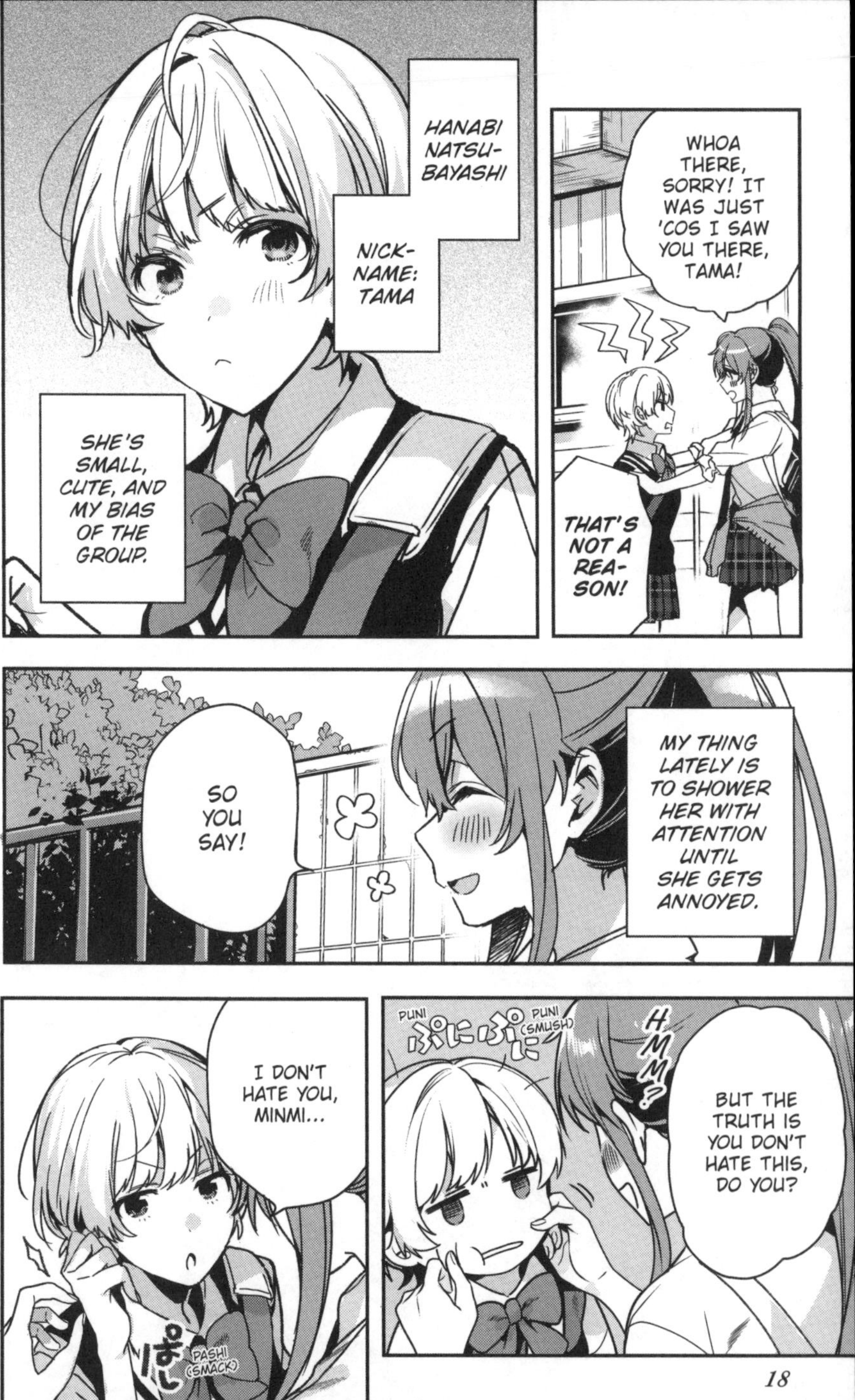
WHOA THERE, SORRY! IT WAS JUST 'COS I SAW YOU THERE, TAMA!
THAT'S NOT A REA-SON!
HANABI NATSU-BAYASHI
NICK-NAME: TAMA
SHE'S SMALL, CUTE, AND MY BIAS OF THE GROUP.
MY THING LATELY IS TO SHOWER HER WITH ATTENTION UNTIL SHE GETS ANNOYED.
SO YOU SAY!
ぷにぷに
PUNI PUNI (SMUSH)
HMM?
BUT THE TRUTH IS YOU DON'T HATE THIS, DO YOU?
I DON'T HATE YOU, MINMI...
ぱし
PASHI (SMACK)

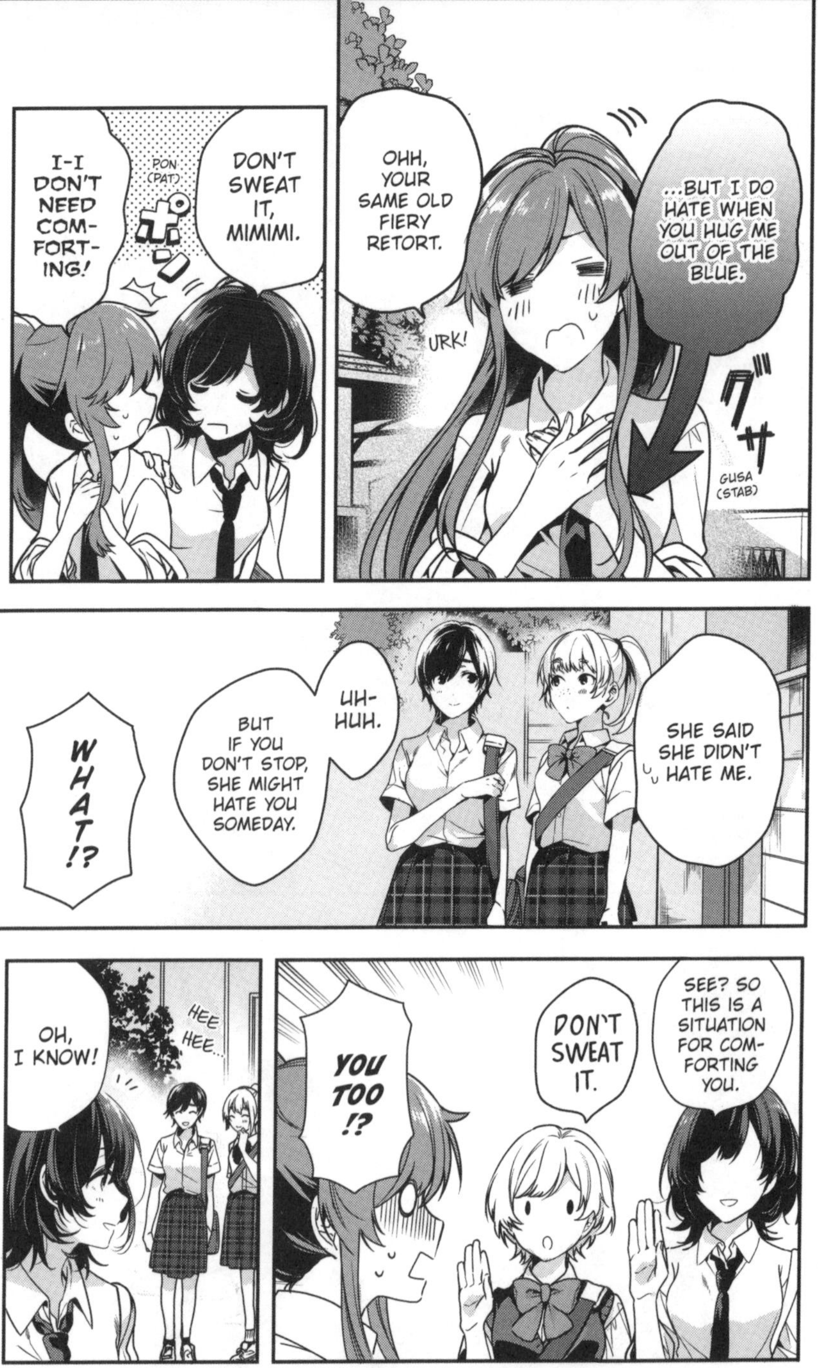
...BUT I DO HATE WHEN YOU HUG ME OUT OF THE BLUE.
OHH, YOUR SAME OLD FIERY RETORT.
URK!
GUSA (STAB)
DON'T SWEAT IT, MIMIMI.
PON (PAT)
I-I DON'T NEED COM-FORT-ING!
SHE SAID SHE DIDN'T HATE ME.
UH-HUH.
BUT IF YOU DON'T STOP, SHE MIGHT HATE YOU SOMEDAY.
WHAT!?
SEE? SO THIS IS A SITUATION FOR COM-FORTING YOU.
DON'T SWEAT IT.
YOU TOO!?
HEE HEE...
OH, I KNOW!

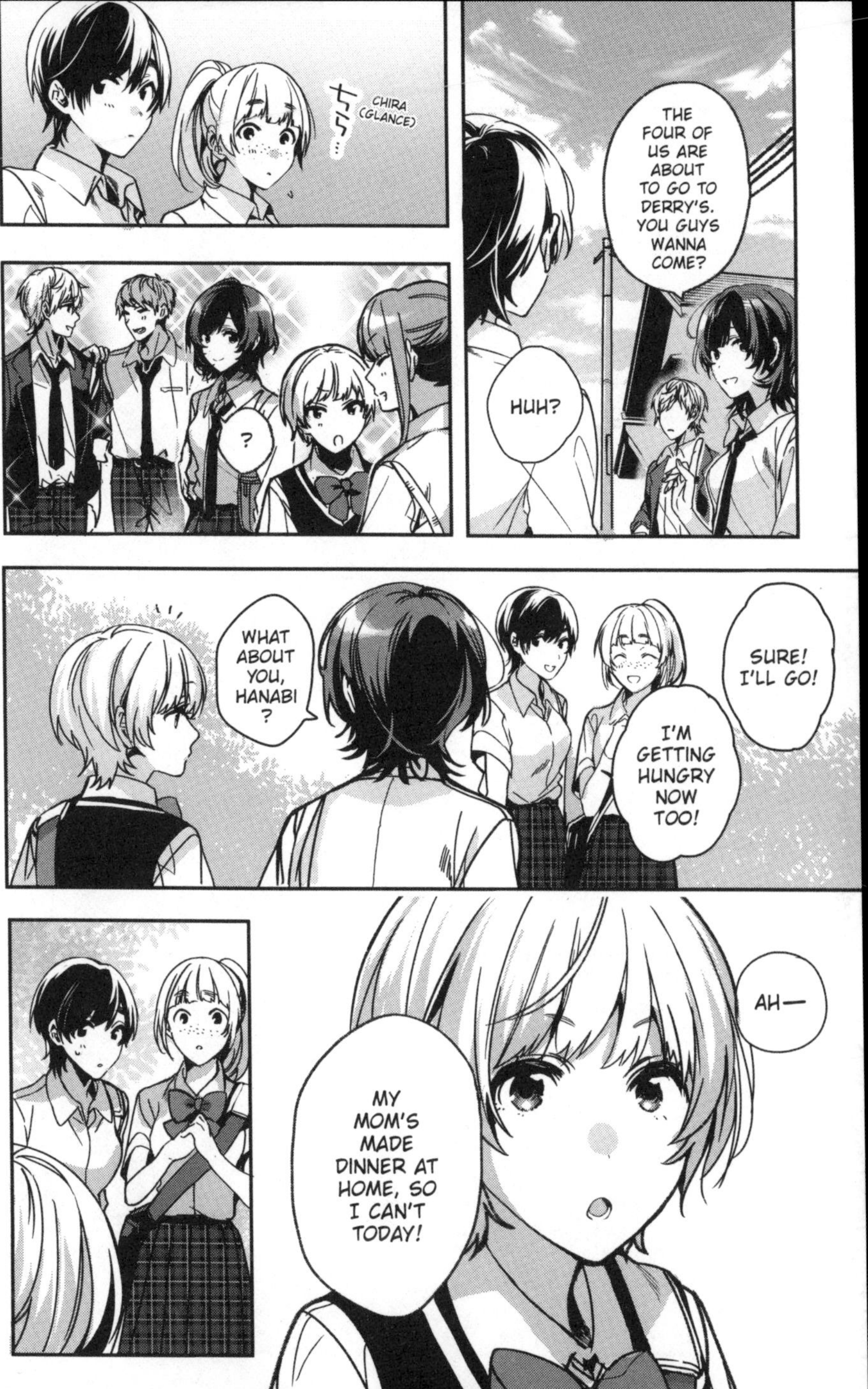
THE FOUR OF US ARE ABOUT TO GO TO DERRY'S. YOU GUYS WANNA COME?
HUH?
ちら…
CHIRA (GLANCE)
?
SURE! I'LL GO!
I'M GETTING HUNGRY NOW TOO!
WHAT ABOUT YOU, HANABI?
AH—
MY MOM'S MADE DINNER AT HOME, SO I CAN'T TODAY!

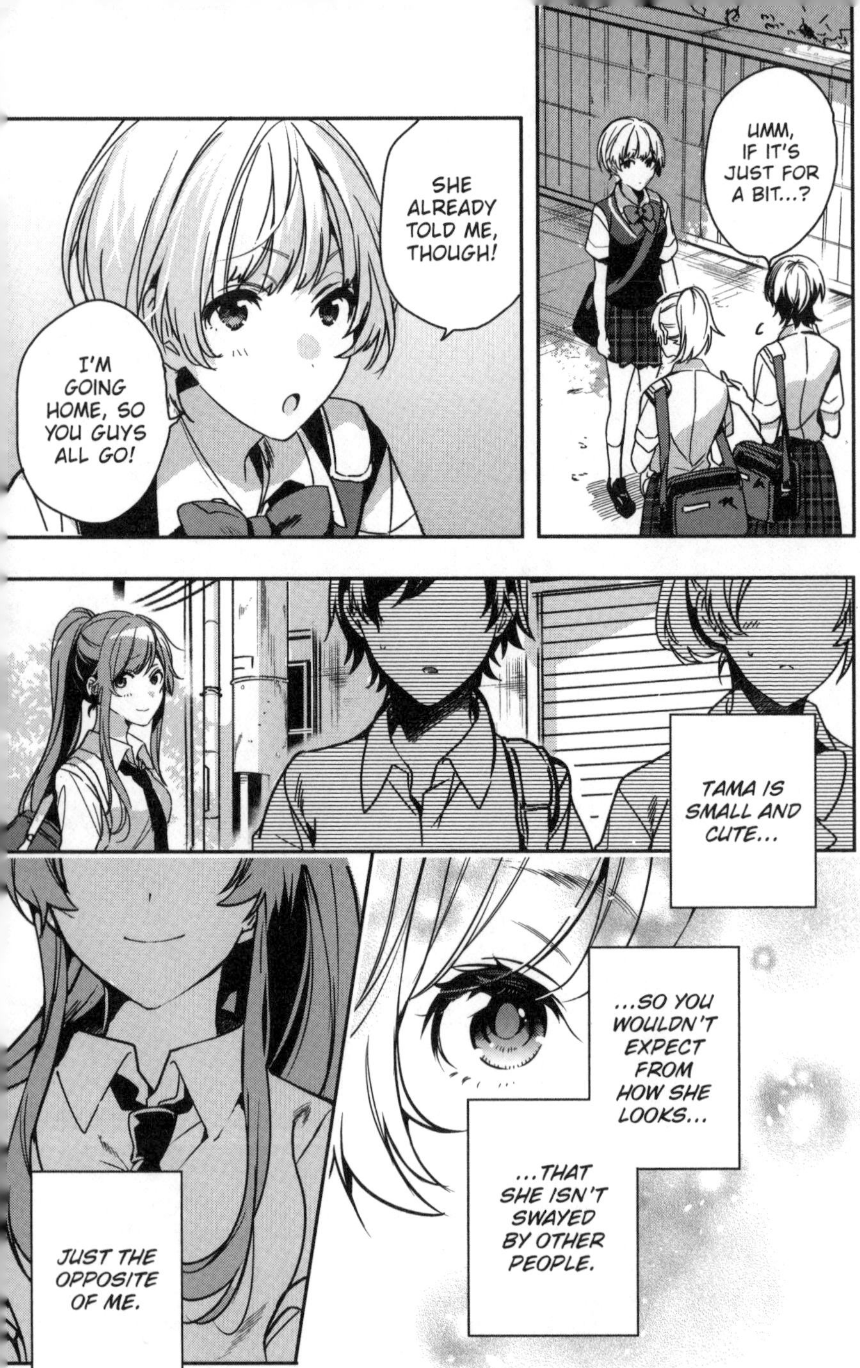
UMM, IF IT'S JUST FOR A BIT...?
SHE ALREADY TOLD ME, THOUGH!
I'M GOING HOME, SO YOU GUYS ALL GO!
TAMA IS SMALL AND CUTE...
...SO YOU WOULDN'T EXPECT FROM HOW SHE LOOKS...
...THAT SHE ISN'T SWAYED BY OTHER PEOPLE.
JUST THE OPPOSITE OF ME.

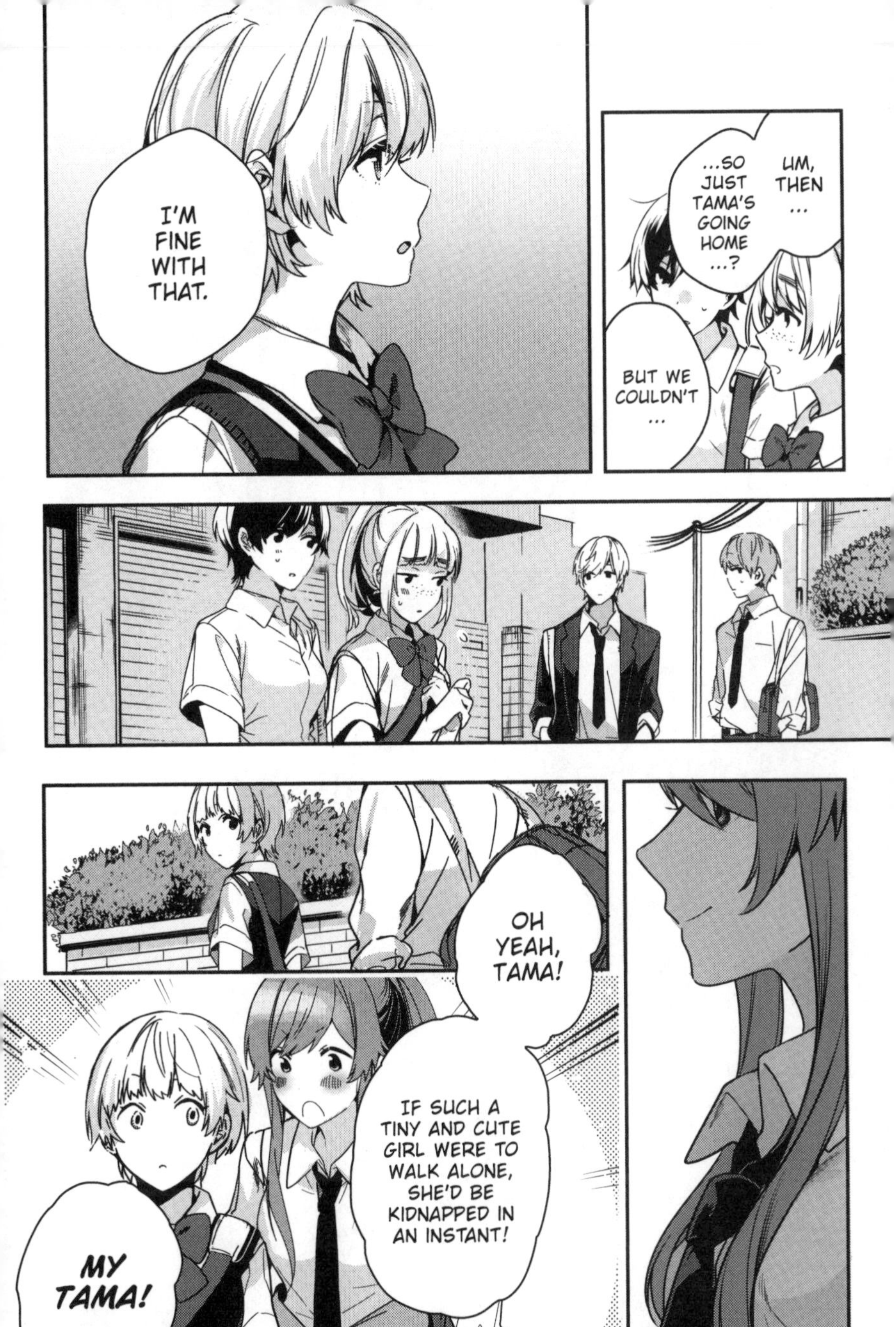
UM, THEN ...
...SO JUST TAMA'S GOING HOME ...?
BUT WE COULDN'T ...
I'M FINE WITH THAT.
OH YEAH, TAMA!
IF SUCH A TINY AND CUTE GIRL WERE TO WALK ALONE, SHE'D BE KIDNAPPED IN AN INSTANT!
MY TAMA!

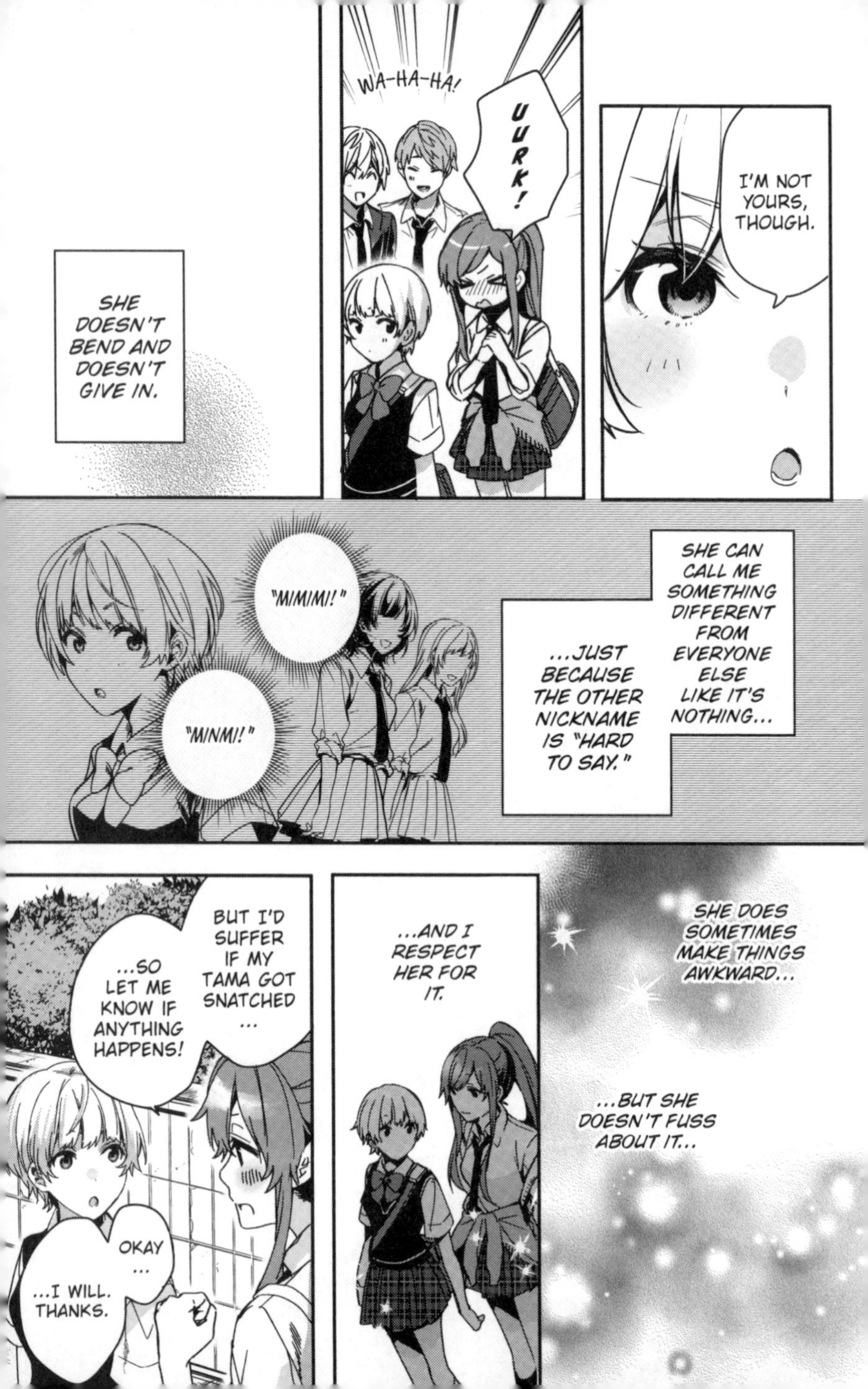
I'M NOT YOURS, THOUGH.
UURK!
WA-HA-HA!
SHE DOESN'T BEND AND DOESN'T GIVE IN.
SHE CAN CALL ME SOMETHING DIFFERENT FROM EVERYONE ELSE LIKE IT'S NOTHING...
...JUST BECAUSE THE OTHER NICKNAME IS "HARD TO SAY."
"MIMIMI!"
"MINMI!"
SHE DOES SOMETIMES MAKE THINGS AWKWARD...
...BUT SHE DOESN'T FUSS ABOUT IT...
...AND I RESPECT HER FOR IT.
BUT I'D SUFFER IF MY TAMA GOT SNATCHED...
...SO LET ME KNOW IF ANYTHING HAPPENS!
OKAY...
...I WILL. THANKS.

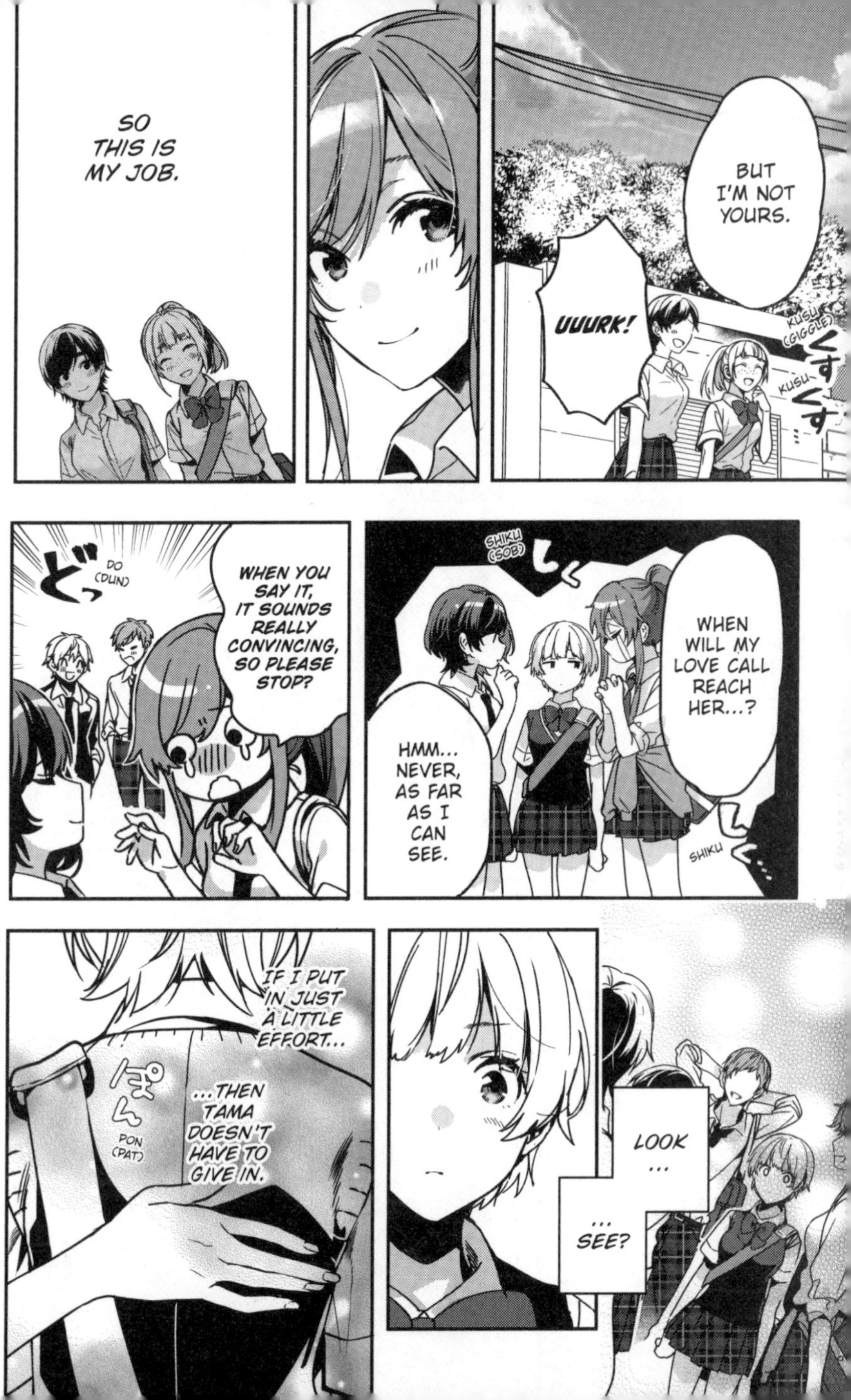
BUT I'M NOT YOURS.
UUURK!
KUSU (GIGGLE)
くす
KUSU
くす
SO THIS IS MY JOB.
WHEN WILL MY LOVE CALL REACH HER...?
SHIKU (SOB)
しく
HMM... NEVER, AS FAR AS I CAN SEE.
SHIKU
しく...
WHEN YOU SAY IT, IT SOUNDS REALLY CONVINCING, SO PLEASE STOP?
どっ
DO (DUN)
LOOK...
...SEE?
IF I PUT IN JUST A LITTLE EFFORT...
...THEN TAMA DOESN'T HAVE TO GIVE IN.
ぽん
PON (PAT)

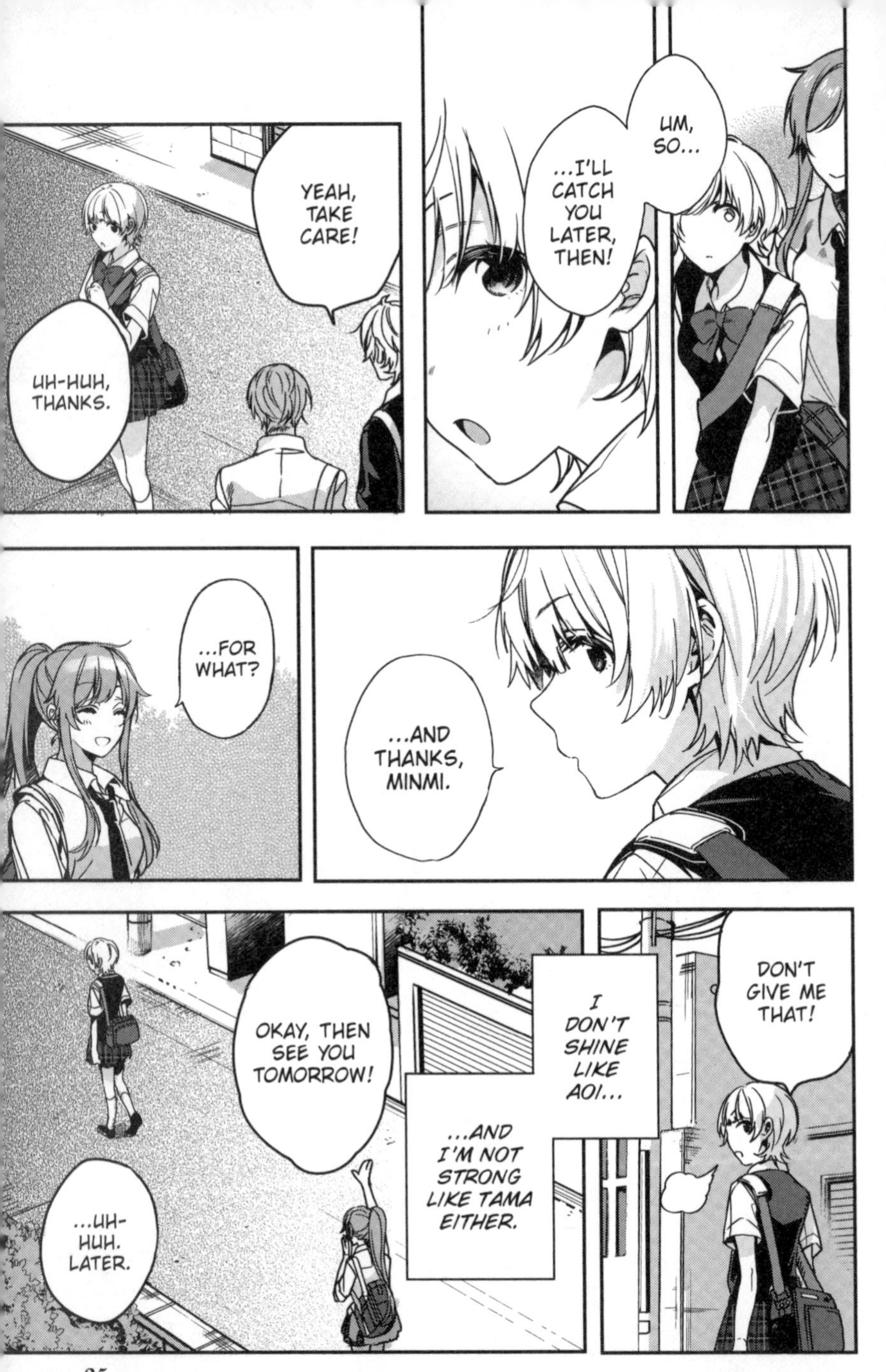
UM, SO...
...I'LL CATCH YOU LATER, THEN!
YEAH, TAKE CARE!
UH-HUH, THANKS.
...AND THANKS, MINMI.
...FOR WHAT?
DON'T GIVE ME THAT!
I DON'T SHINE LIKE AOI...
...AND I'M NOT STRONG LIKE TAMA EITHER.
OKAY, THEN SEE YOU TOMORROW!
...UH-HUH. LATER.

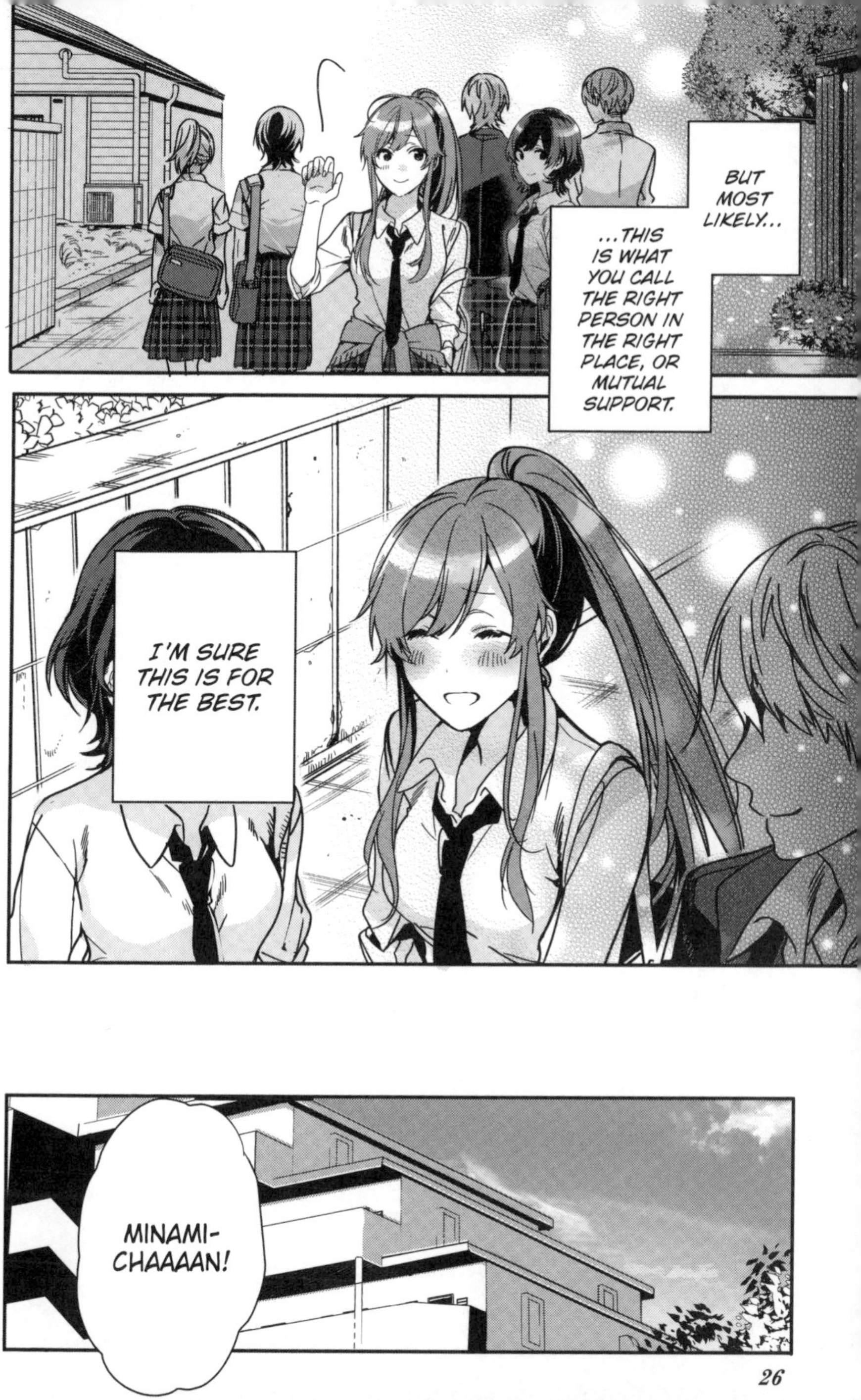
BUT MOST LIKELY...
...THIS IS WHAT YOU CALL THE RIGHT PERSON IN THE RIGHT PLACE, OR MUTUAL SUPPORT.
I'M SURE THIS IS FOR THE BEST.
MINAMI-CHAAAAN!

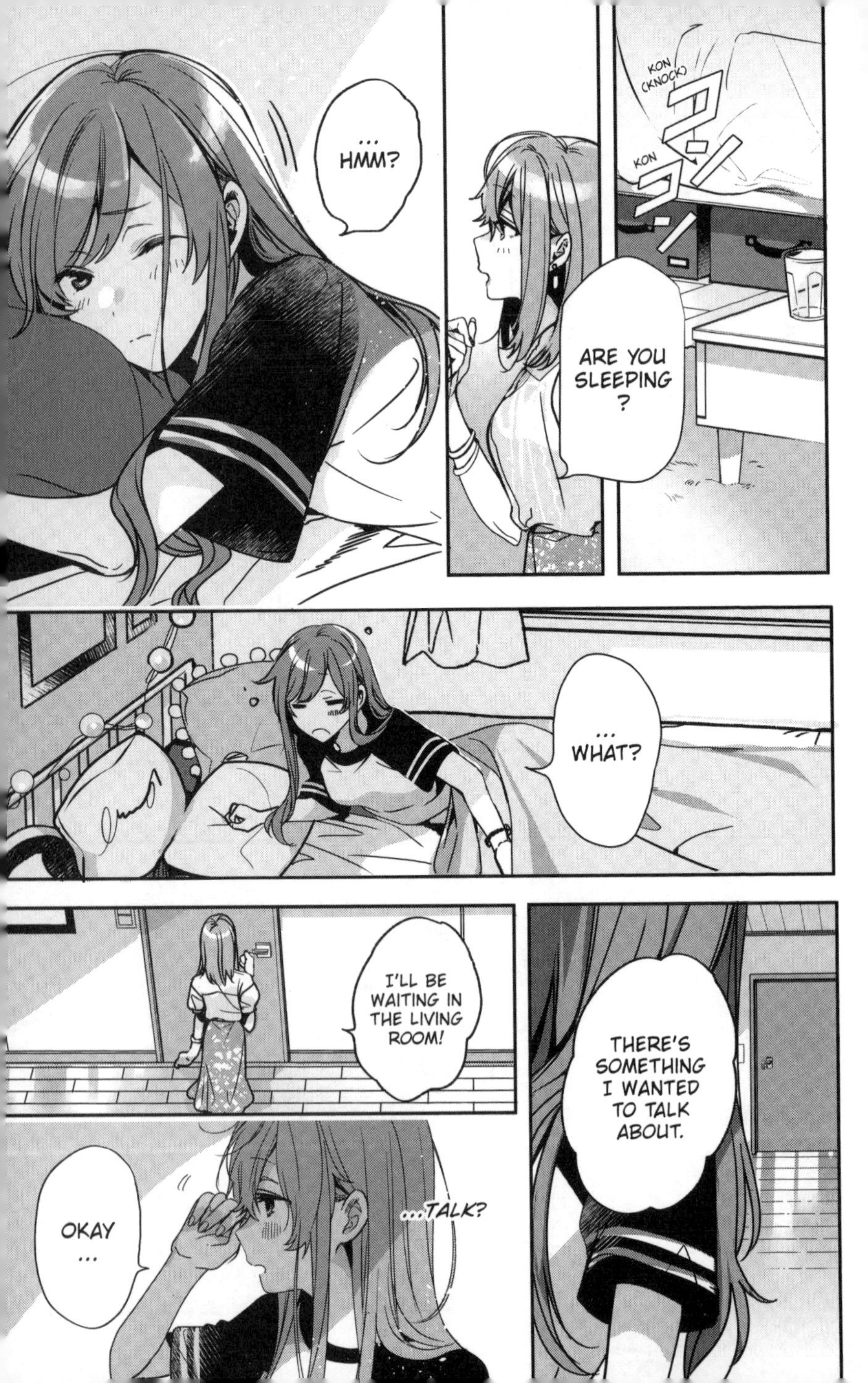
KON (KNOCK)
KON
ARE YOU SLEEPING?
... HMM?
... WHAT?
THERE'S SOMETHING I WANTED TO TALK ABOUT.
I'LL BE WAITING IN THE LIVING ROOM!
...TALK?
OKAY ...

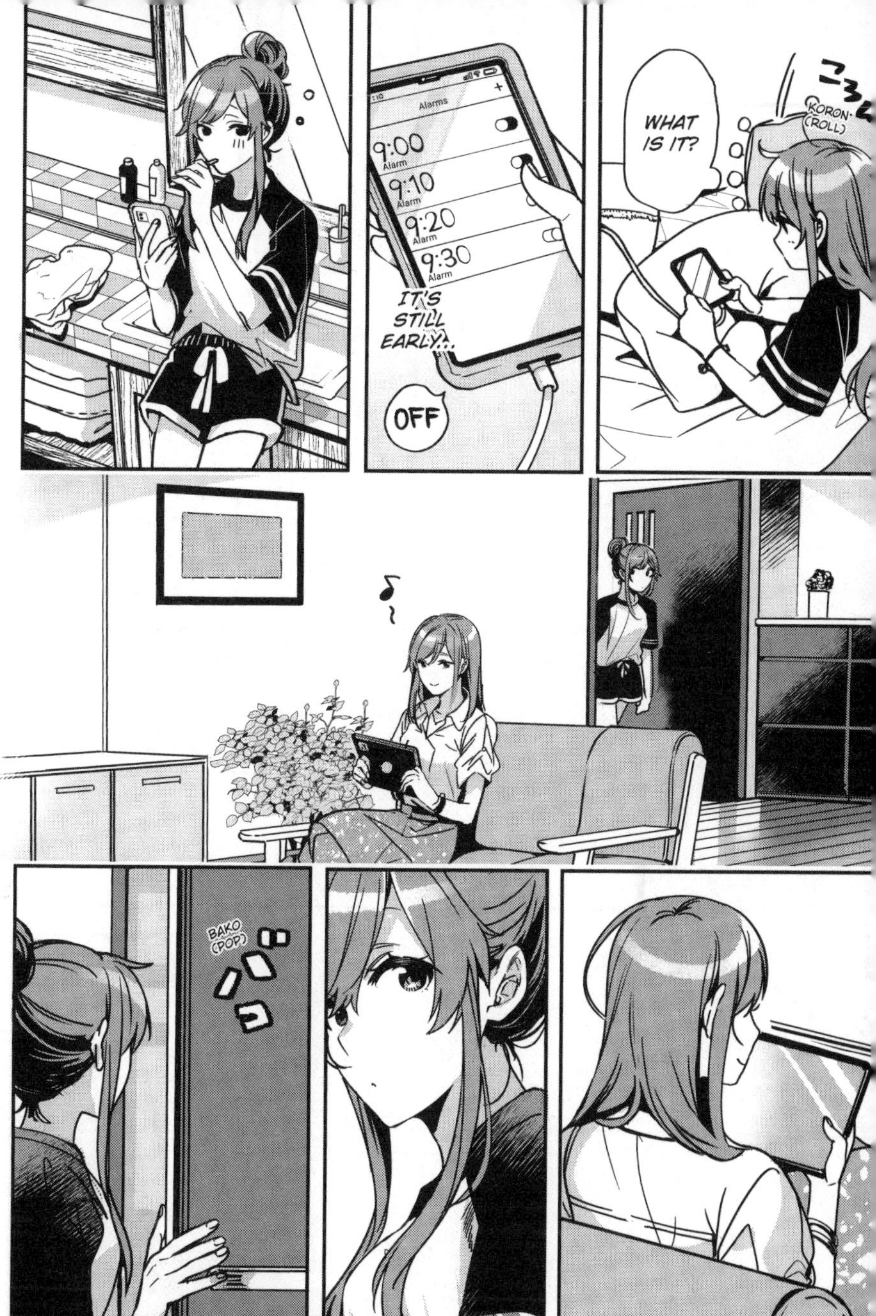
WHAT IS IT?
KORON (ROLL)
Alarms
9:00 Alarm
9:10 Alarm
9:20 Alarm
9:30 Alarm
IT'S STILL EARLY...
OFF
BAKO (POP)

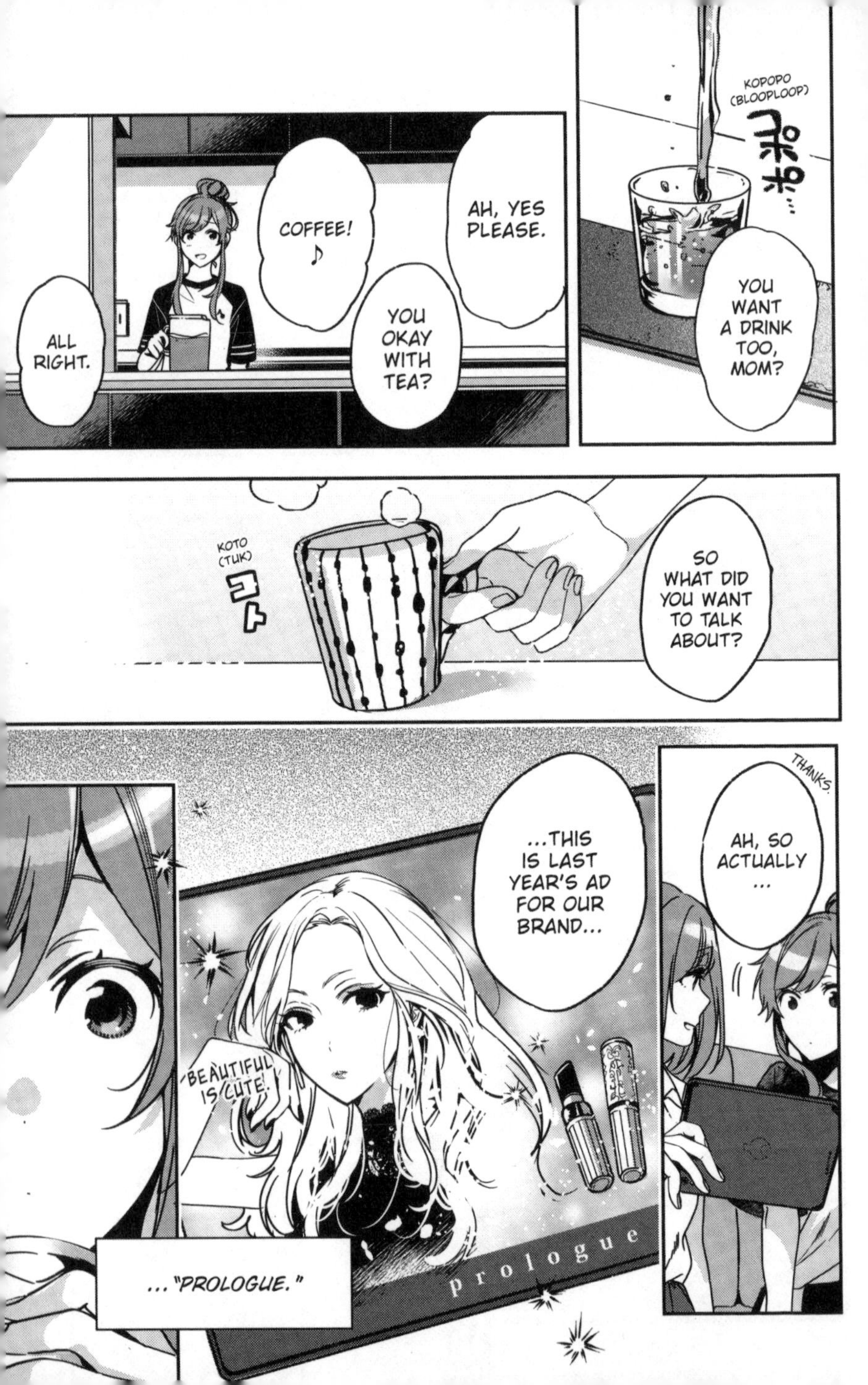
KOPOPO (BLOOPLOOP)
コポポ…
YOU WANT A DRINK TOO, MOM?
AH, YES PLEASE.
YOU OKAY WITH TEA?
COFFEE! ♪
ALL RIGHT.
SO WHAT DID YOU WANT TO TALK ABOUT?
KOTO (TUK)
コト
THANKS.
AH, SO ACTUALLY …
…THIS IS LAST YEAR'S AD FOR OUR BRAND…
BEAUTIFUL IS CUTE.
prologue
…"PROLOGUE."

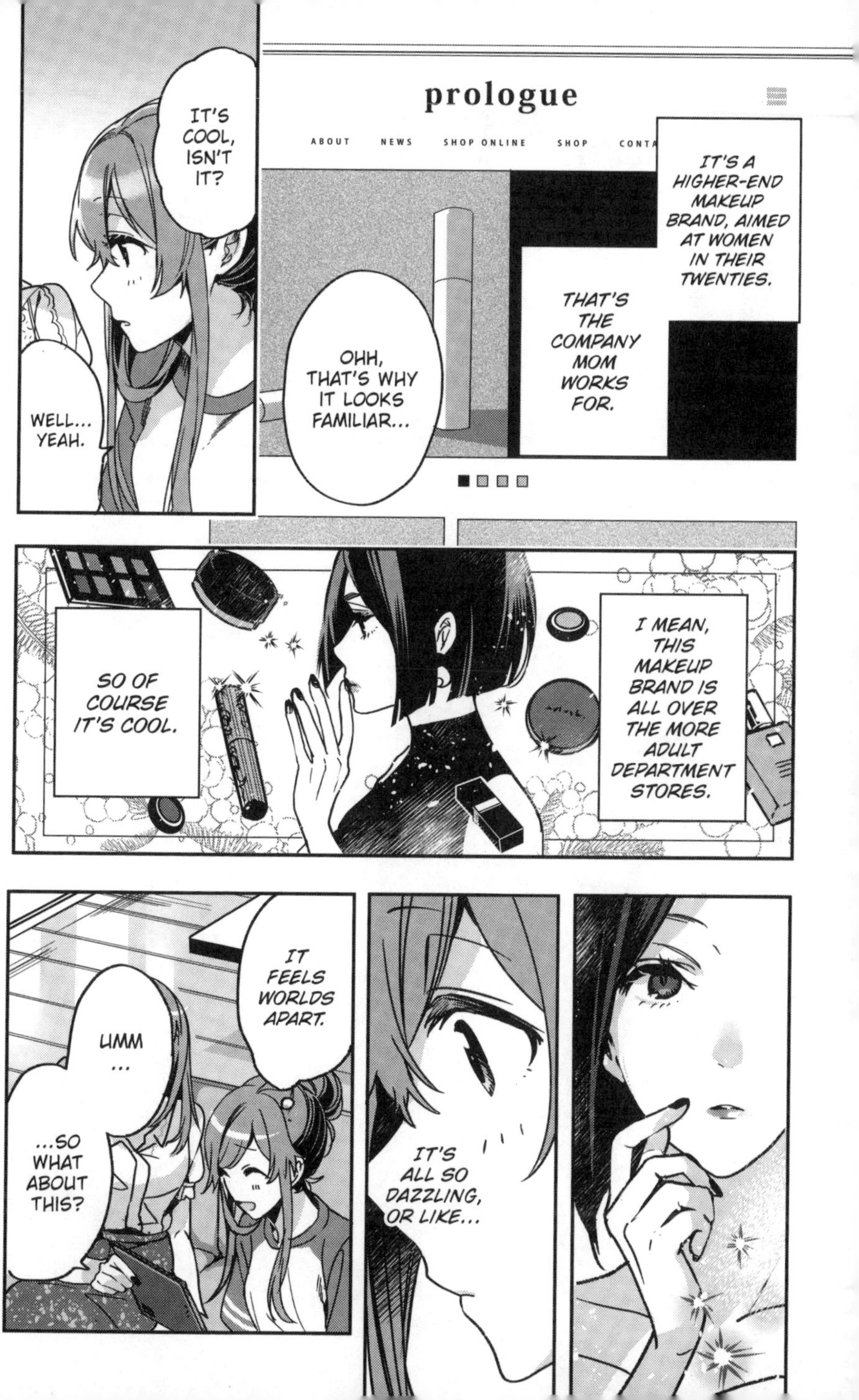

prologue
ABOUT
NEWS
SHOP ONLINE
SHOP
CONTA
IT'S A HIGHER-END MAKEUP BRAND, AIMED AT WOMEN IN THEIR TWENTIES.
THAT'S THE COMPANY MOM WORKS FOR.
OHH, THAT'S WHY IT LOOKS FAMILIAR...
IT'S COOL, ISN'T IT?
WELL... YEAH.
I MEAN, THIS MAKEUP BRAND IS ALL OVER THE MORE ADULT DEPARTMENT STORES.
SO OF COURSE IT'S COOL.
IT'S ALL SO DAZZLING, OR LIKE...
IT FEELS WORLDS APART.
UMM...
...SO WHAT ABOUT THIS?

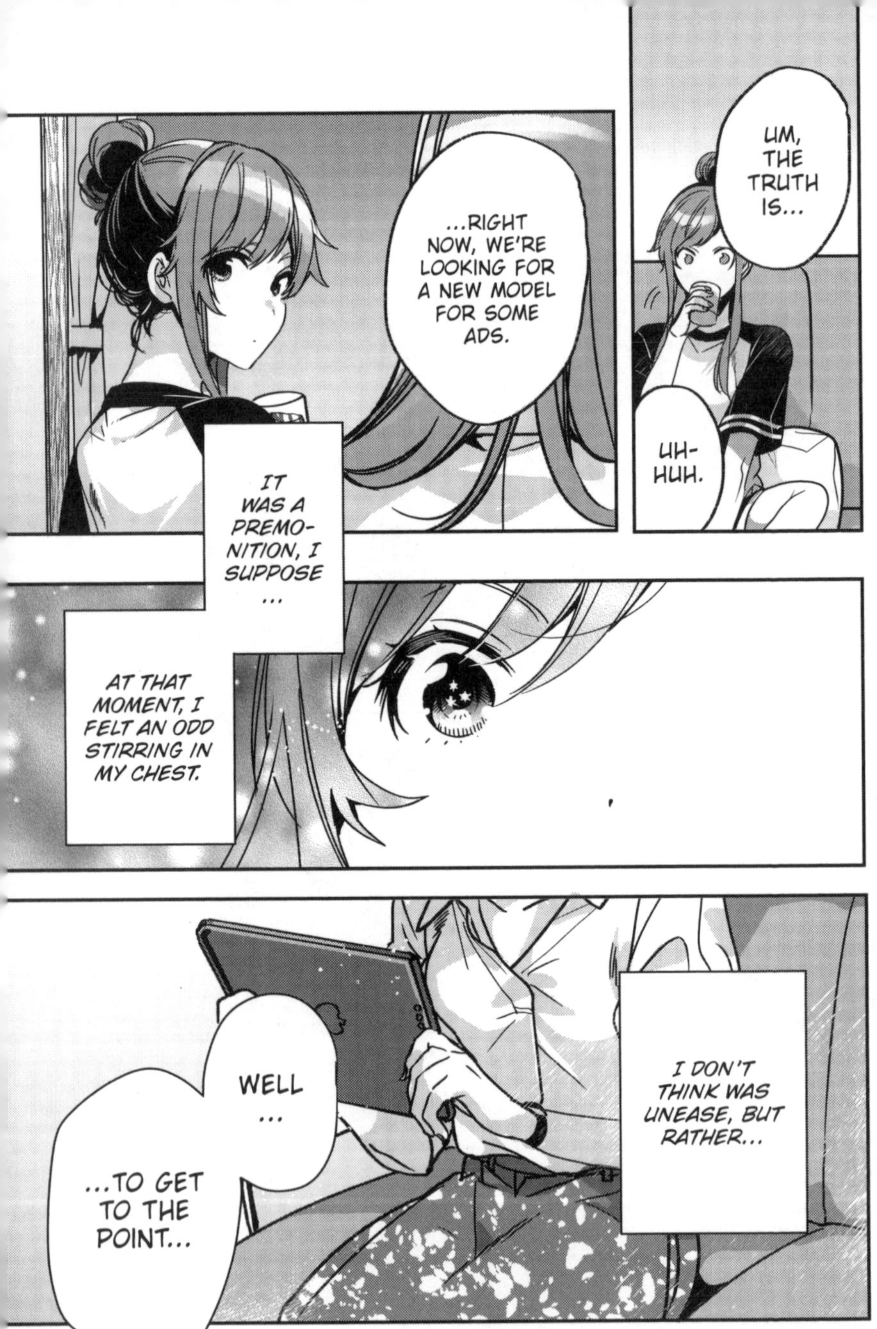
UM, THE TRUTH IS...
UH-HUH.
...RIGHT NOW, WE'RE LOOKING FOR A NEW MODEL FOR SOME ADS.
IT WAS A PREMONITION, I SUPPOSE...
AT THAT MOMENT, I FELT AN ODD STIRRING IN MY CHEST.
I DON'T THINK WAS UNEASE, BUT RATHER...
WELL...
...TO GET TO THE POINT...

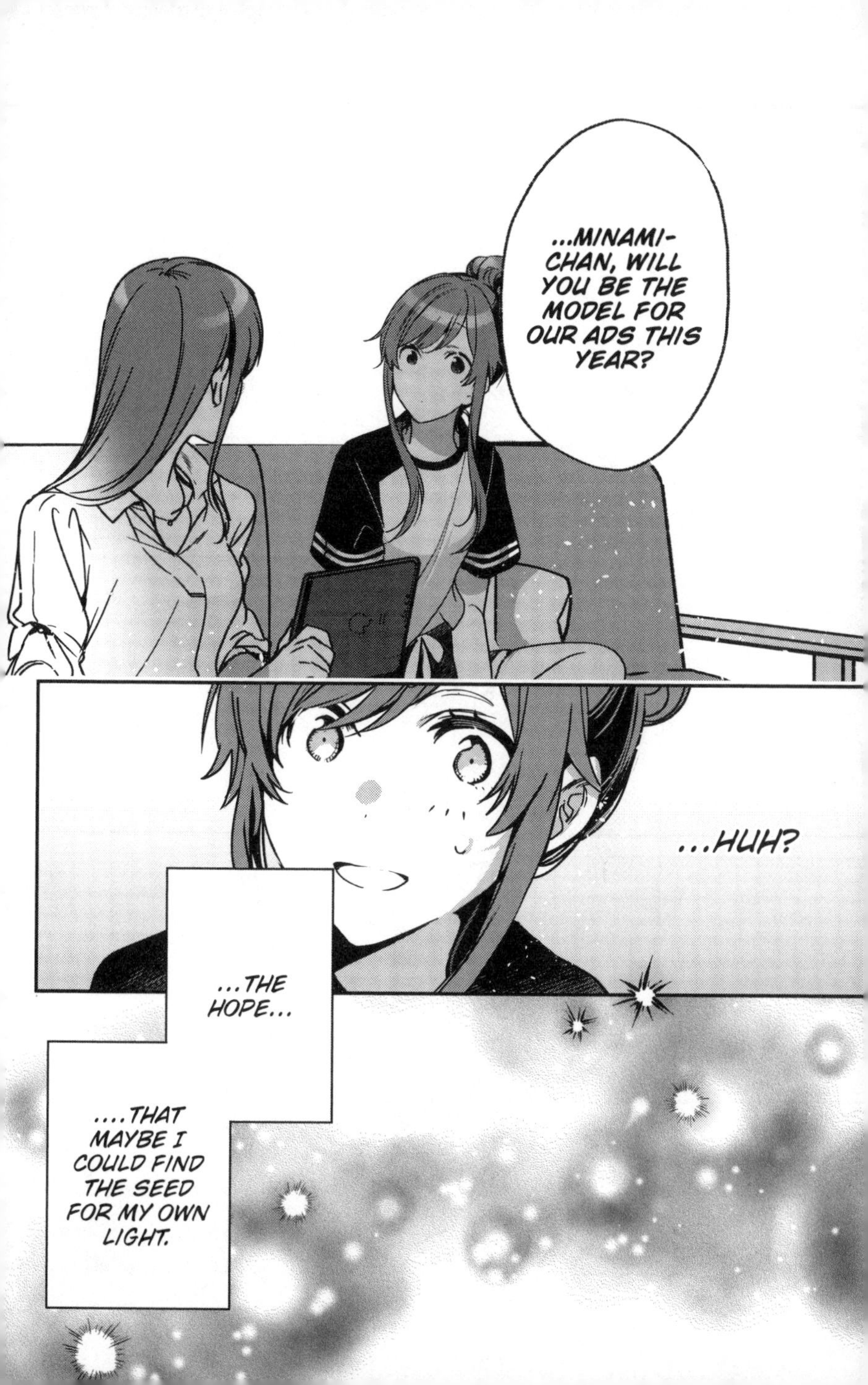
...MINAMI-CHAN, WILL YOU BE THE MODEL FOR OUR ADS THIS YEAR?
...HUH?
...THE HOPE...
....THAT MAYBE I COULD FIND THE SEED FOR MY OWN LIGHT.

Chapter 2
SHINING PROLOGUE

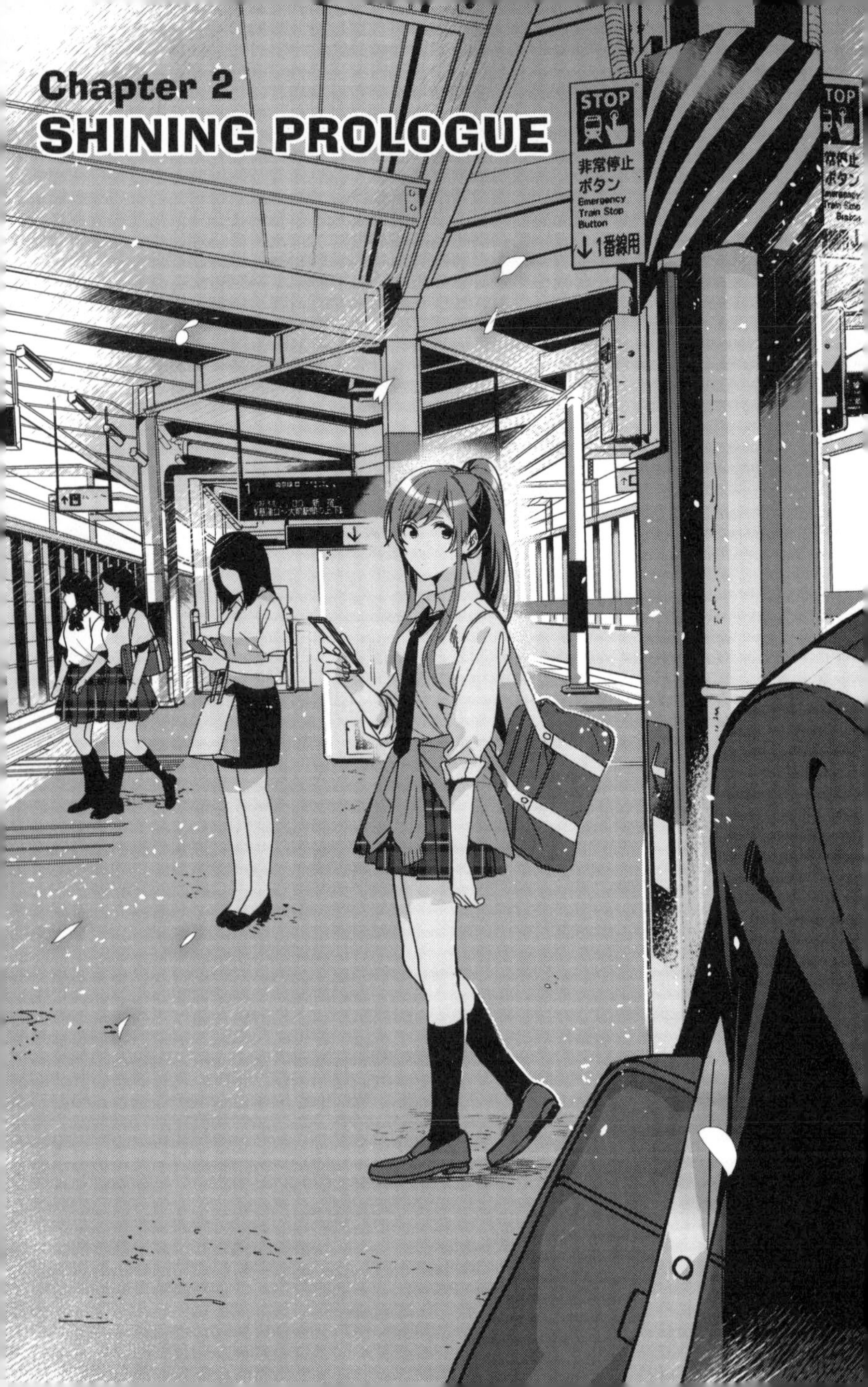
STOP
非常停止
ボタン
Emergency
Train Stop
Button
↓1番線用

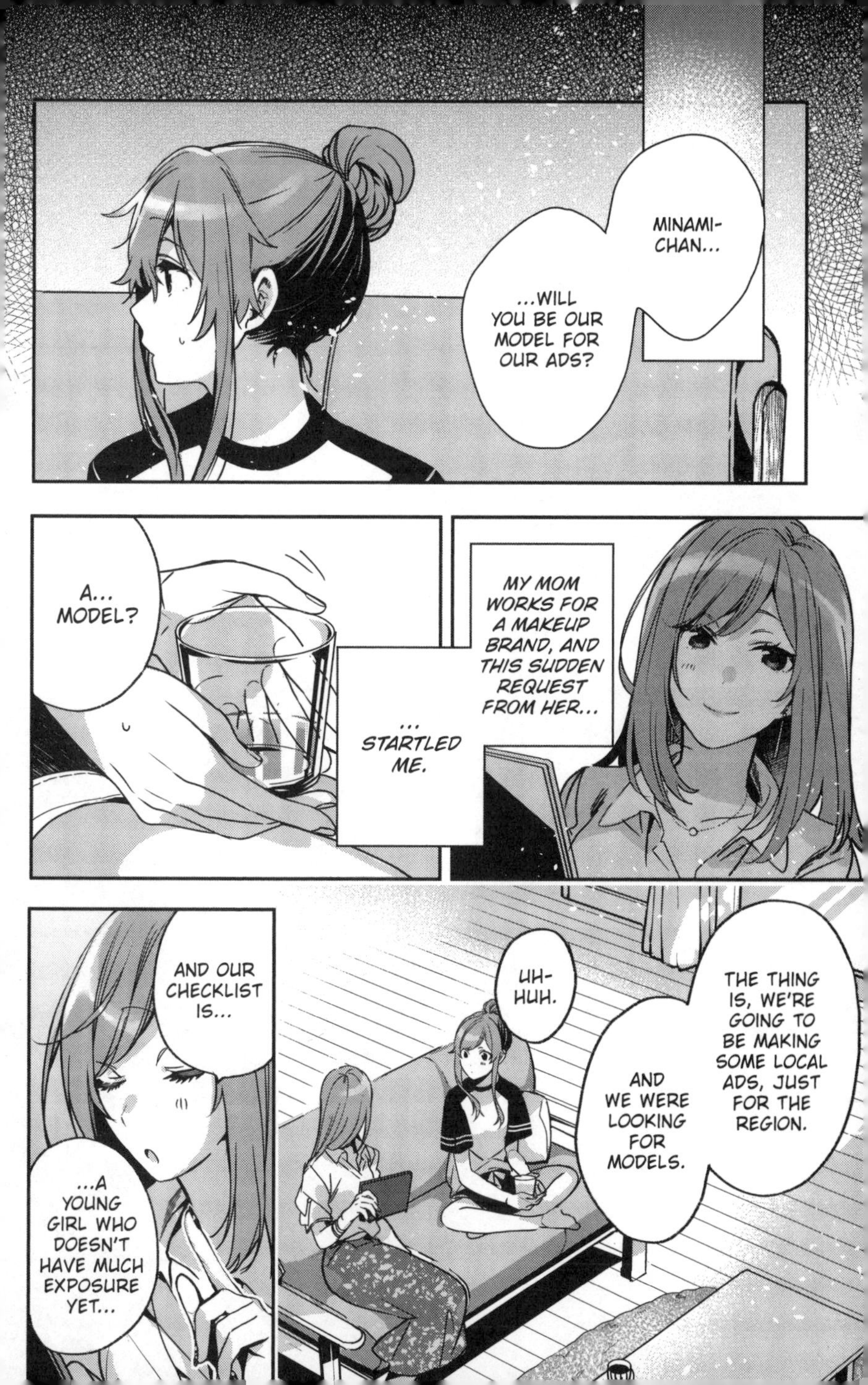
MINAMI-CHAN...
...WILL YOU BE OUR MODEL FOR OUR ADS?
MY MOM WORKS FOR A MAKEUP BRAND, AND THIS SUDDEN REQUEST FROM HER...
...STARTLED ME.
A... MODEL?
THE THING IS, WE'RE GOING TO BE MAKING SOME LOCAL ADS, JUST FOR THE REGION.
AND WE WERE LOOKING FOR MODELS.
UH-HUH.
AND OUR CHECKLIST IS...
...A YOUNG GIRL WHO DOESN'T HAVE MUCH EXPOSURE YET...

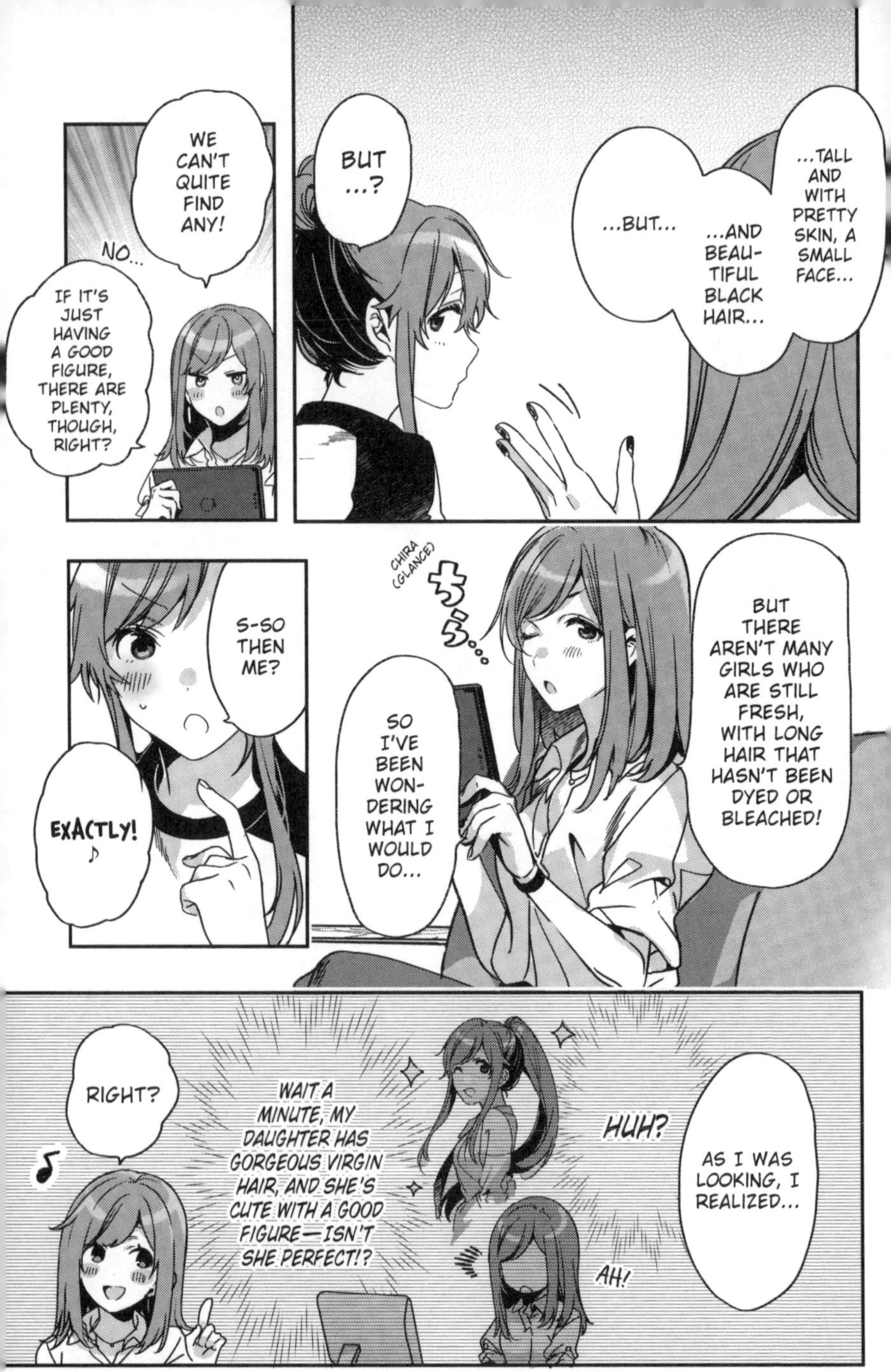
...TALL AND WITH PRETTY SKIN, A SMALL FACE...
...AND BEAUTIFUL BLACK HAIR...
...BUT...
BUT ...?
WE CAN'T QUITE FIND ANY!
NO...
IF IT'S JUST HAVING A GOOD FIGURE, THERE ARE PLENTY, THOUGH, RIGHT?
CHIRA (GLANCE)
ちら…
BUT THERE AREN'T MANY GIRLS WHO ARE STILL FRESH, WITH LONG HAIR THAT HASN'T BEEN DYED OR BLEACHED!
SO I'VE BEEN WONDERING WHAT I WOULD DO...
S-SO THEN ME?
EXACTLY! ♪
AS I WAS LOOKING, I REALIZED...
HUH?
AH!
WAIT A MINUTE, MY DAUGHTER HAS GORGEOUS VIRGIN HAIR, AND SHE'S CUTE WITH A GOOD FIGURE—ISN'T SHE PERFECT!?
RIGHT? ♪

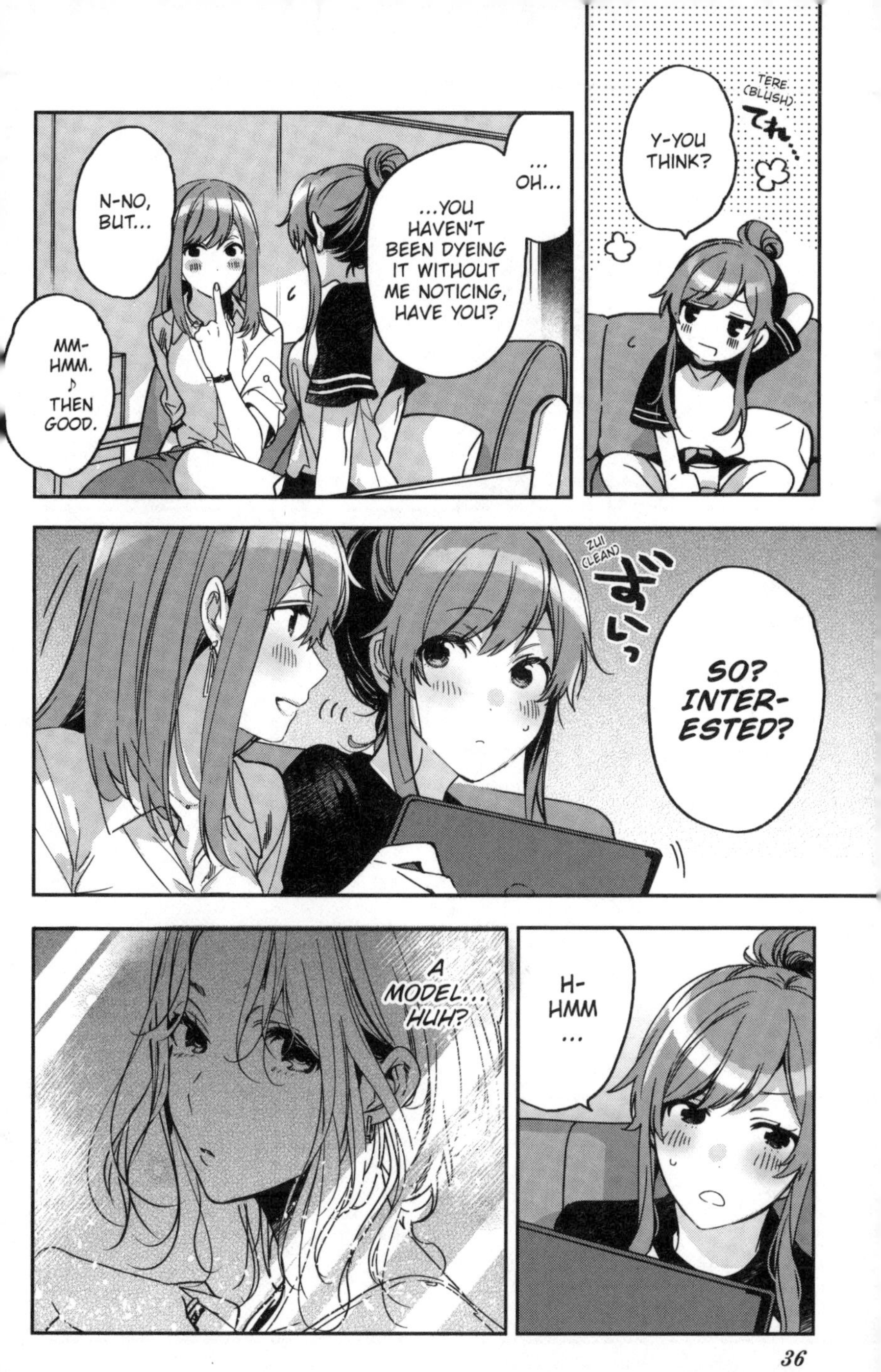
TERE (BLUSH)
てれ…
Y-YOU THINK?
... OH...
...YOU HAVEN'T BEEN DYEING IT WITHOUT ME NOTICING, HAVE YOU?
N-NO, BUT...
MM-HMM. ♪ THEN GOOD.
ZUI (CLEAN)
ずいっ
SO? INTER-ESTED?
H-HMM ...
A MODEL... HUH?

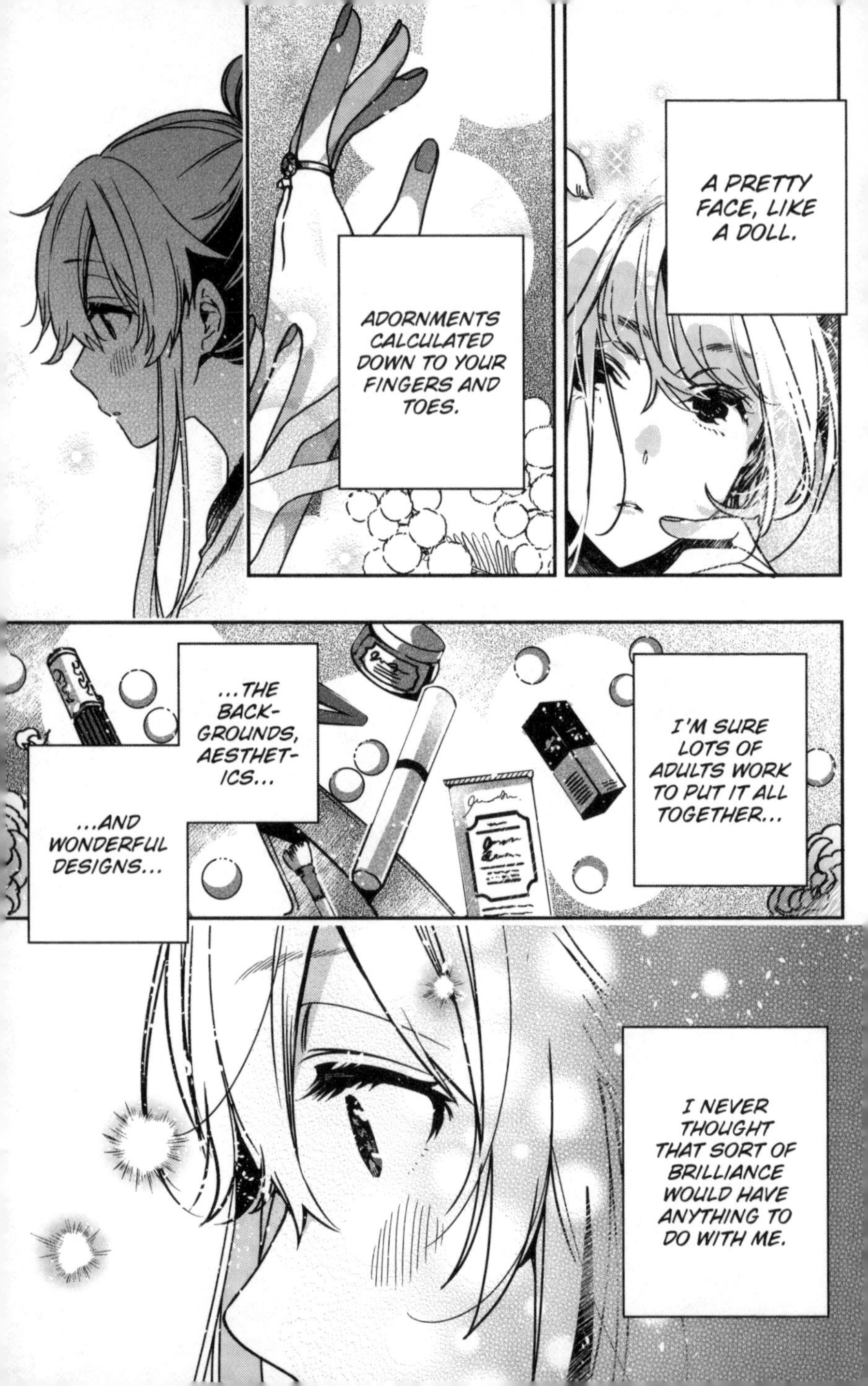
A PRETTY FACE, LIKE A DOLL.
ADORNMENTS CALCULATED DOWN TO YOUR FINGERS AND TOES.
I'M SURE LOTS OF ADULTS WORK TO PUT IT ALL TOGETHER...
...THE BACK-GROUNDS, AESTHET-ICS...
...AND WONDERFUL DESIGNS...
I NEVER THOUGHT THAT SORT OF BRILLIANCE WOULD HAVE ANYTHING TO DO WITH ME.

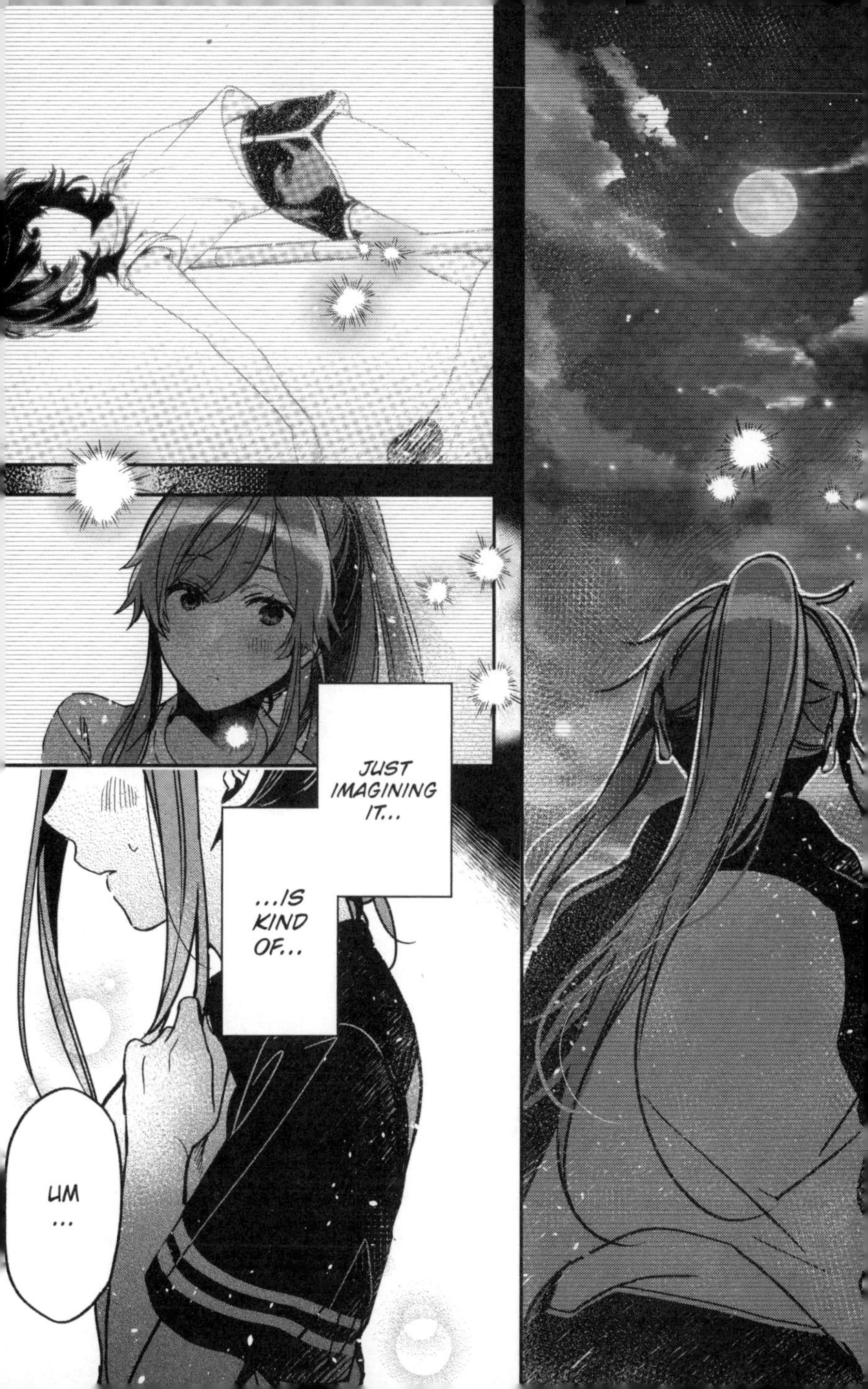
JUST IMAGINING IT...
...IS KIND OF...
UM ...

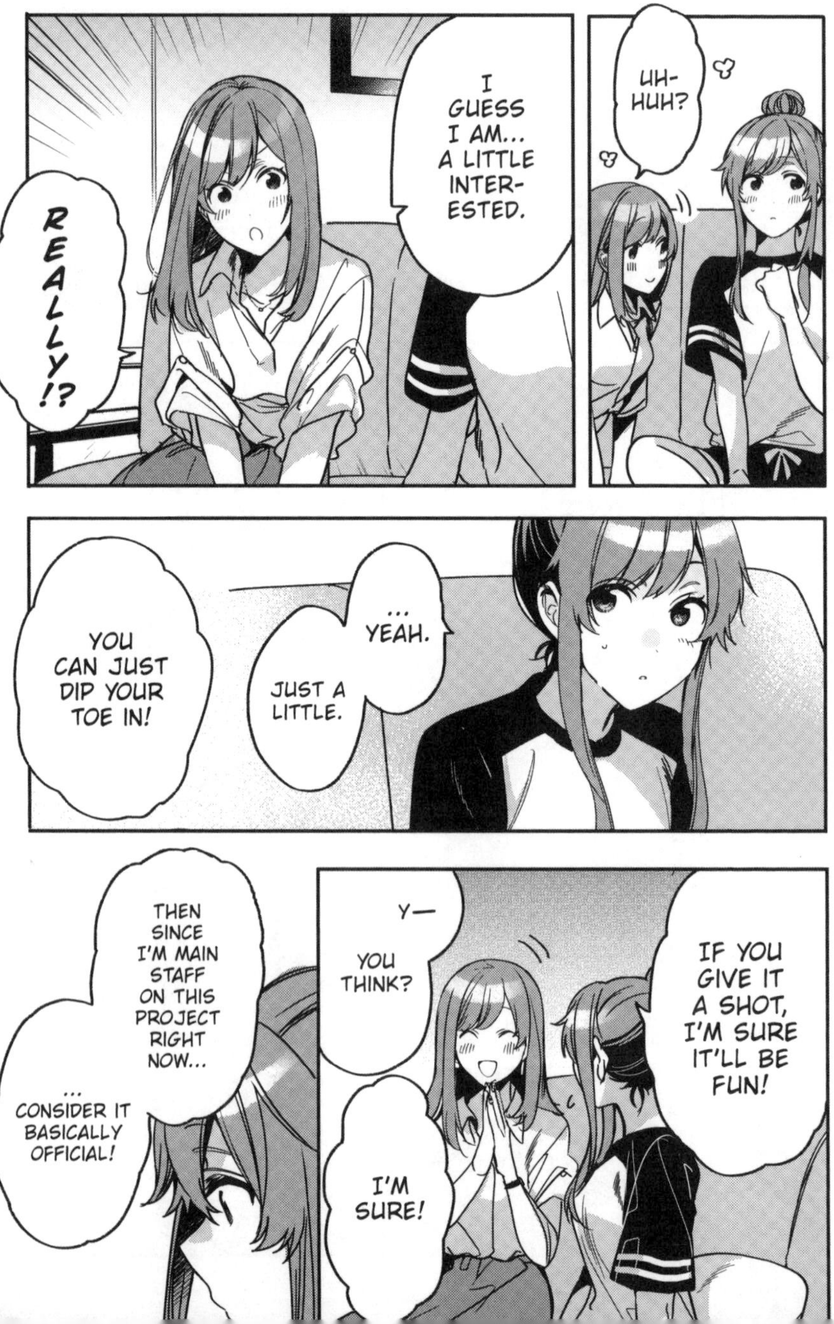
UH-HUH?
I GUESS I AM... A LITTLE INTERESTED.
REALLY!?
...YEAH.
JUST A LITTLE.
YOU CAN JUST DIP YOUR TOE IN!
IF YOU GIVE IT A SHOT, I'M SURE IT'LL BE FUN!
Y—
YOU THINK?
I'M SURE!
THEN SINCE I'M MAIN STAFF ON THIS PROJECT RIGHT NOW...
...CONSIDER IT BASICALLY OFFICIAL!

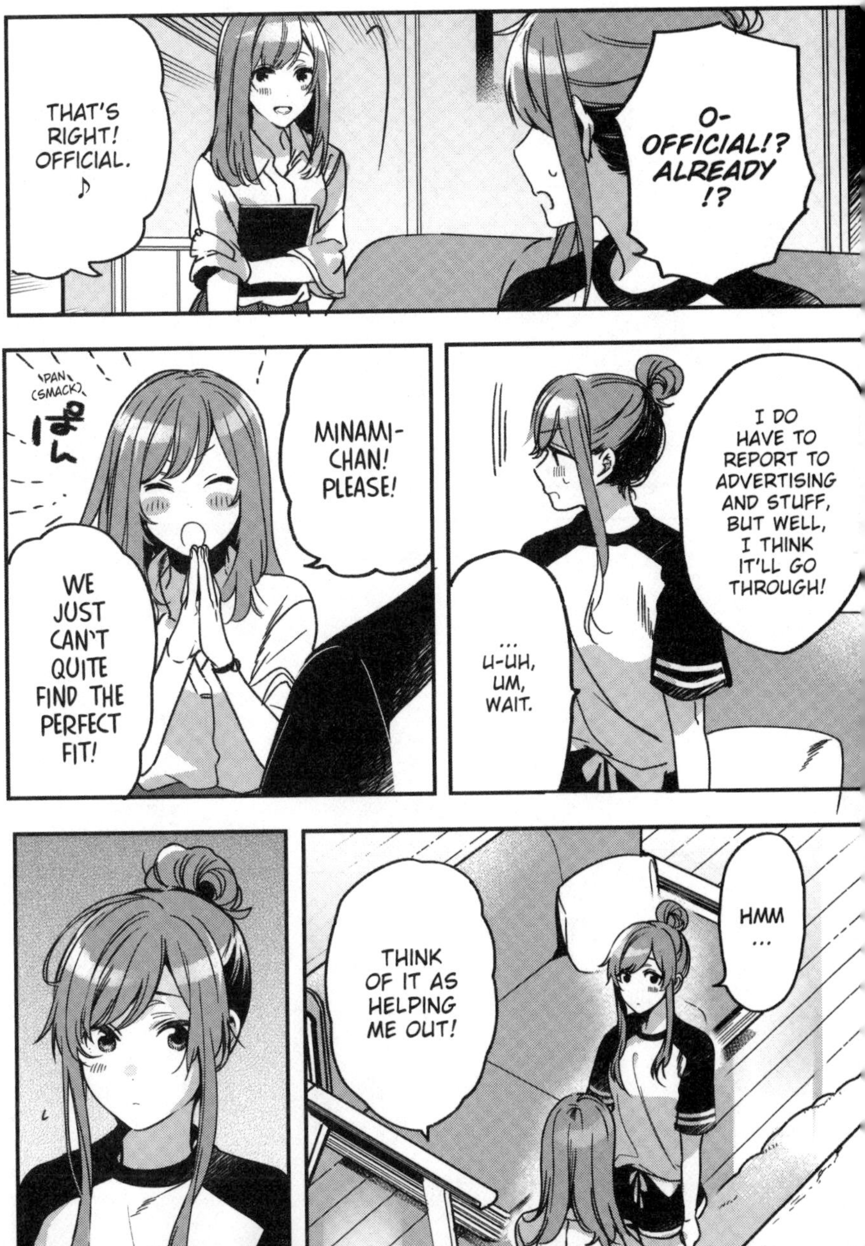
O-OFFICIAL!? ALREADY!?
THAT'S RIGHT! OFFICIAL. ♪
I DO HAVE TO REPORT TO ADVERTISING AND STUFF, BUT WELL, I THINK IT'LL GO THROUGH!
... U-UH, UM, WAIT.
MINAMI-CHAN! PLEASE!
PAN (SMACK) ぱん
WE JUST CAN'T QUITE FIND THE PERFECT FIT!
HMM ...
THINK OF IT AS HELPING ME OUT!

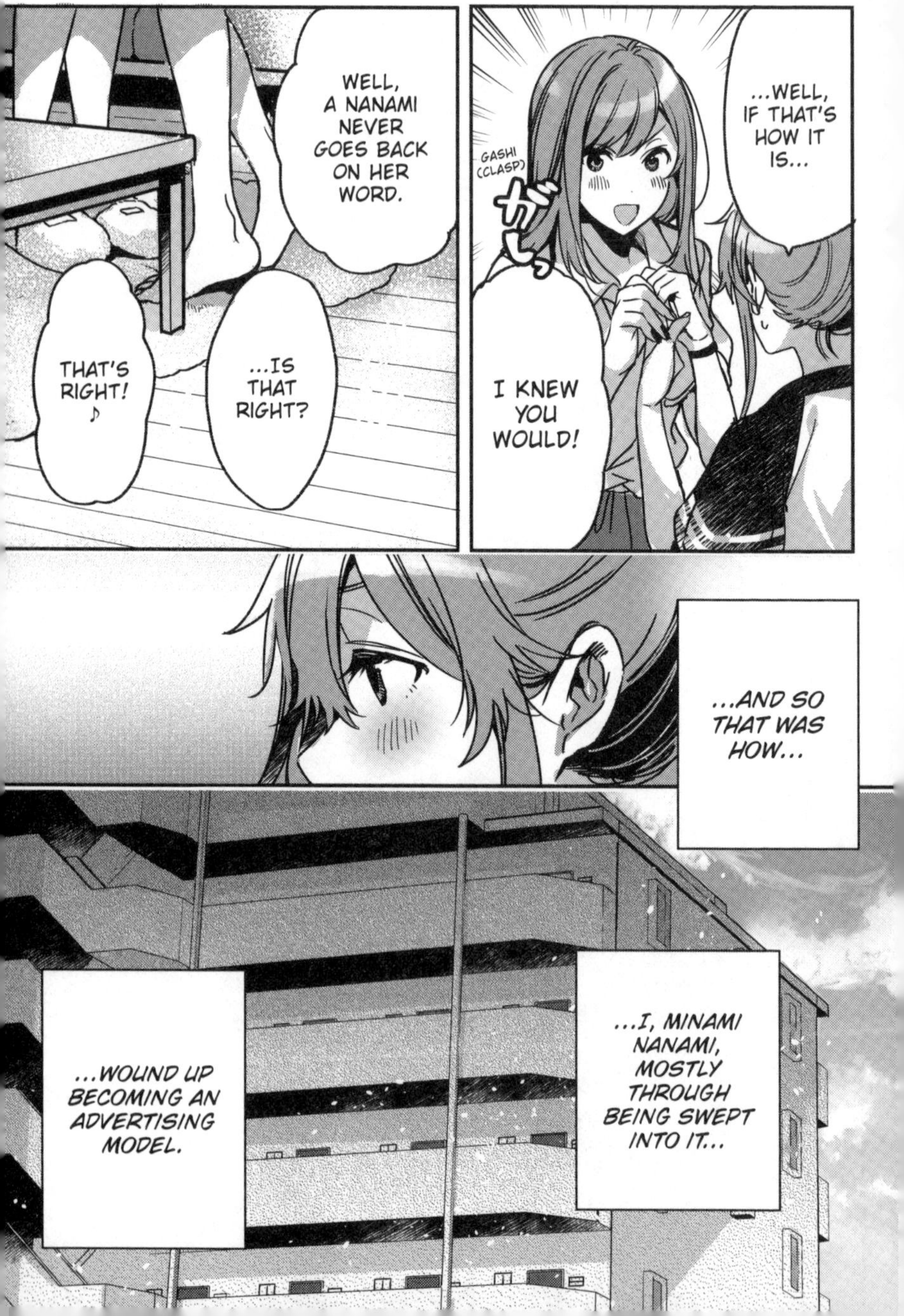
...WELL, IF THAT'S HOW IT IS...
GASHI (CLASP)
がしっ
I KNEW YOU WOULD!
WELL, A NANAMI NEVER GOES BACK ON HER WORD.
...IS THAT RIGHT?
THAT'S RIGHT! ♪
...AND SO THAT WAS HOW...
...I, MINAMI NANAMI, MOSTLY THROUGH BEING SWEPT INTO IT...
...WOUND UP BECOMING AN ADVERTISING MODEL.

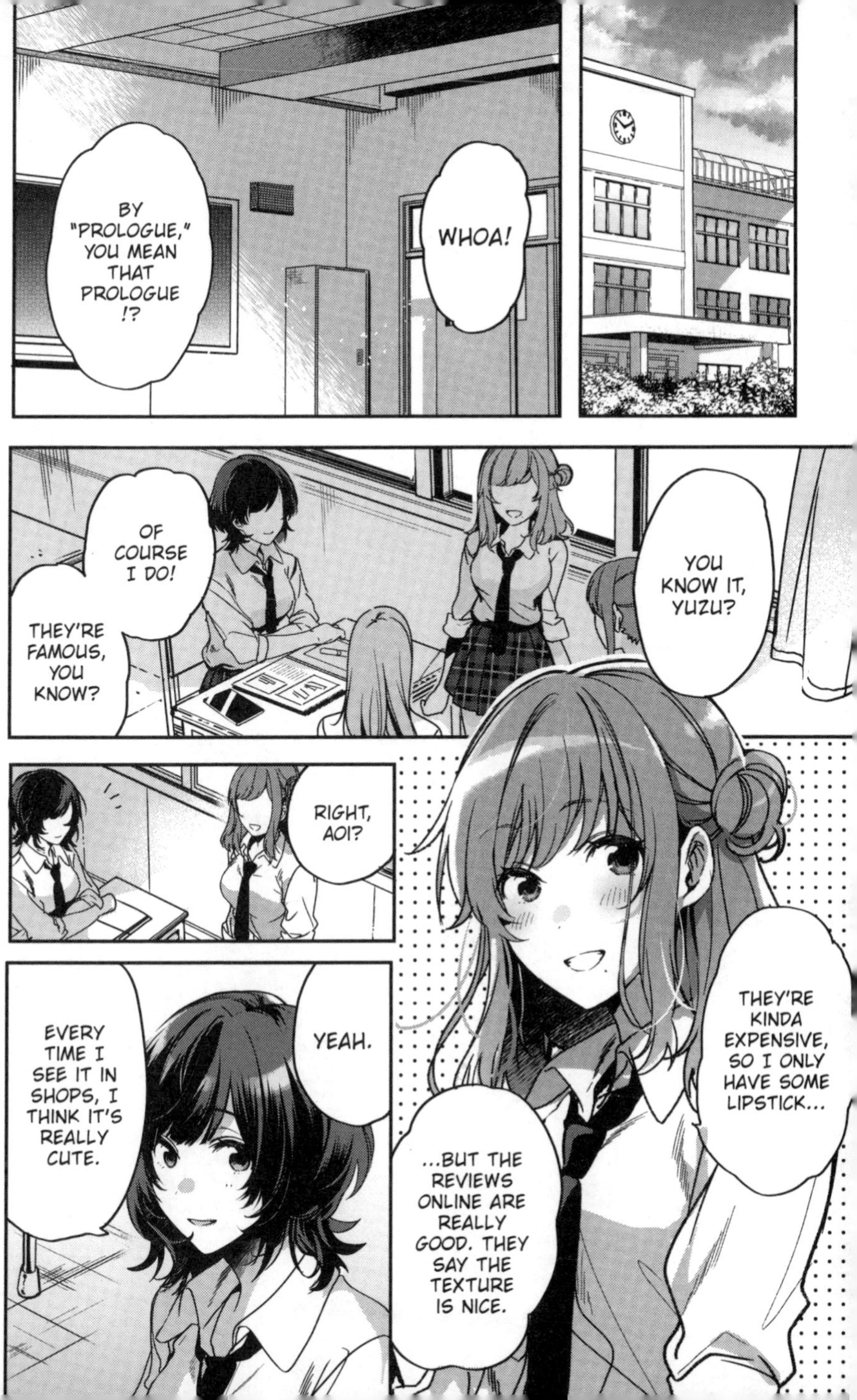
WHOA!
BY "PROLOGUE," YOU MEAN THAT PROLOGUE!?
YOU KNOW IT, YUZU?
OF COURSE I DO!
THEY'RE FAMOUS, YOU KNOW?
THEY'RE KINDA EXPENSIVE, SO I ONLY HAVE SOME LIPSTICK...
...BUT THE REVIEWS ONLINE ARE REALLY GOOD. THEY SAY THE TEXTURE IS NICE.
RIGHT, AOI?
YEAH.
EVERY TIME I SEE IT IN SHOPS, I THINK IT'S REALLY CUTE.

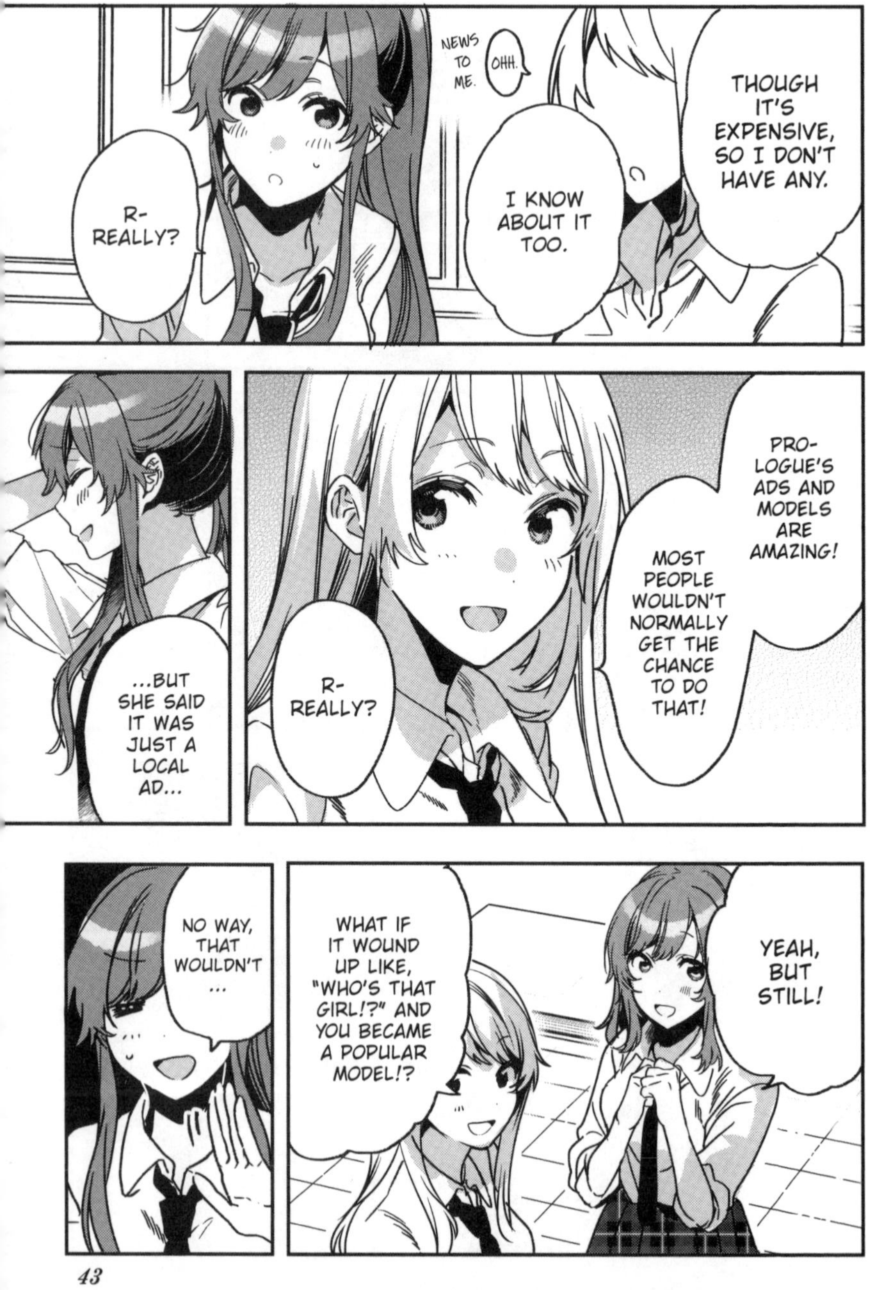
THOUGH IT'S EXPENSIVE, SO I DON'T HAVE ANY.
OHH.
NEWS TO ME.
I KNOW ABOUT IT TOO.
R-REALLY?
PRO-LOGUE'S ADS AND MODELS ARE AMAZING!
MOST PEOPLE WOULDN'T NORMALLY GET THE CHANCE TO DO THAT!
R-REALLY?
...BUT SHE SAID IT WAS JUST A LOCAL AD...
YEAH, BUT STILL!
WHAT IF IT WOUND UP LIKE, "WHO'S THAT GIRL!?" AND YOU BECAME A POPULAR MODEL!?
NO WAY, THAT WOULDN'T ...

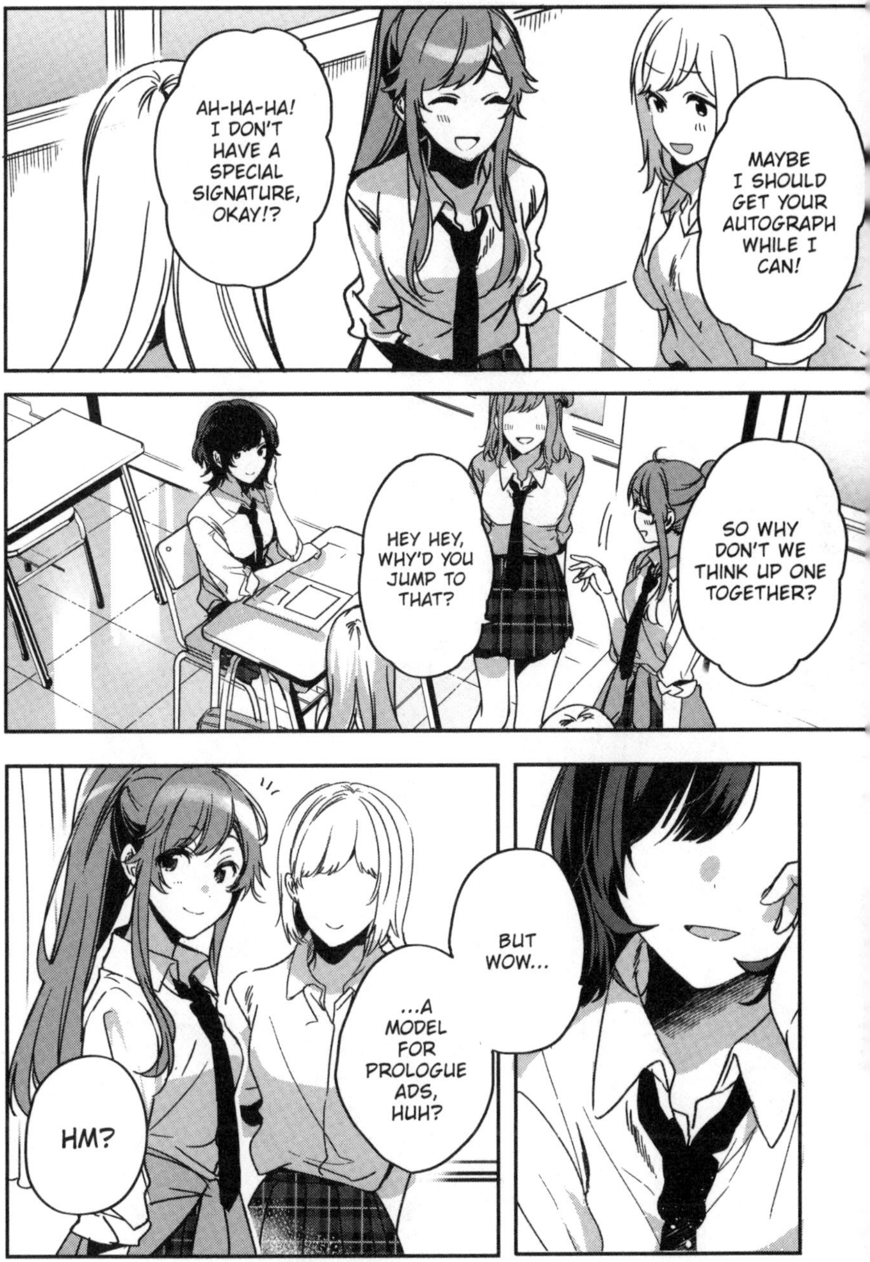
MAYBE I SHOULD GET YOUR AUTOGRAPH WHILE I CAN!
AH-HA-HA! I DON'T HAVE A SPECIAL SIGNATURE, OKAY!?
SO WHY DON'T WE THINK UP ONE TOGETHER?
HEY HEY, WHY'D YOU JUMP TO THAT?
BUT WOW...
...A MODEL FOR PROLOGUE ADS, HUH?
HM?

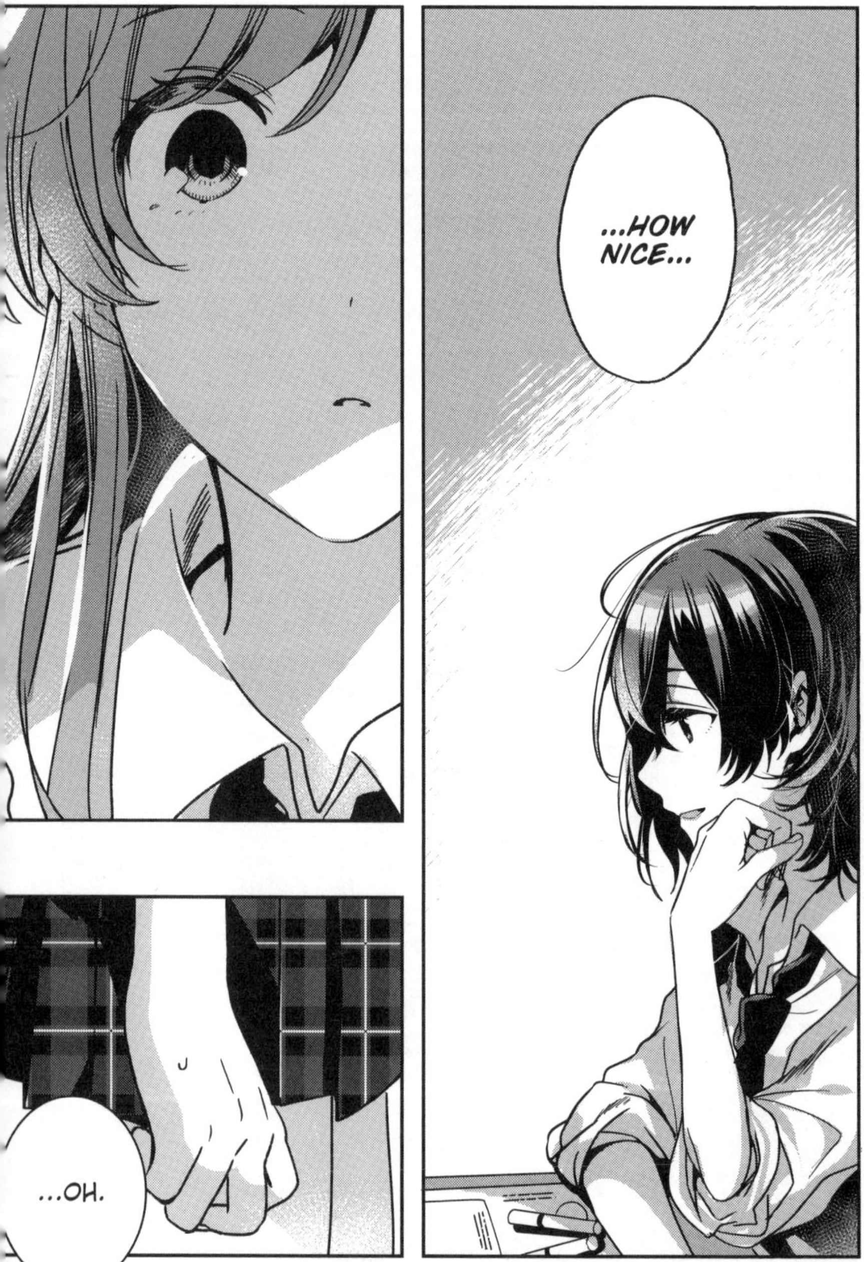
...HOW NICE...
...OH.

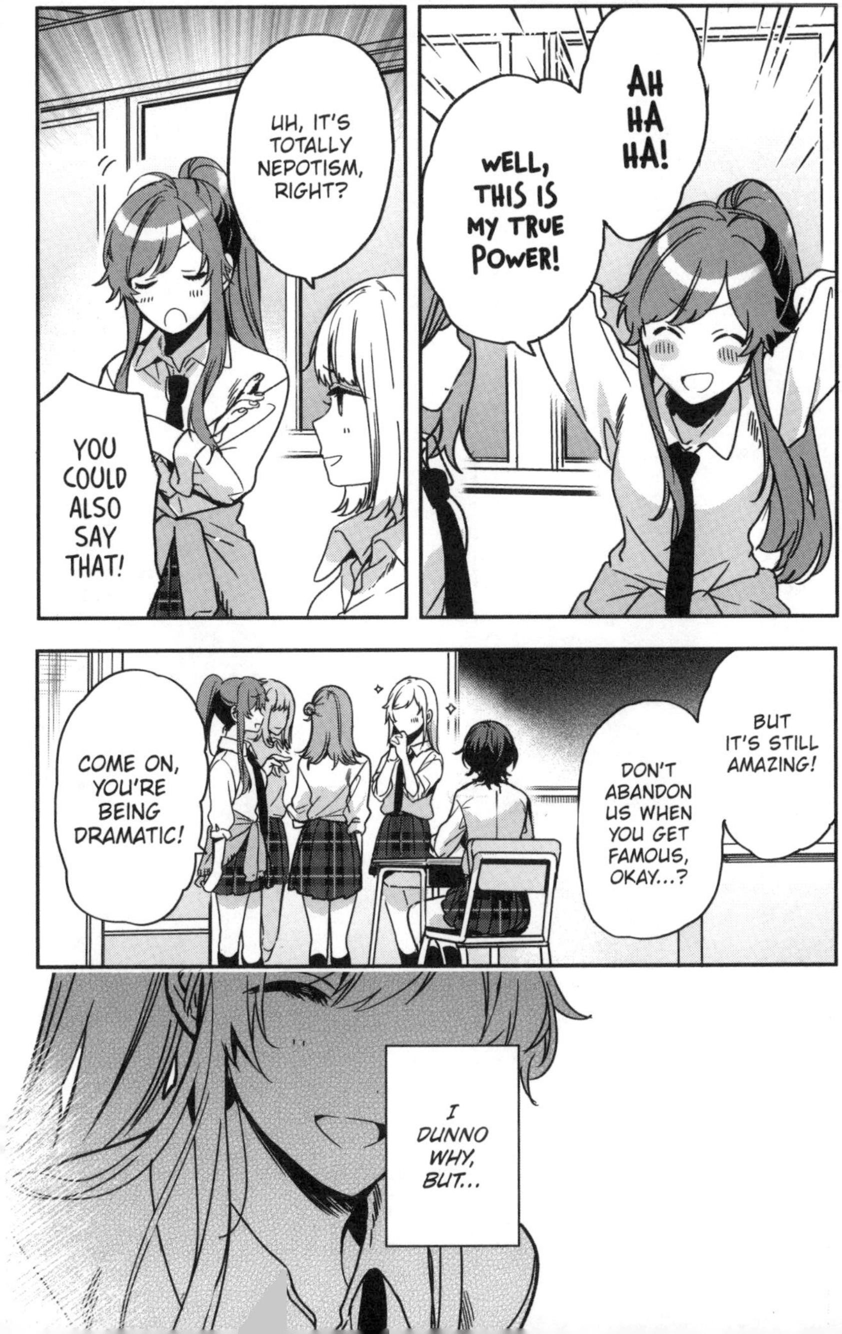
AH HA HA!
WELL, THIS IS MY TRUE POWER!
UH, IT'S TOTALLY NEPOTISM, RIGHT?
YOU COULD ALSO SAY THAT!
BUT IT'S STILL AMAZING!
DON'T ABANDON US WHEN YOU GET FAMOUS, OKAY...?
COME ON, YOU'RE BEING DRAMATIC!
I DUNNO WHY, BUT...

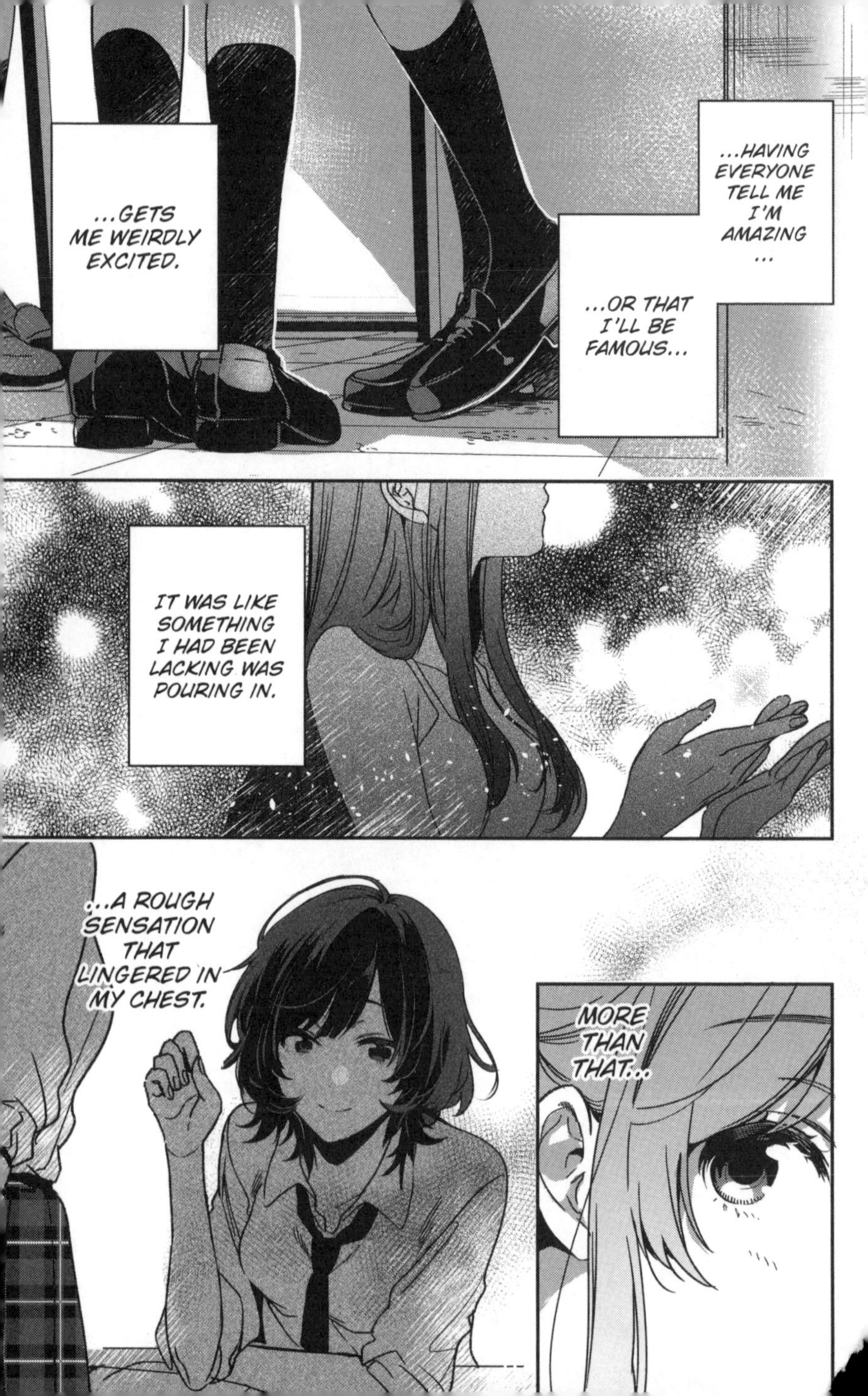
...HAVING EVERYONE TELL ME I'M AMAZING ...
...OR THAT I'LL BE FAMOUS...
...GETS ME WEIRDLY EXCITED.
IT WAS LIKE SOMETHING I HAD BEEN LACKING WAS POURING IN.
MORE THAN THAT...
...A ROUGH SENSATION THAT LINGERED IN MY CHEST.

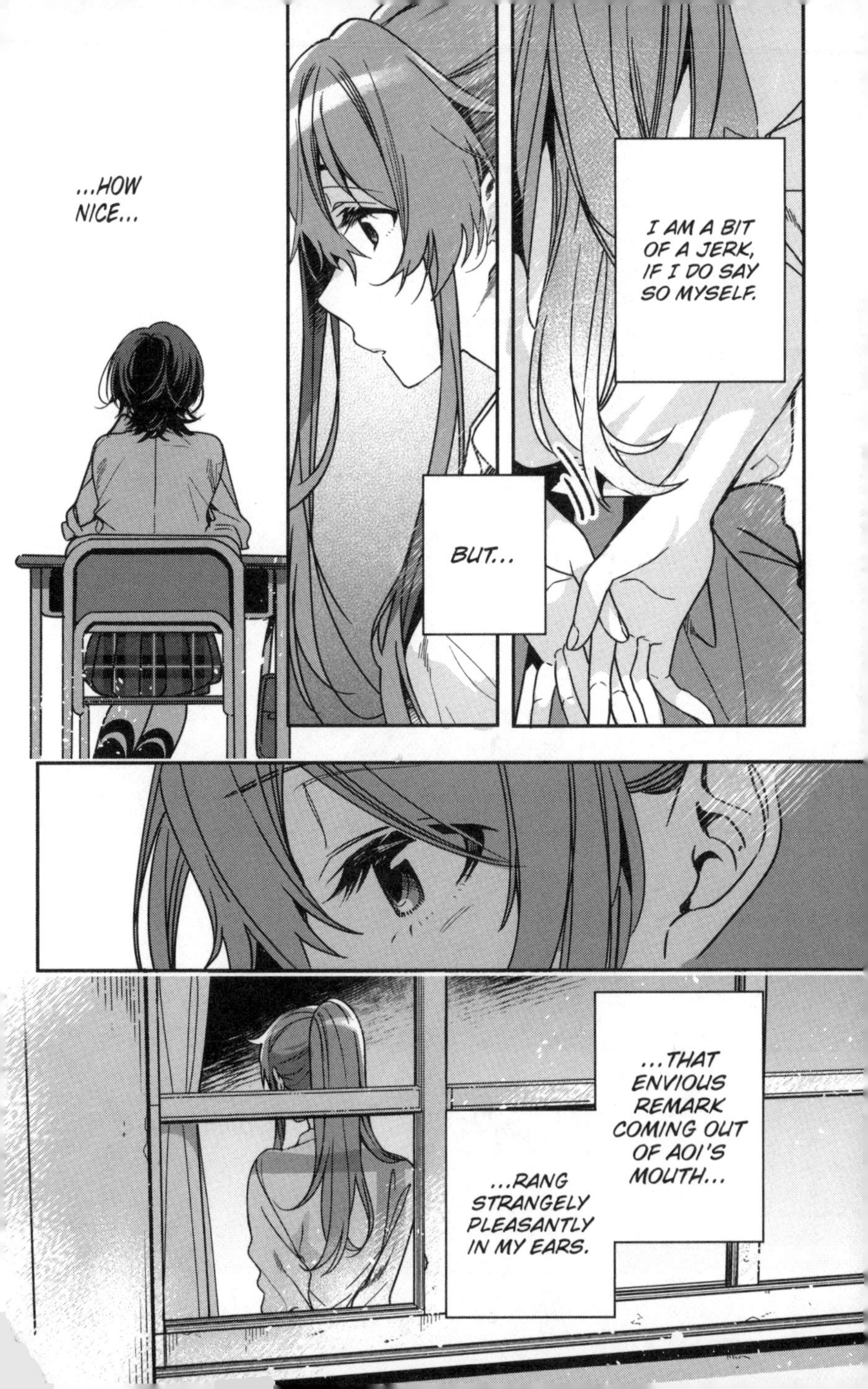
I AM A BIT OF A JERK, IF I DO SAY SO MYSELF.
BUT...
...HOW NICE...
...THAT ENVIOUS REMARK COMING OUT OF AOI'S MOUTH...
...RANG STRANGELY PLEASANTLY IN MY EARS.

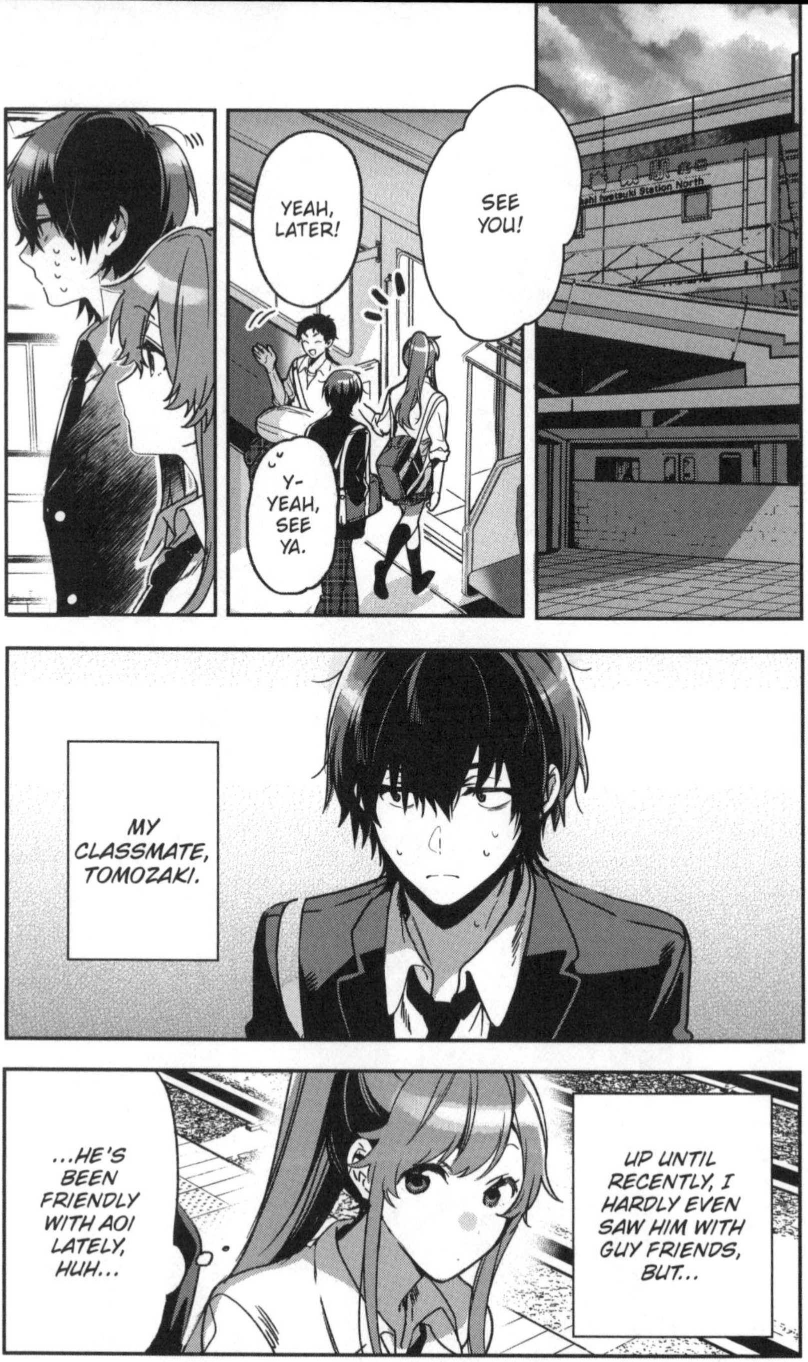
Station North
SEE YOU!
YEAH, LATER!
Y-YEAH, SEE YA.
MY CLASSMATE, TOMOZAKI.
UP UNTIL RECENTLY, I HARDLY EVEN SAW HIM WITH GUY FRIENDS, BUT...
...HE'S BEEN FRIENDLY WITH AOI LATELY, HUH...

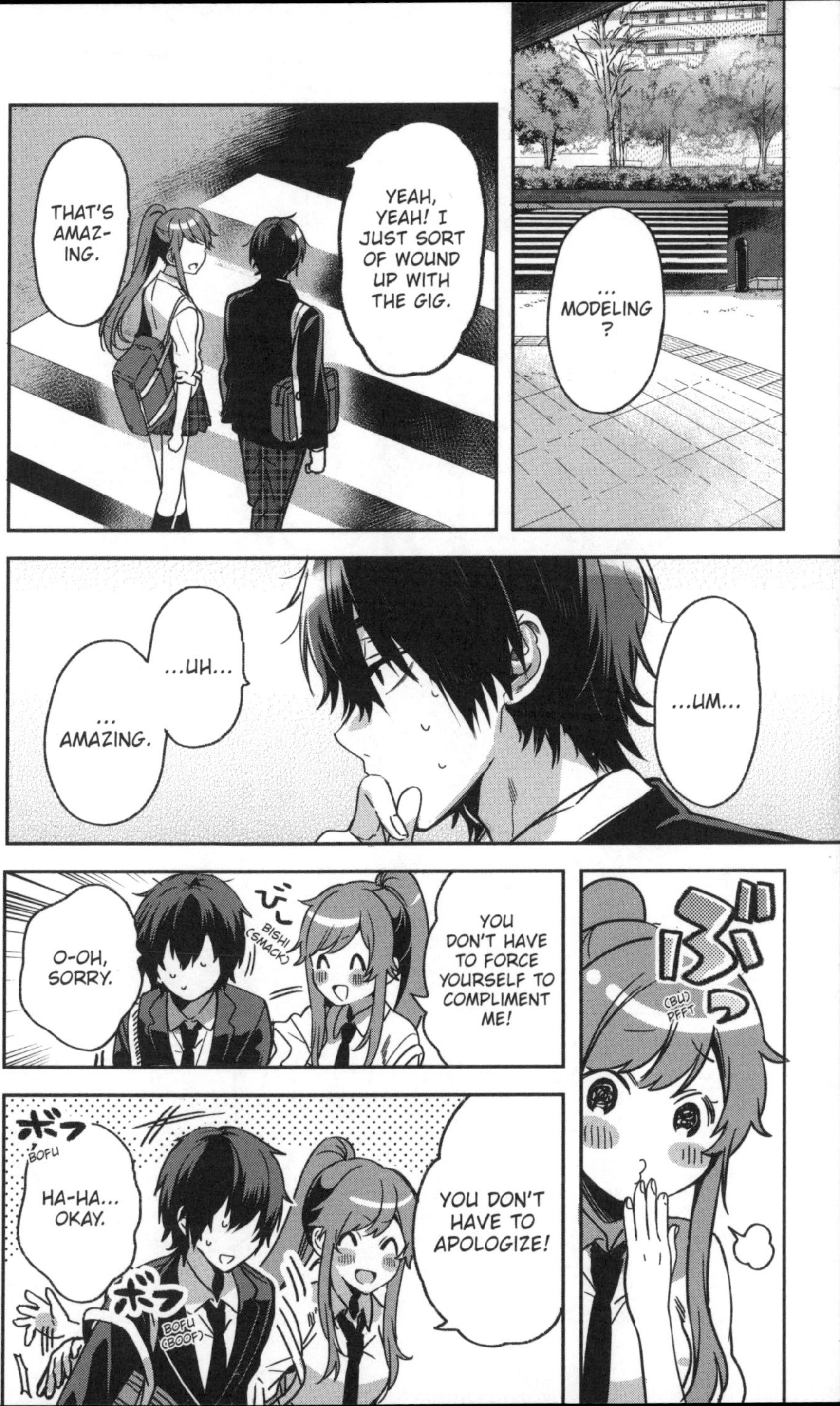
...MODELING?
YEAH, YEAH! I JUST SORT OF WOUND UP WITH THE GIG.
THAT'S AMAZ-ING.
...UM...
...UH...
...AMAZING.
ぶっ
(BU) PFFT
YOU DON'T HAVE TO FORCE YOURSELF TO COMPLIMENT ME!
びし
BISHI (SMACK)
O-OH, SORRY.
YOU DON'T HAVE TO APOLOGIZE!
ボフ
BOFU (BOOF)
ボフ
BOFU
HA-HA... OKAY.

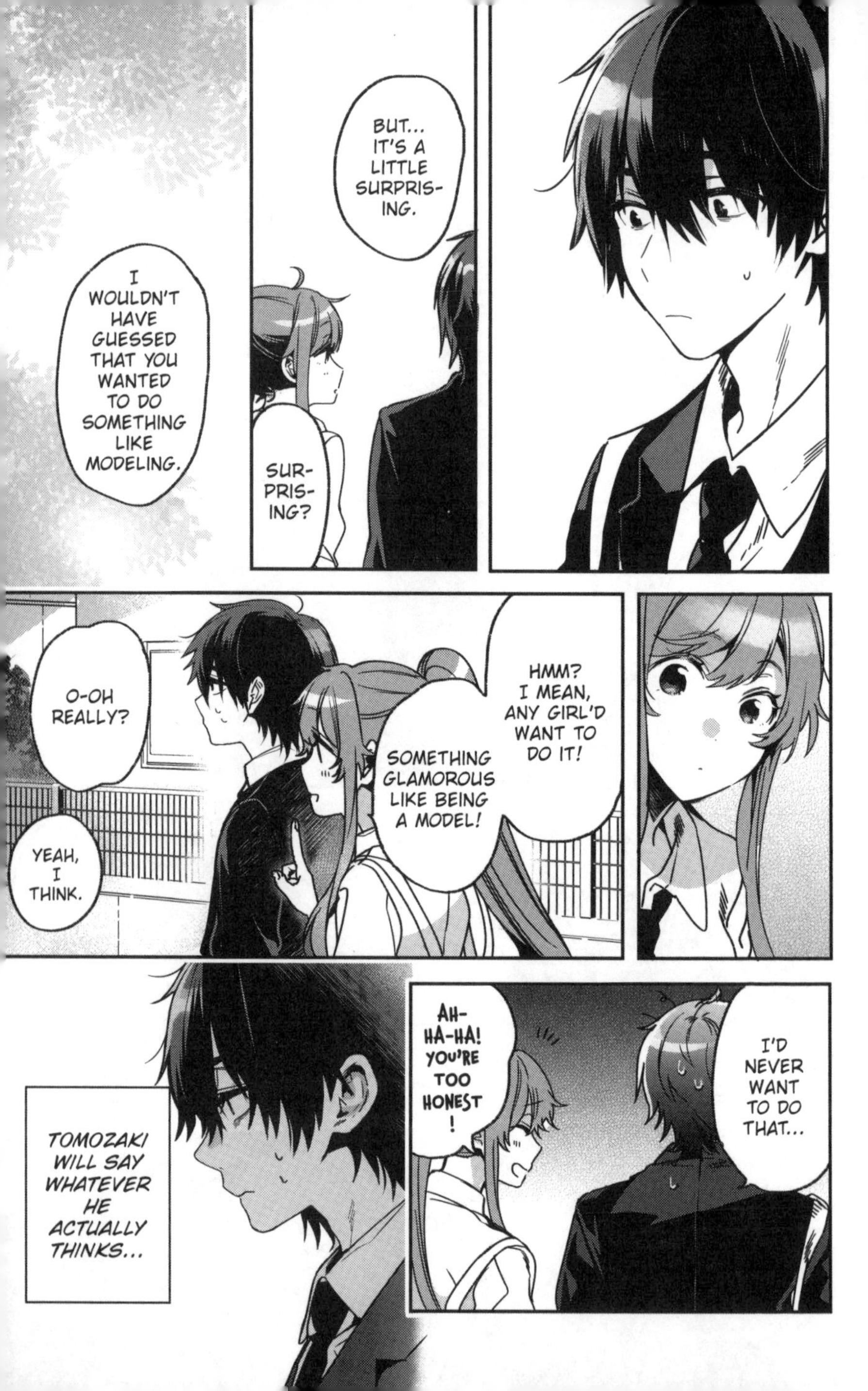
BUT... IT'S A LITTLE SURPRIS-ING.
SUR-PRIS-ING?
I WOULDN'T HAVE GUESSED THAT YOU WANTED TO DO SOMETHING LIKE MODELING.
HMM? I MEAN, ANY GIRL'D WANT TO DO IT!
SOMETHING GLAMOROUS LIKE BEING A MODEL!
O-OH REALLY?
YEAH, I THINK.
I'D NEVER WANT TO DO THAT...
AH-HA-HA! YOU'RE TOO HONEST!
TOMOZAKI WILL SAY WHATEVER HE ACTUALLY THINKS...

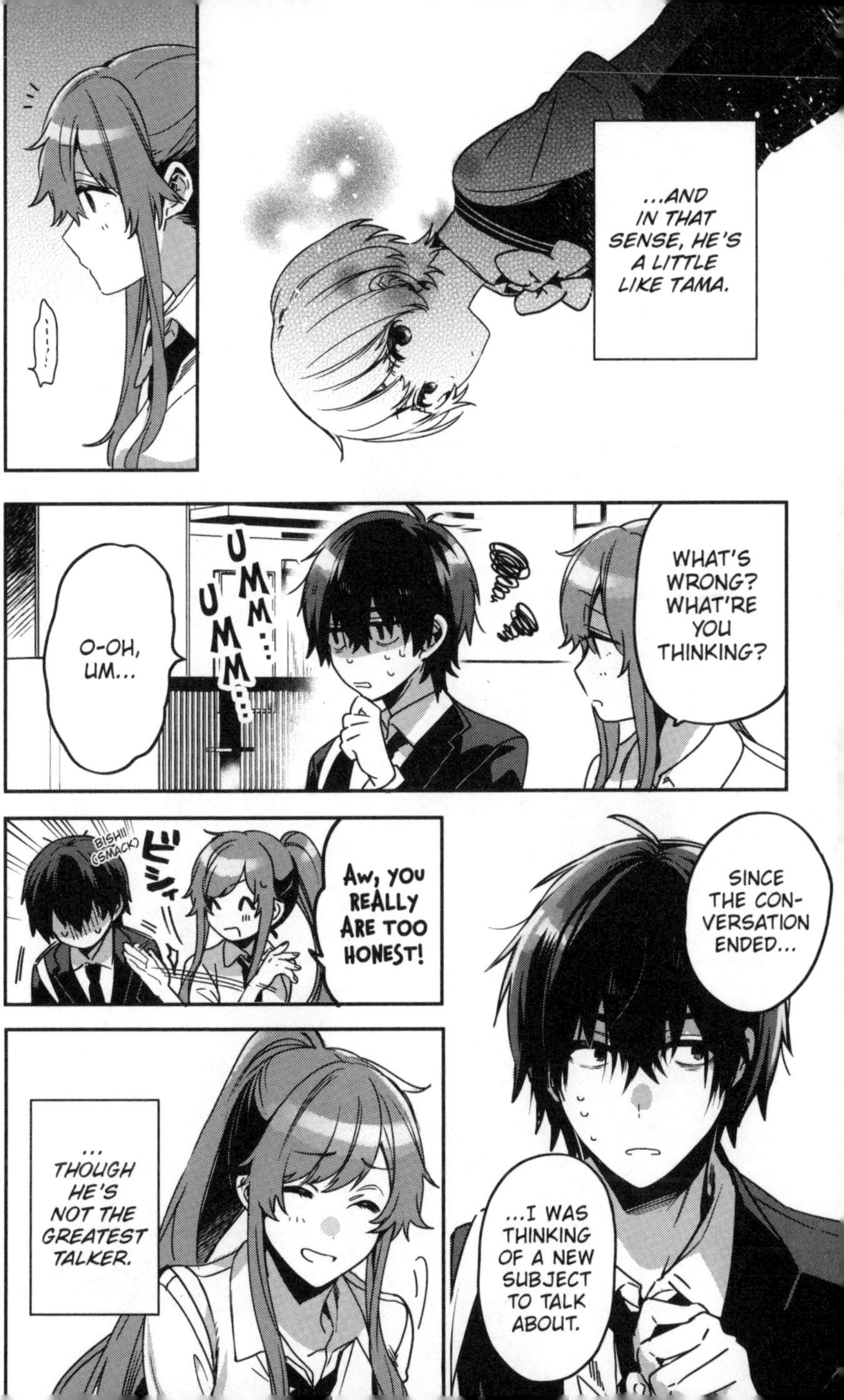
...AND IN THAT SENSE, HE'S A LITTLE LIKE TAMA.
......
WHAT'S WRONG? WHAT'RE YOU THINKING?
UMM...
UMM...
O-OH, UM...
SINCE THE CON-VERSATION ENDED...
...I WAS THINKING OF A NEW SUBJECT TO TALK ABOUT.
BISHII (SMACK)
Aw, YOU REALLY ARE TOO HONEST!
...THOUGH HE'S NOT THE GREATEST TALKER.

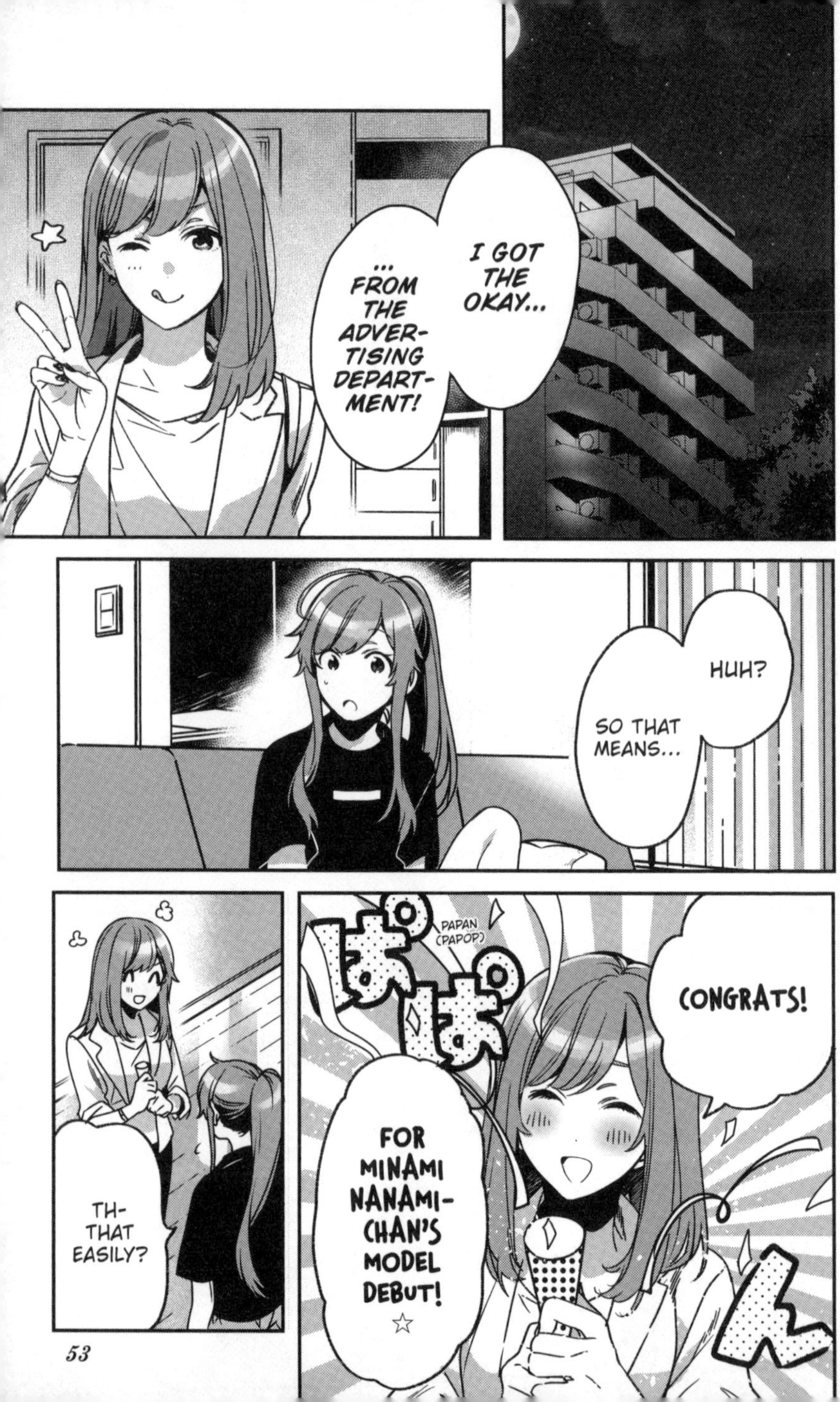
I GOT THE OKAY...
...FROM THE ADVERTISING DEPARTMENT!
HUH?
SO THAT MEANS...
PAPAN (PAPOP)
CONGRATS!
FOR MINAMI NANAMI-CHAN'S MODEL DEBUT! ☆
TH-THAT EASILY?

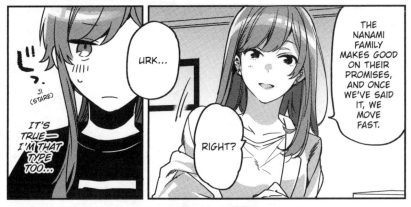

JI (STARE)

URK...

IT'S TRUE — I'M THAT TYPE TOO...

THE NANAMI FAMILY MAKES GOOD ON THEIR PROMISES, AND ONCE WE'VE SAID IT, WE MOVE FAST.

RIGHT?

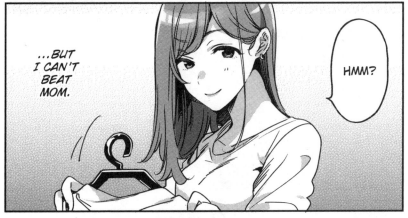

...BUT I CAN'T BEAT MOM.

HMM?

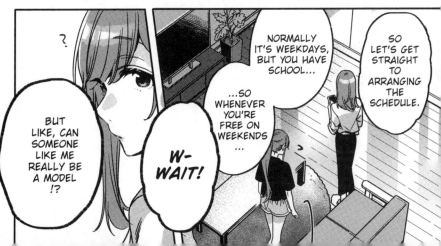

?

NORMALLY IT'S WEEKDAYS, BUT YOU HAVE SCHOOL...

SO LET'S GET STRAIGHT TO ARRANGING THE SCHEDULE.

...SO WHENEVER YOU'RE FREE ON WEEKENDS...

BUT LIKE, CAN SOMEONE LIKE ME REALLY BE A MODEL!?

W-WAIT!

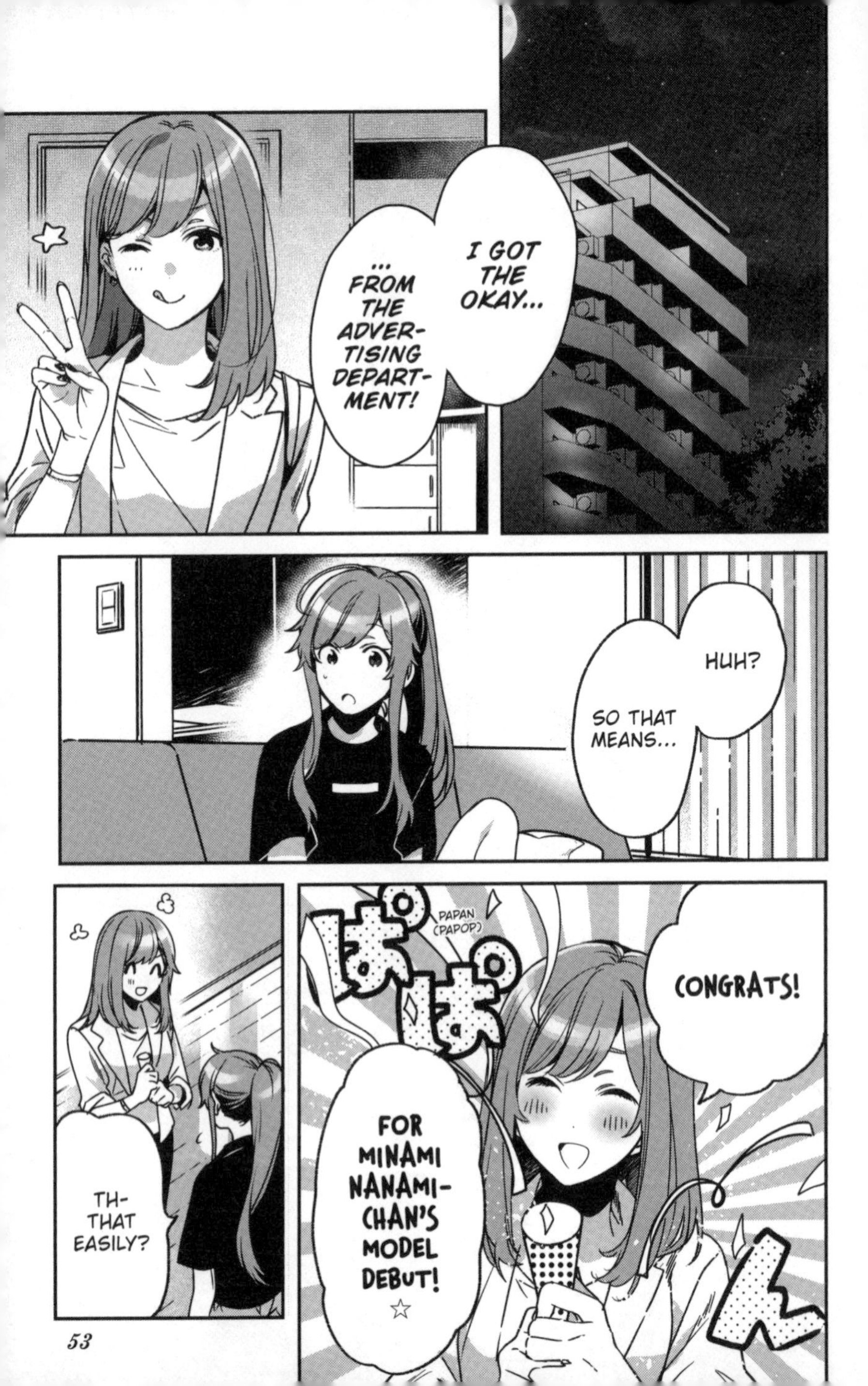
I GOT THE OKAY...
... FROM THE ADVERTISING DEPARTMENT!
HUH?
SO THAT MEANS...
PAPAN (PAPOP)
CONGRATS!
FOR MINAMI NANAMI-CHAN'S MODEL DEBUT! ☆
TH-THAT EASILY?

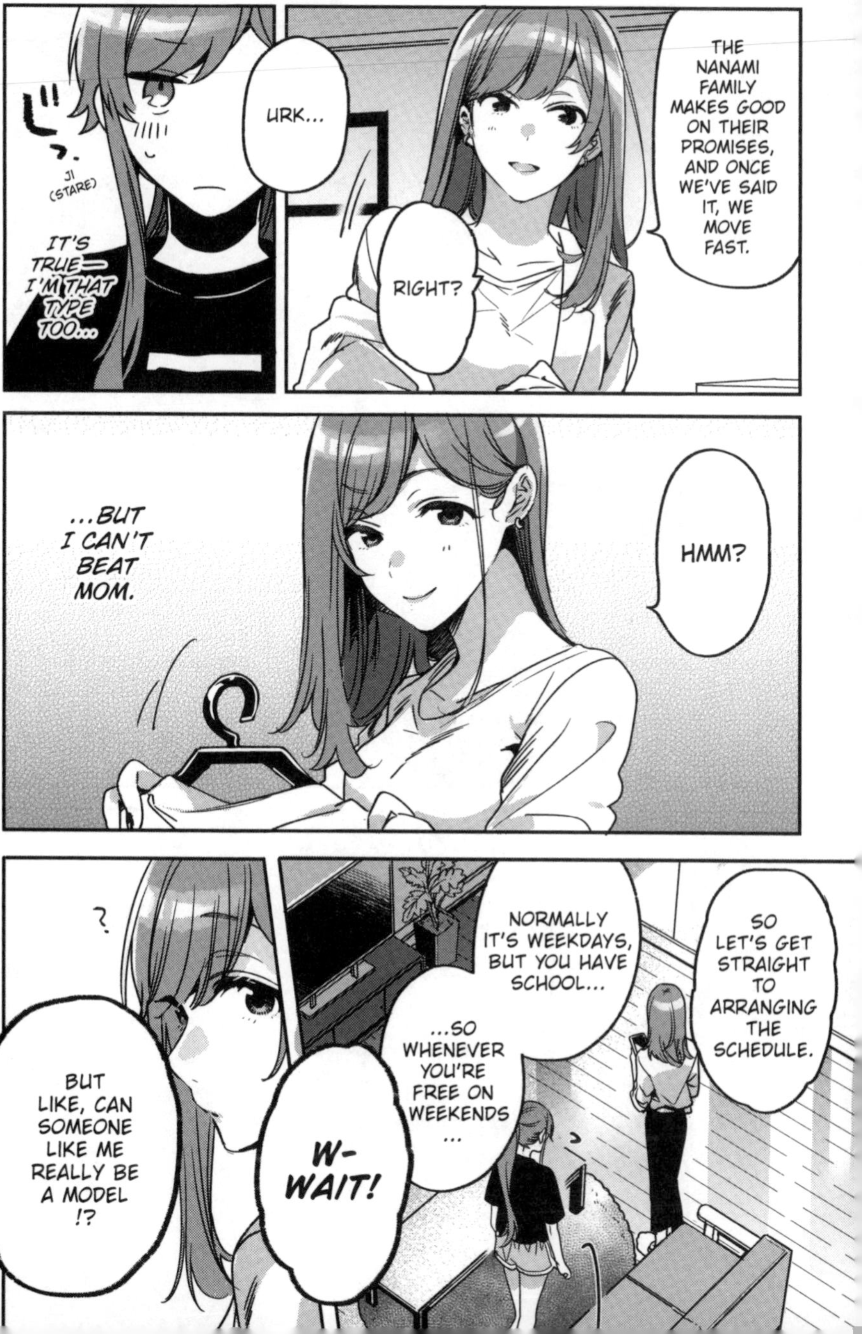
THE NANAMI FAMILY MAKES GOOD ON THEIR PROMISES, AND ONCE WE'VE SAID IT, WE MOVE FAST.
RIGHT?
URK...
JI (STARE)
IT'S TRUE— I'M THAT TYPE TOO...
HMM?
...BUT I CAN'T BEAT MOM.
SO LET'S GET STRAIGHT TO ARRANGING THE SCHEDULE.
NORMALLY IT'S WEEKDAYS, BUT YOU HAVE SCHOOL...
...SO WHENEVER YOU'RE FREE ON WEEKENDS...
?
W-WAIT!
BUT LIKE, CAN SOMEONE LIKE ME REALLY BE A MODEL!?

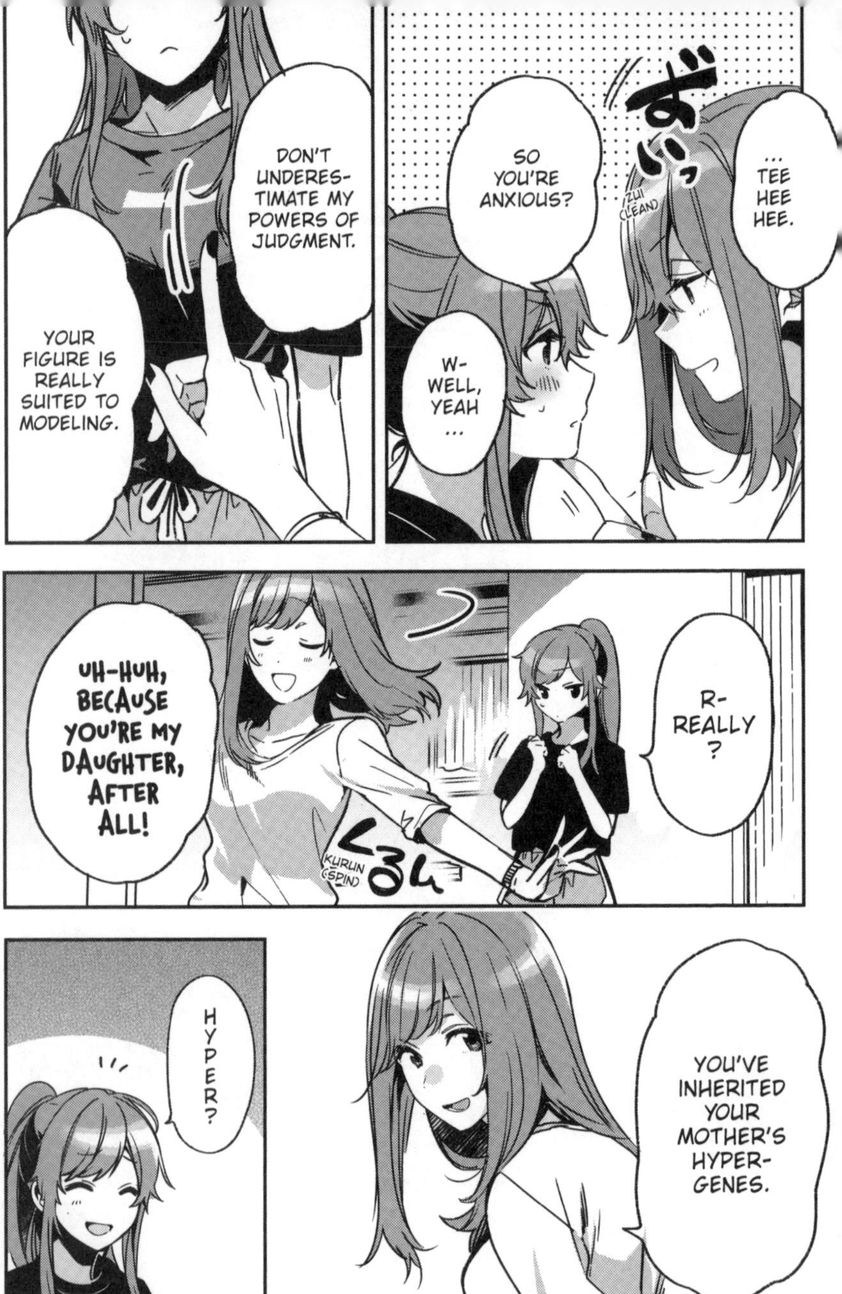

... TEE HEE HEE.
ZUI (LEAN)
SO YOU'RE ANXIOUS?
W-WELL, YEAH ...
DON'T UNDERESTIMATE MY POWERS OF JUDGMENT.
YOUR FIGURE IS REALLY SUITED TO MODELING.
R-REALLY?
UH-HUH, BECAUSE YOU'RE MY DAUGHTER, AFTER ALL!
KURUN (SPIN)
YOU'VE INHERITED YOUR MOTHER'S HYPER-GENES.
HYPER?

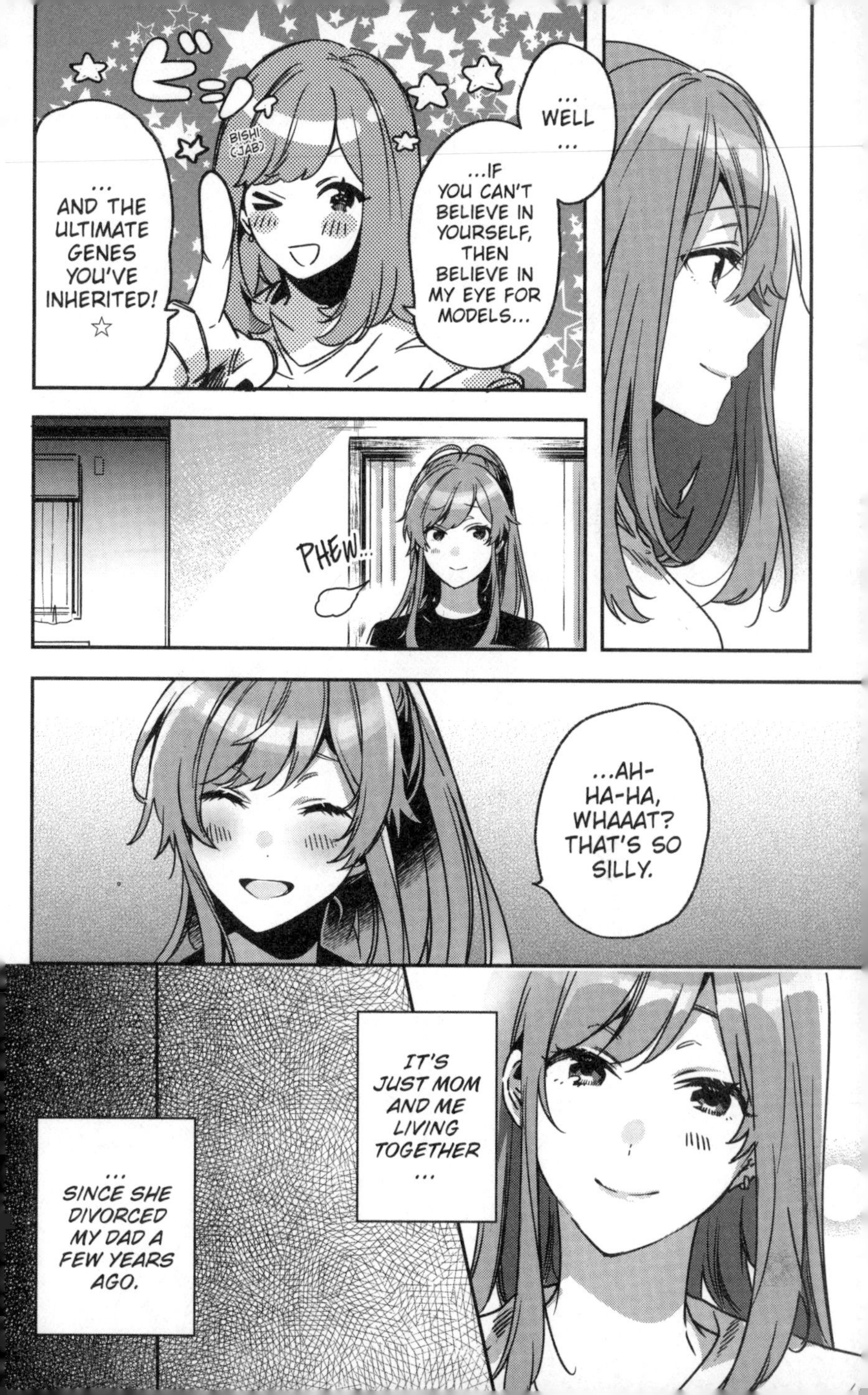
... WELL ...
...IF YOU CAN'T BELIEVE IN YOURSELF, THEN BELIEVE IN MY EYE FOR MODELS...
BISHI (JAB)
... AND THE ULTIMATE GENES YOU'VE INHERITED! ☆
PHEW...
...AH-HA-HA, WHAAAT? THAT'S SO SILLY.
IT'S JUST MOM AND ME LIVING TOGETHER ...
... SINCE SHE DIVORCED MY DAD A FEW YEARS AGO.

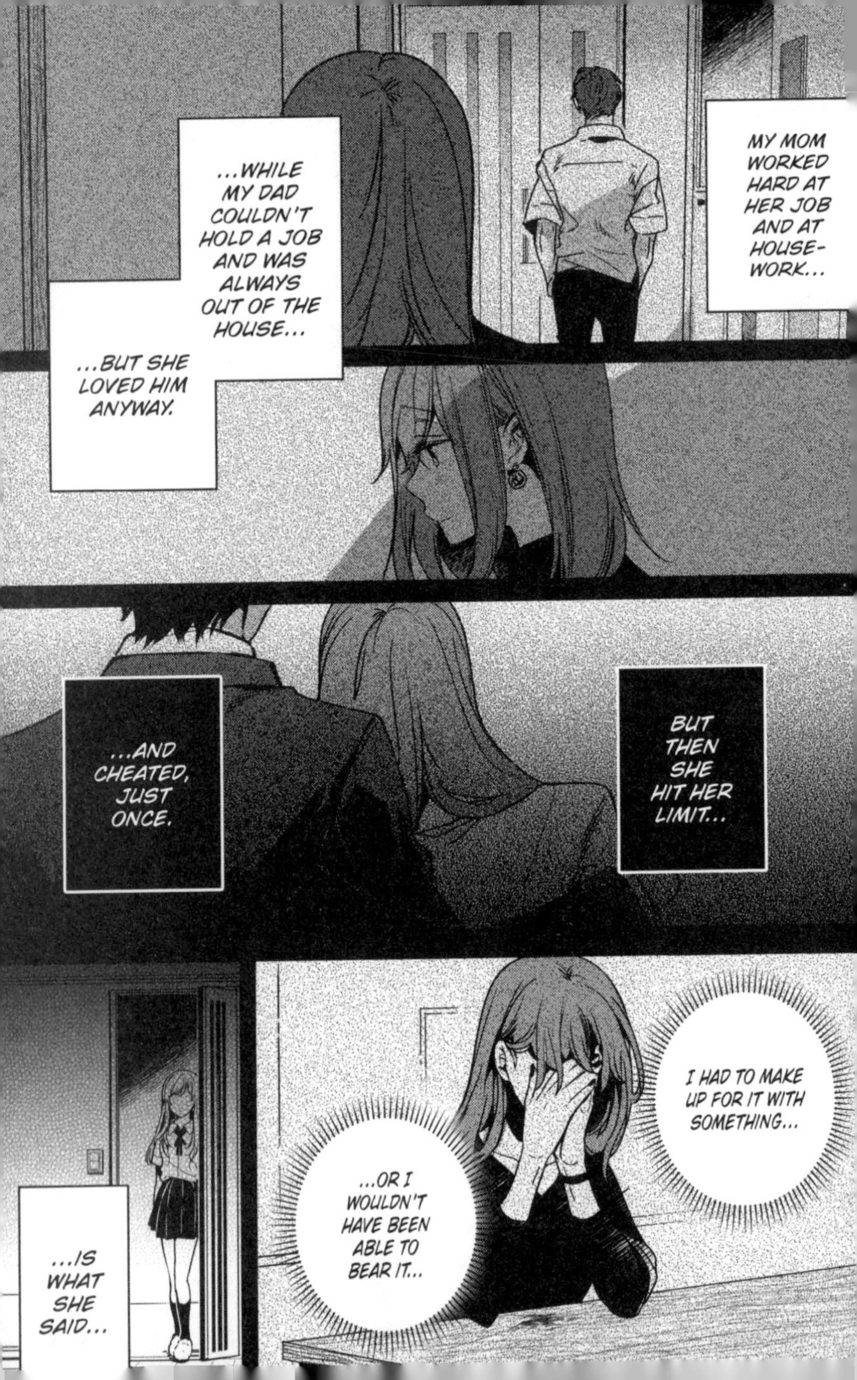

MY MOM WORKED HARD AT HER JOB AND AT HOUSE-WORK...
...WHILE MY DAD COULDN'T HOLD A JOB AND WAS ALWAYS OUT OF THE HOUSE...
...BUT SHE LOVED HIM ANYWAY.
BUT THEN SHE HIT HER LIMIT...
...AND CHEATED, JUST ONCE.
I HAD TO MAKE UP FOR IT WITH SOMETHING...
...OR I WOULDN'T HAVE BEEN ABLE TO BEAR IT...
...IS WHAT SHE SAID...

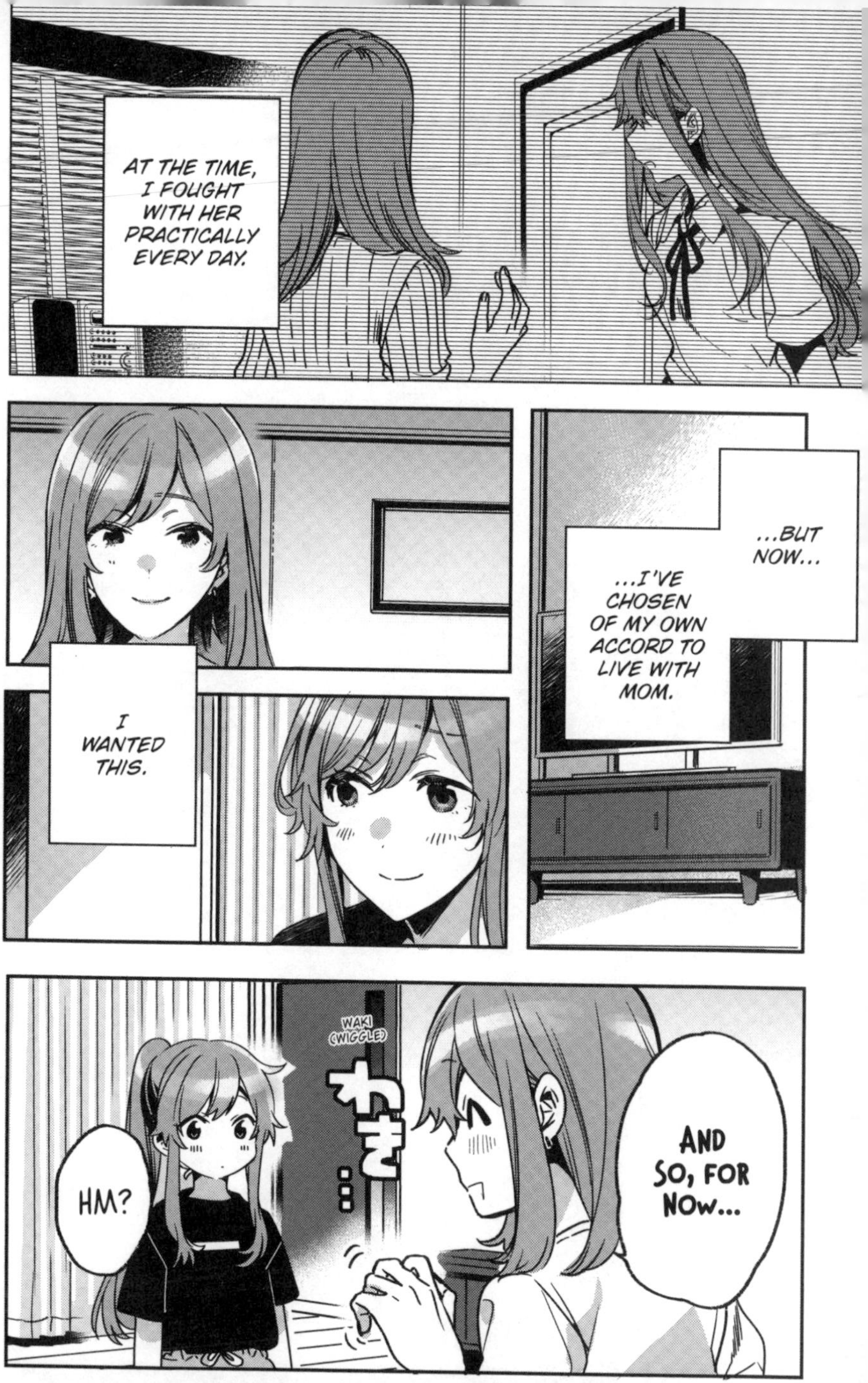
AT THE TIME, I FOUGHT WITH HER PRACTICALLY EVERY DAY.
...BUT NOW...
...I'VE CHOSEN OF MY OWN ACCORD TO LIVE WITH MOM.
I WANTED THIS.
AND SO, FOR NOW...
わき…
WAKI (WIGGLE)
HM?

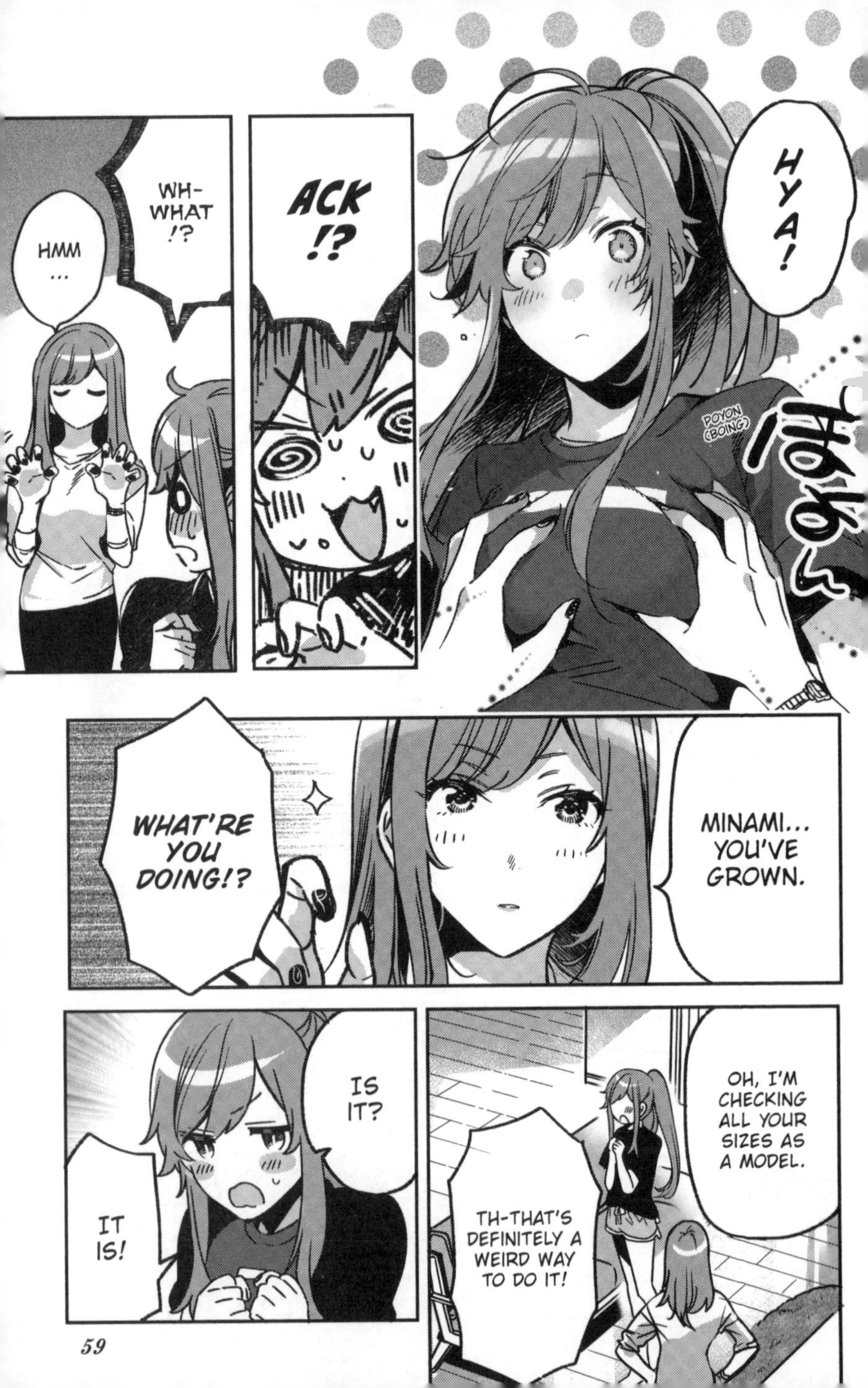
HYA!
ぽよん
POYON (BOING)
ACK!?
WH-WHAT!?
HMM...
MINAMI... YOU'VE GROWN.
WHAT'RE YOU DOING!?
OH, I'M CHECKING ALL YOUR SIZES AS A MODEL.
TH-THAT'S DEFINITELY A WEIRD WAY TO DO IT!
IS IT?
IT IS!

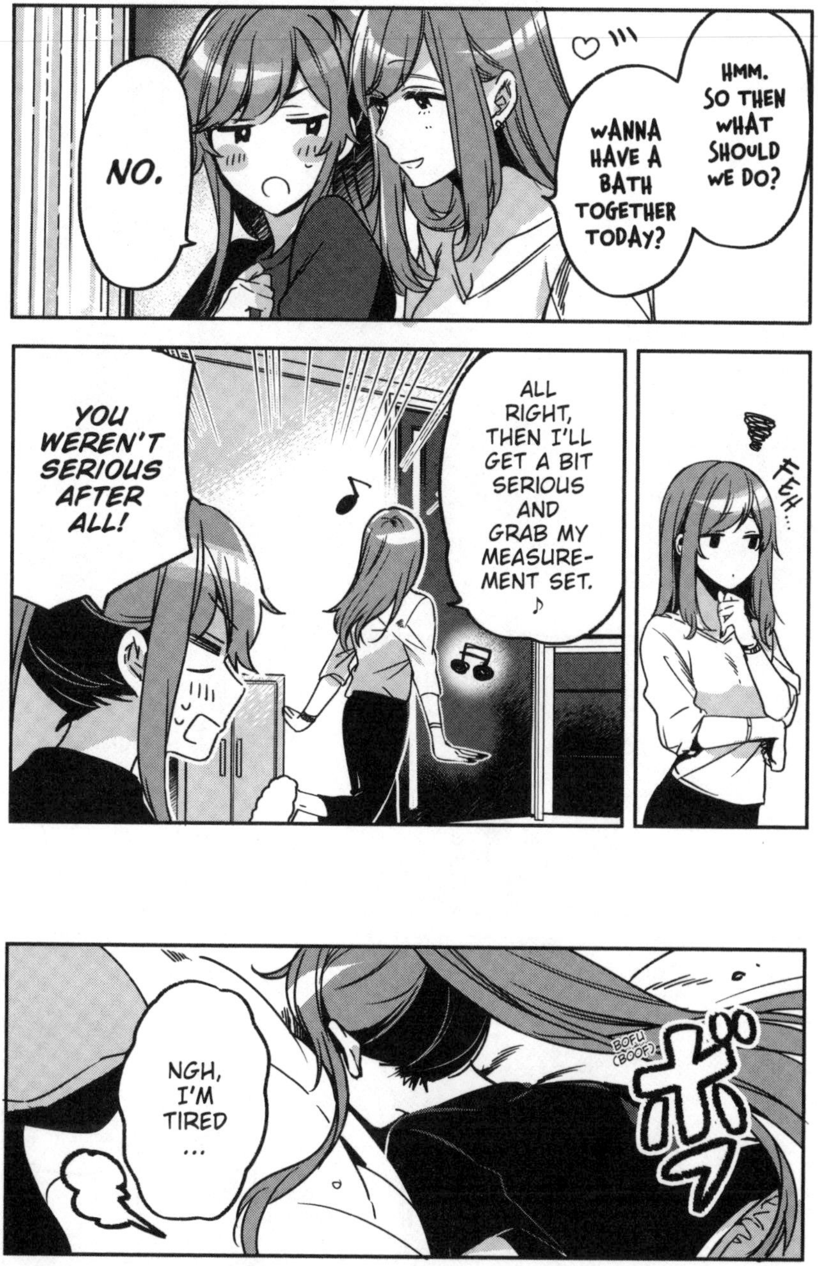
HMM. SO THEN WHAT SHOULD WE DO?
WANNA HAVE A BATH TOGETHER TODAY?
NO.
FEH...
ALL RIGHT, THEN I'LL GET A BIT SERIOUS AND GRAB MY MEASUREMENT SET. ♪
YOU WEREN'T SERIOUS AFTER ALL!
ボフッ
BOFU (BOOF)
NGH, I'M TIRED ...

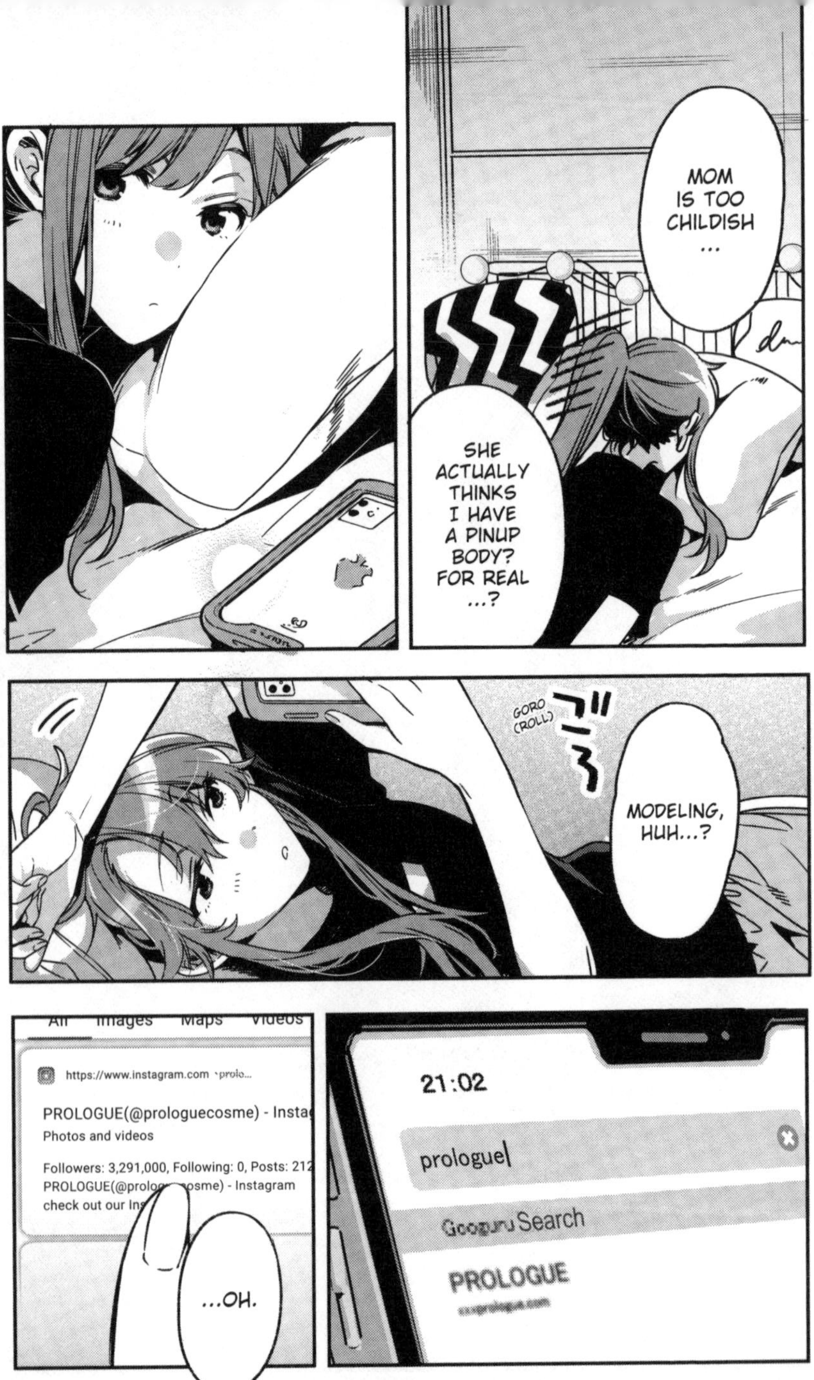
MOM IS TOO CHILDISH ...
SHE ACTUALLY THINKS I HAVE A PINUP BODY? FOR REAL ...?
GORO (ROLL)
MODELING, HUH...?
21:02
prologue
Googuru Search
PROLOGUE
https://www.instagram.com › prolo...
PROLOGUE(@prologuecosme) - Instag
Photos and videos
Followers: 3,291,000, Following: 0, Posts: 212
PROLOGUE(@prolo osme) - Instagram
check out our Ins
...OH.

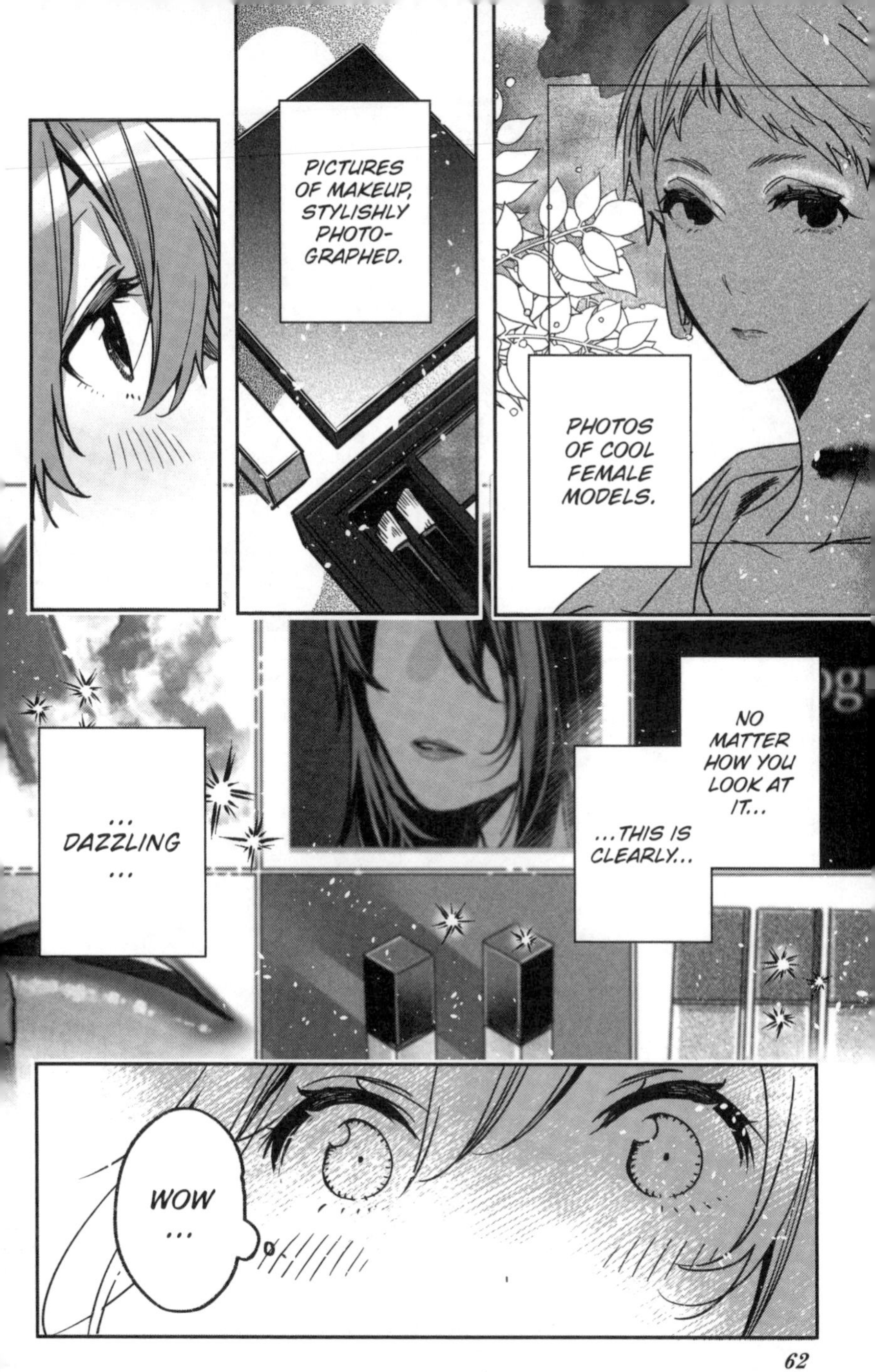
PHOTOS OF COOL FEMALE MODELS.
PICTURES OF MAKEUP, STYLISHLY PHOTO-GRAPHED.
NO MATTER HOW YOU LOOK AT IT...
...THIS IS CLEARLY...
...DAZZLING...
WOW...

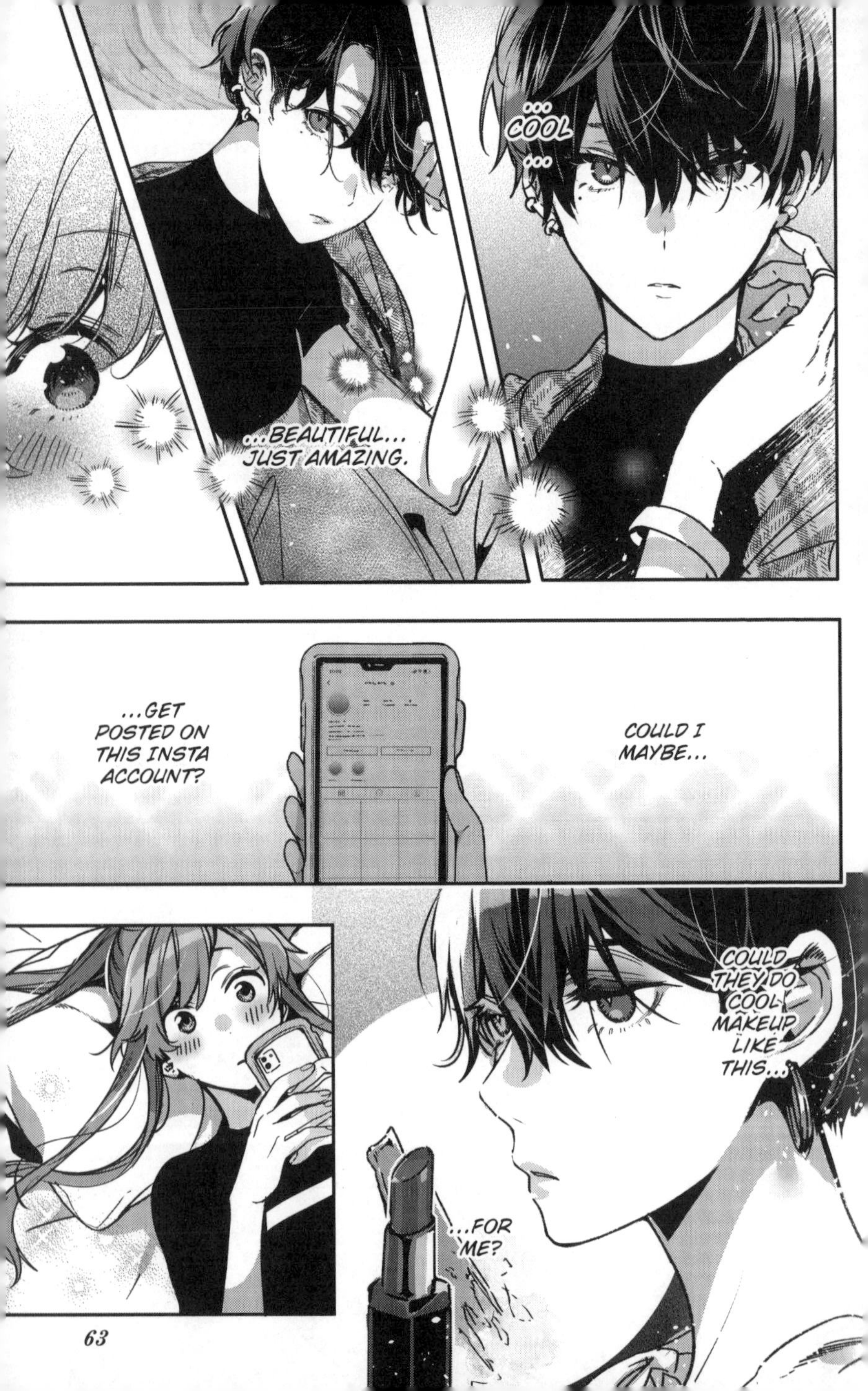
...COOL...
...BEAUTIFUL... JUST AMAZING.
COULD I MAYBE...
...GET POSTED ON THIS INSTA ACCOUNT?
COULD THEY DO COOL MAKEUP LIKE THIS...
...FOR ME?

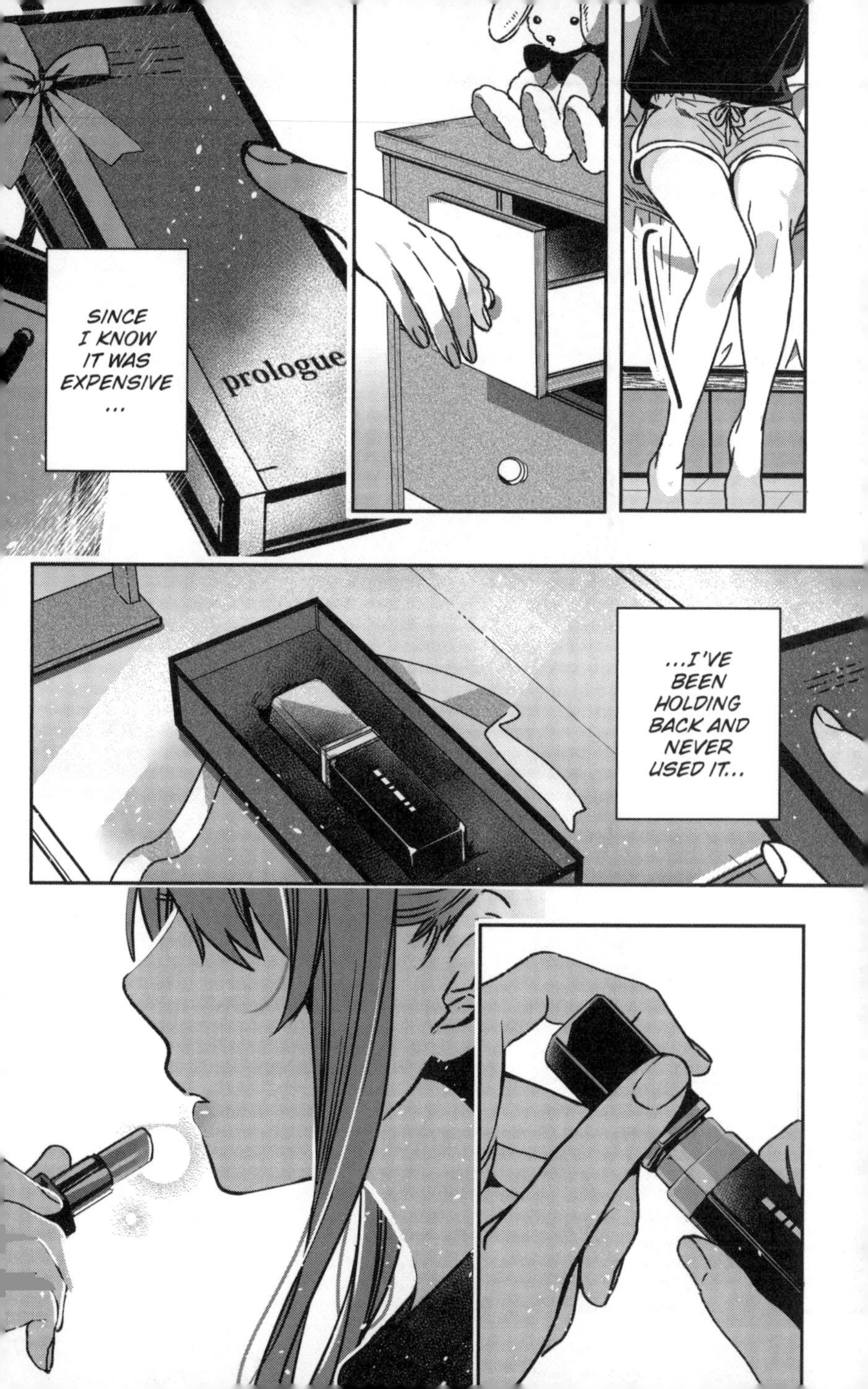
SINCE I KNOW IT WAS EXPENSIVE ...
prologue
...I'VE BEEN HOLDING BACK AND NEVER USED IT...

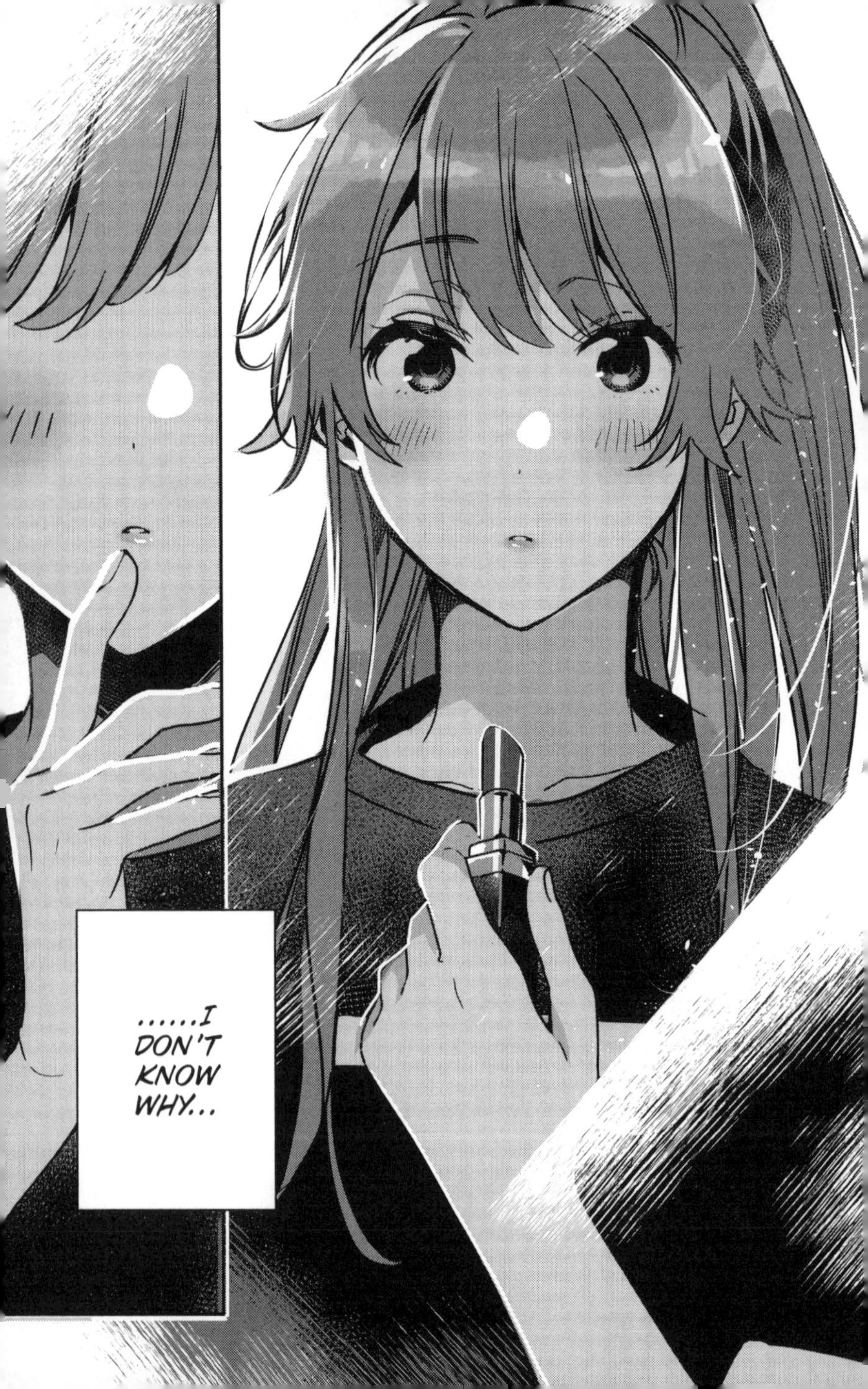
......I DON'T KNOW WHY...

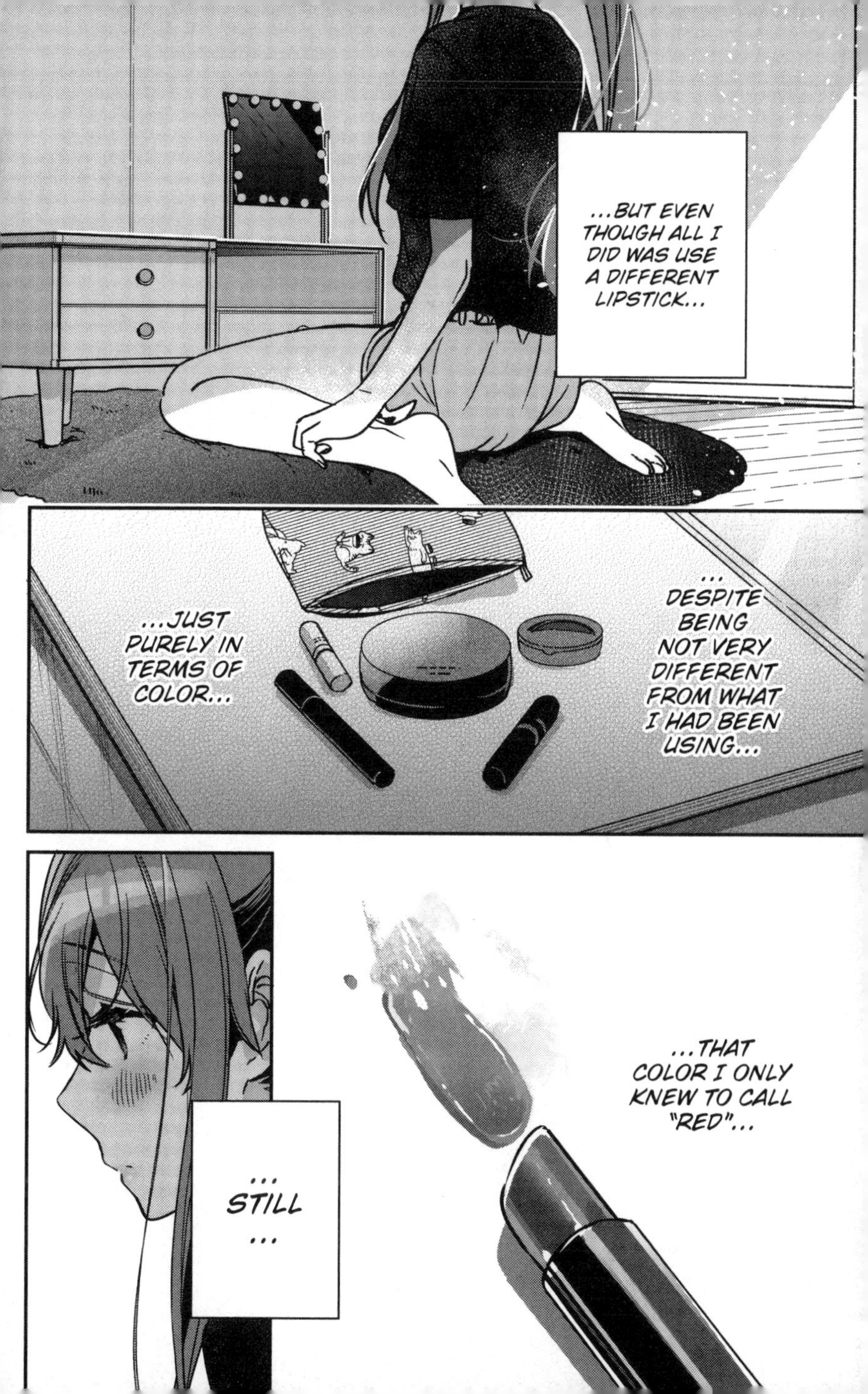
...BUT EVEN THOUGH ALL I DID WAS USE A DIFFERENT LIPSTICK...
...DESPITE BEING NOT VERY DIFFERENT FROM WHAT I HAD BEEN USING...
...JUST PURELY IN TERMS OF COLOR...
...THAT COLOR I ONLY KNEW TO CALL "RED"...
... STILL ...

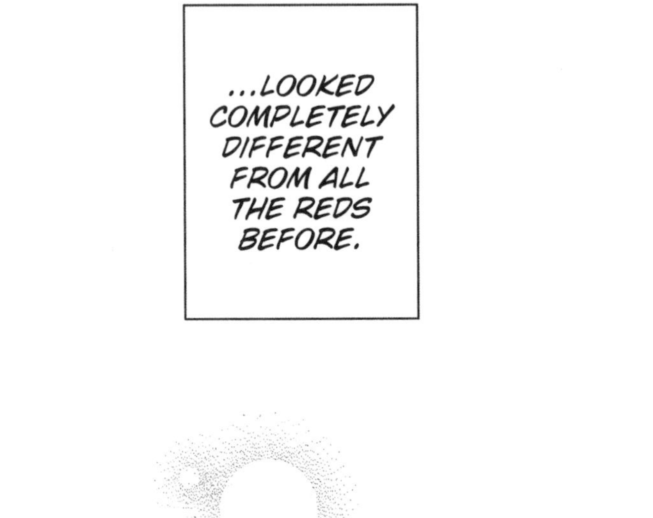

...LOOKED COMPLETELY DIFFERENT FROM ALL THE REDS BEFORE.

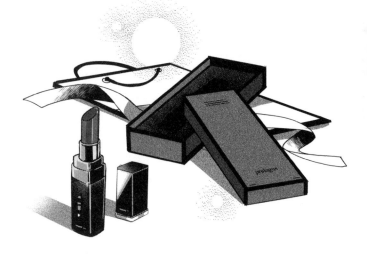

prologue

Minami Nanami
Wants to SHINE

Chapter 3 NEW SELF

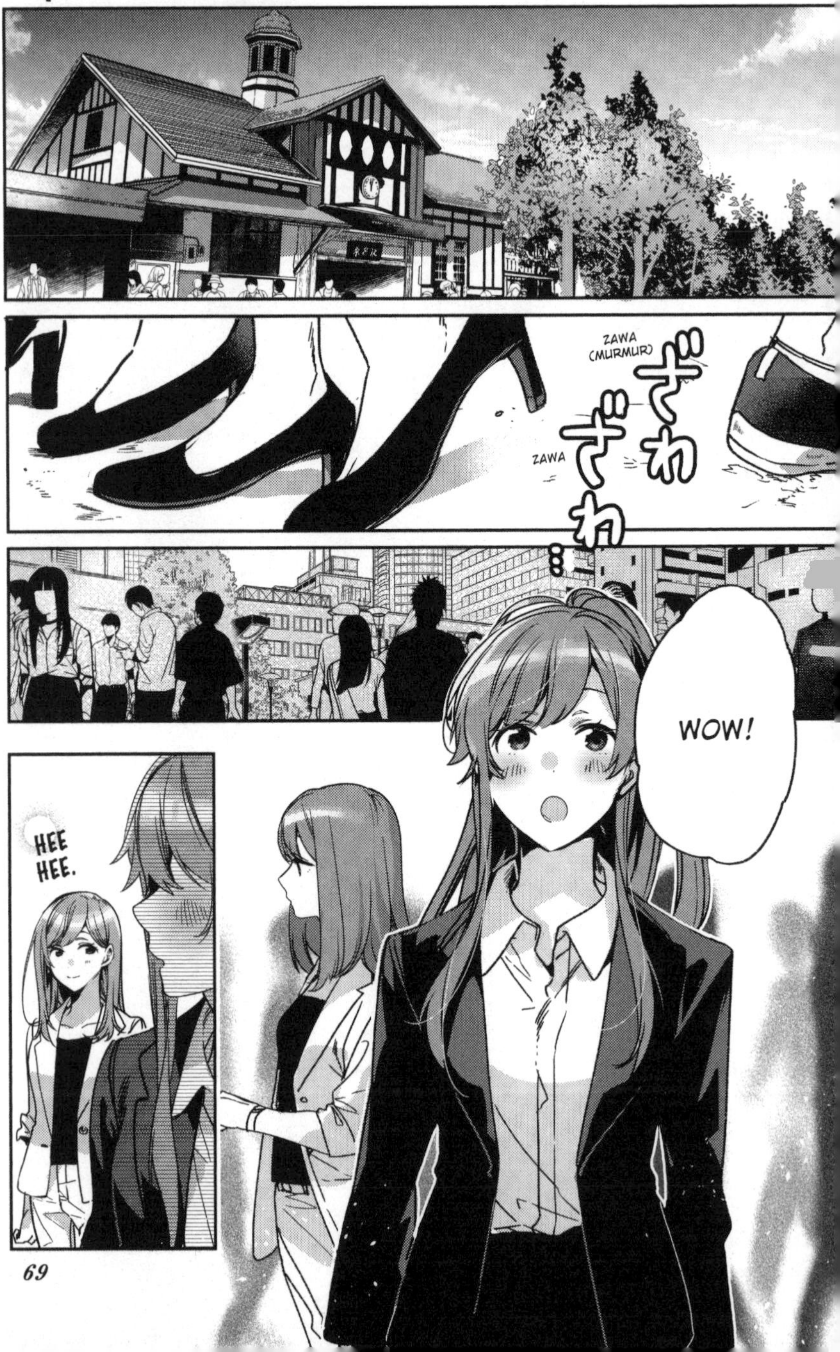
ざわざわ…
ZAWA (MURMUR)
ZAWA
WOW!
HEE HEE.

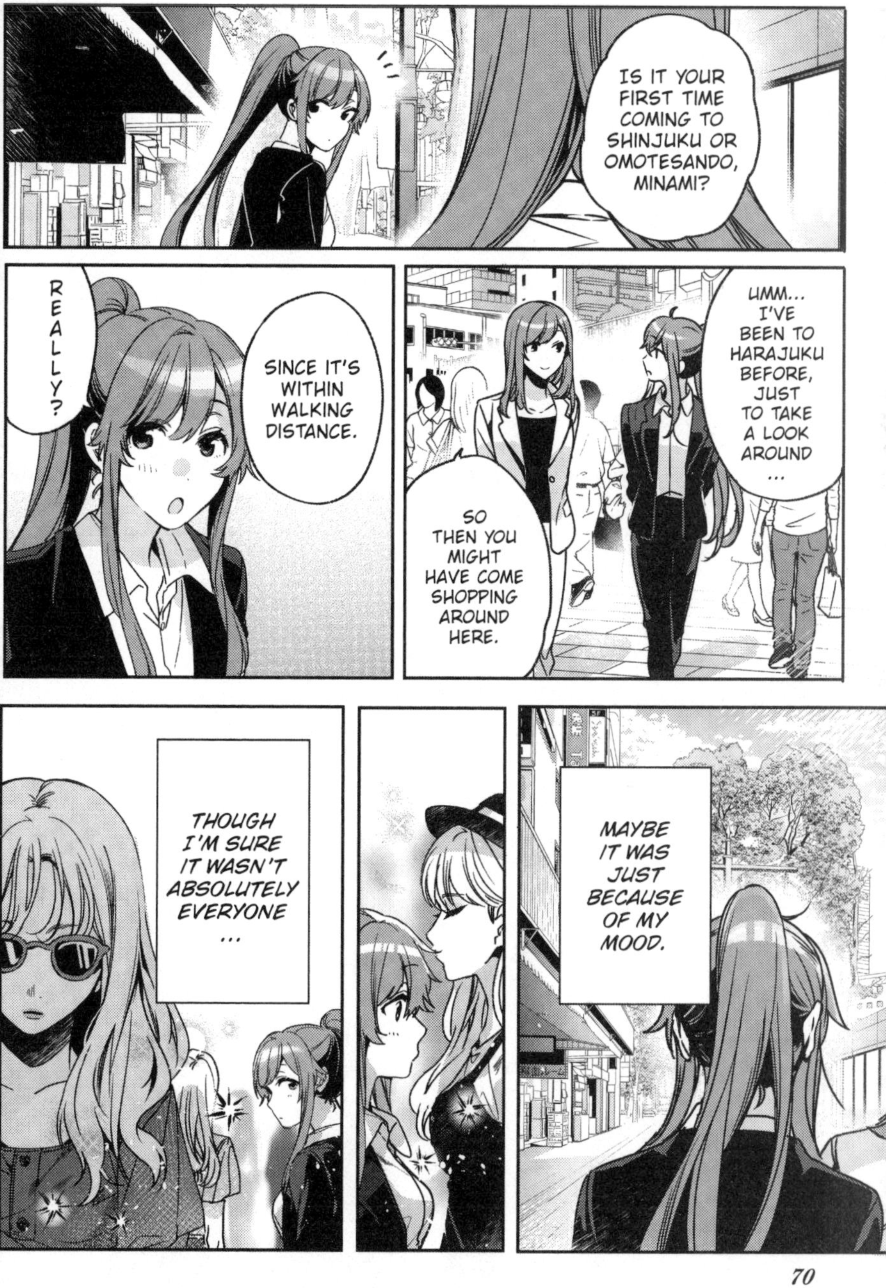
IS IT YOUR FIRST TIME COMING TO SHINJUKU OR OMOTESANDO, MINAMI?
UMM... I'VE BEEN TO HARAJUKU BEFORE, JUST TO TAKE A LOOK AROUND...
SO THEN YOU MIGHT HAVE COME SHOPPING AROUND HERE.
SINCE IT'S WITHIN WALKING DISTANCE.
REALLY?
MAYBE IT WAS JUST BECAUSE OF MY MOOD.
THOUGH I'M SURE IT WASN'T ABSOLUTELY EVERYONE...

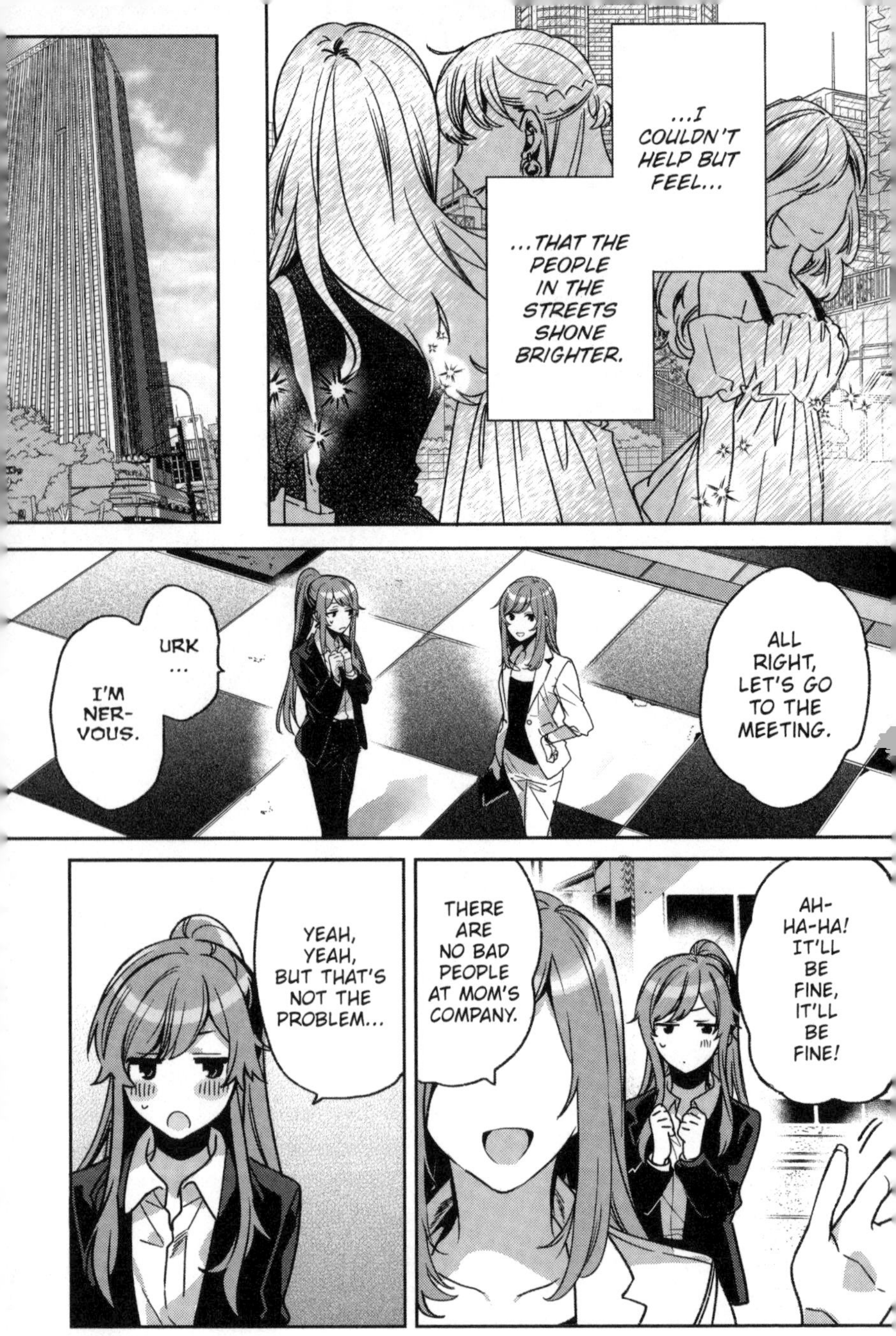
...I COULDN'T HELP BUT FEEL...
...THAT THE PEOPLE IN THE STREETS SHONE BRIGHTER.
ALL RIGHT, LET'S GO TO THE MEETING.
URK... I'M NERVOUS.
AH-HA-HA! IT'LL BE FINE, IT'LL BE FINE!
THERE ARE NO BAD PEOPLE AT MOM'S COMPANY.
YEAH, YEAH, BUT THAT'S NOT THE PROBLEM...

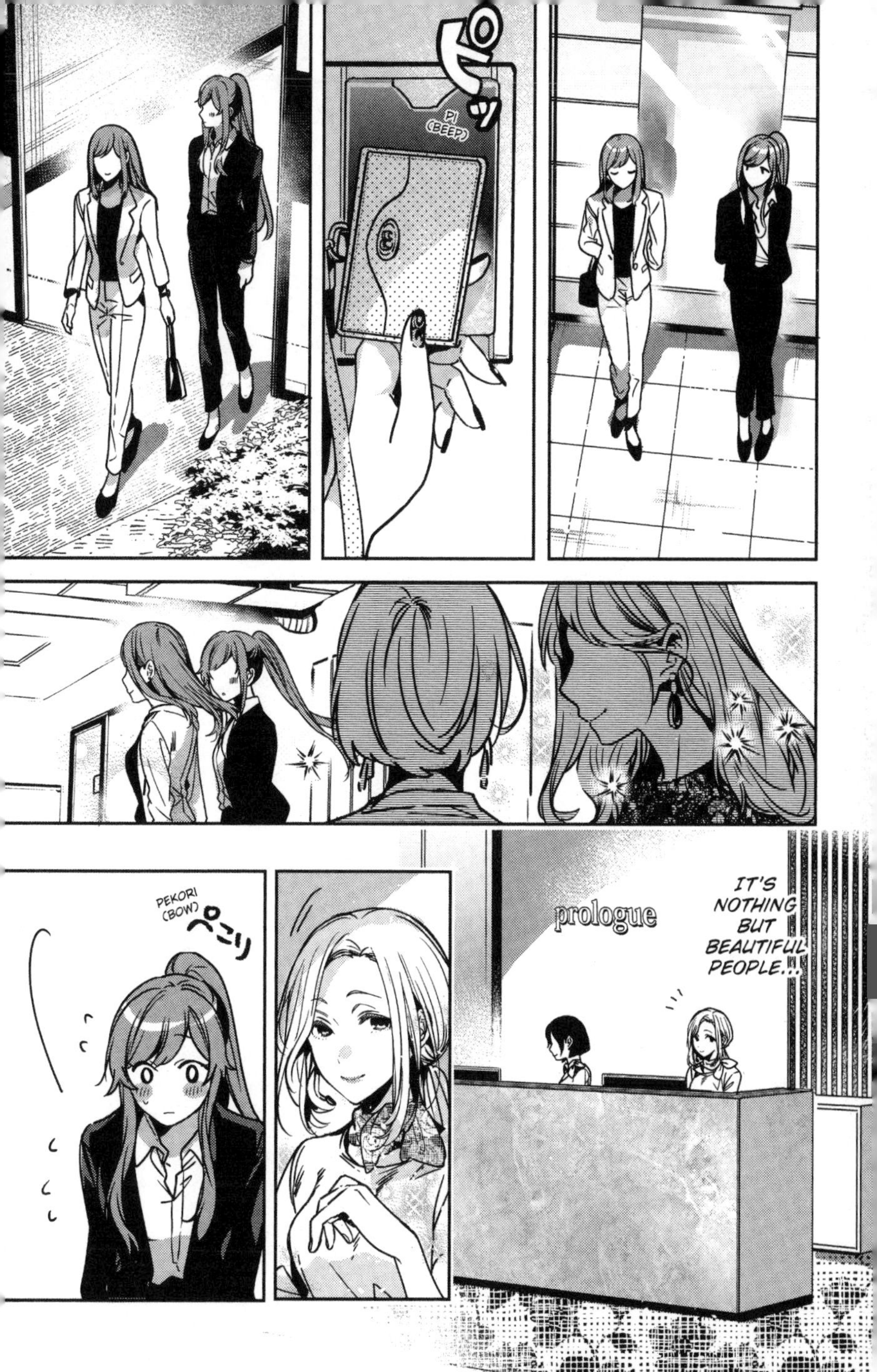
ピッ
PI (BEEP)
IT'S NOTHING BUT BEAUTIFUL PEOPLE...
prologue
ぺこり
PEKORI (BOW)

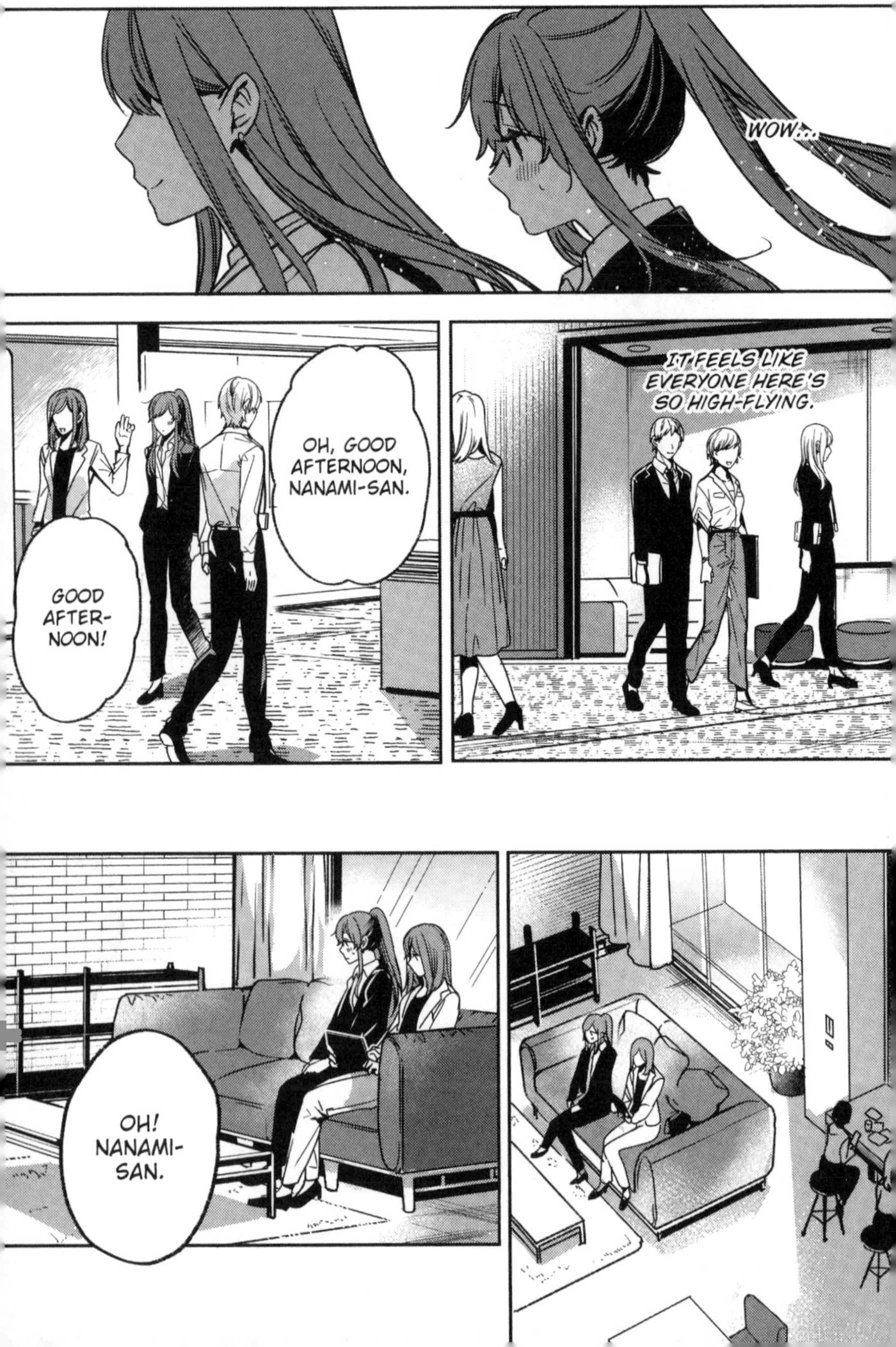
WOW...
IT FEELS LIKE EVERYONE HERE'S SO HIGH-FLYING.
OH, GOOD AFTERNOON, NANAMI-SAN.
GOOD AFTER-NOON!
OH! NANAMI-SAN.

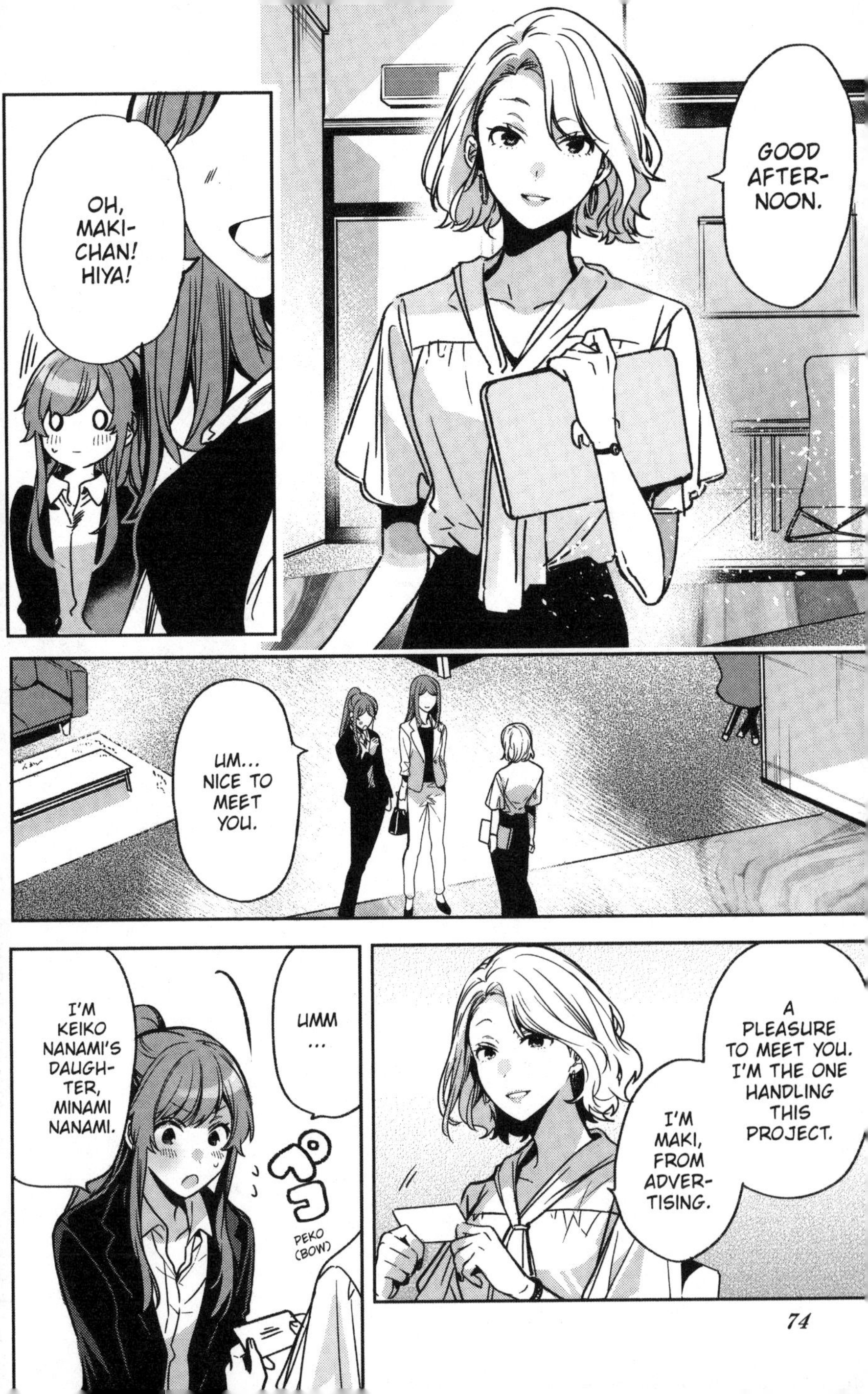
GOOD AFTER-NOON.
OH, MAKI-CHAN! HIYA!
UM... NICE TO MEET YOU.
A PLEASURE TO MEET YOU. I'M THE ONE HANDLING THIS PROJECT.
I'M MAKI, FROM ADVER-TISING.
UMM ...
I'M KEIKO NANAMI'S DAUGH-TER, MINAMI NANAMI.
PEKO (BOW)

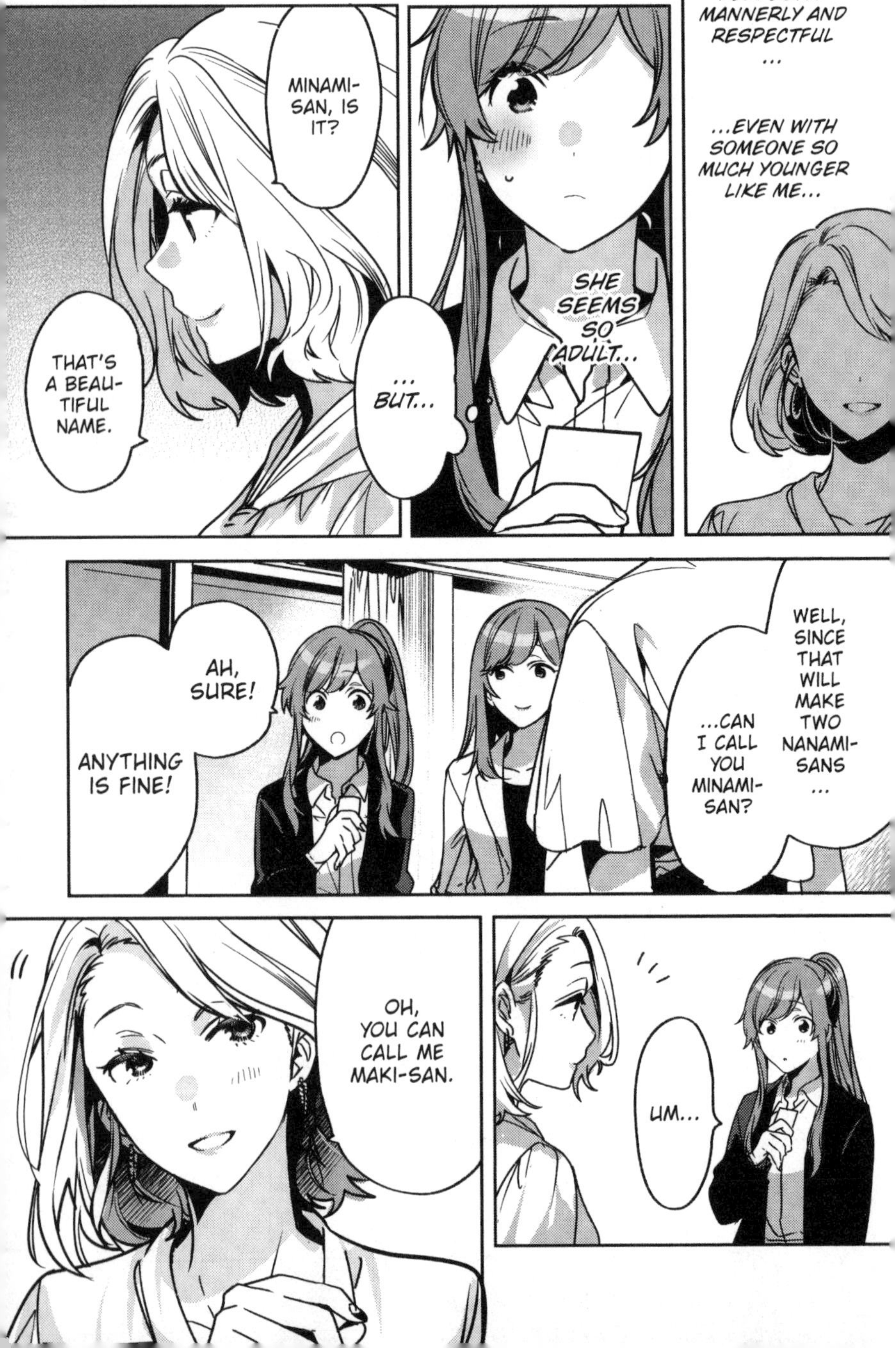
SHE'S SO PERFECTLY MANNERLY AND RESPECTFUL ...
...EVEN WITH SOMEONE SO MUCH YOUNGER LIKE ME...
SHE SEEMS SO ADULT...
... BUT...
MINAMI-SAN, IS IT?
THAT'S A BEAUTIFUL NAME.
WELL, SINCE THAT WILL MAKE TWO NANAMI-SANS ...
...CAN I CALL YOU MINAMI-SAN?
AH, SURE!
ANYTHING IS FINE!
UM...
OH, YOU CAN CALL ME MAKI-SAN.

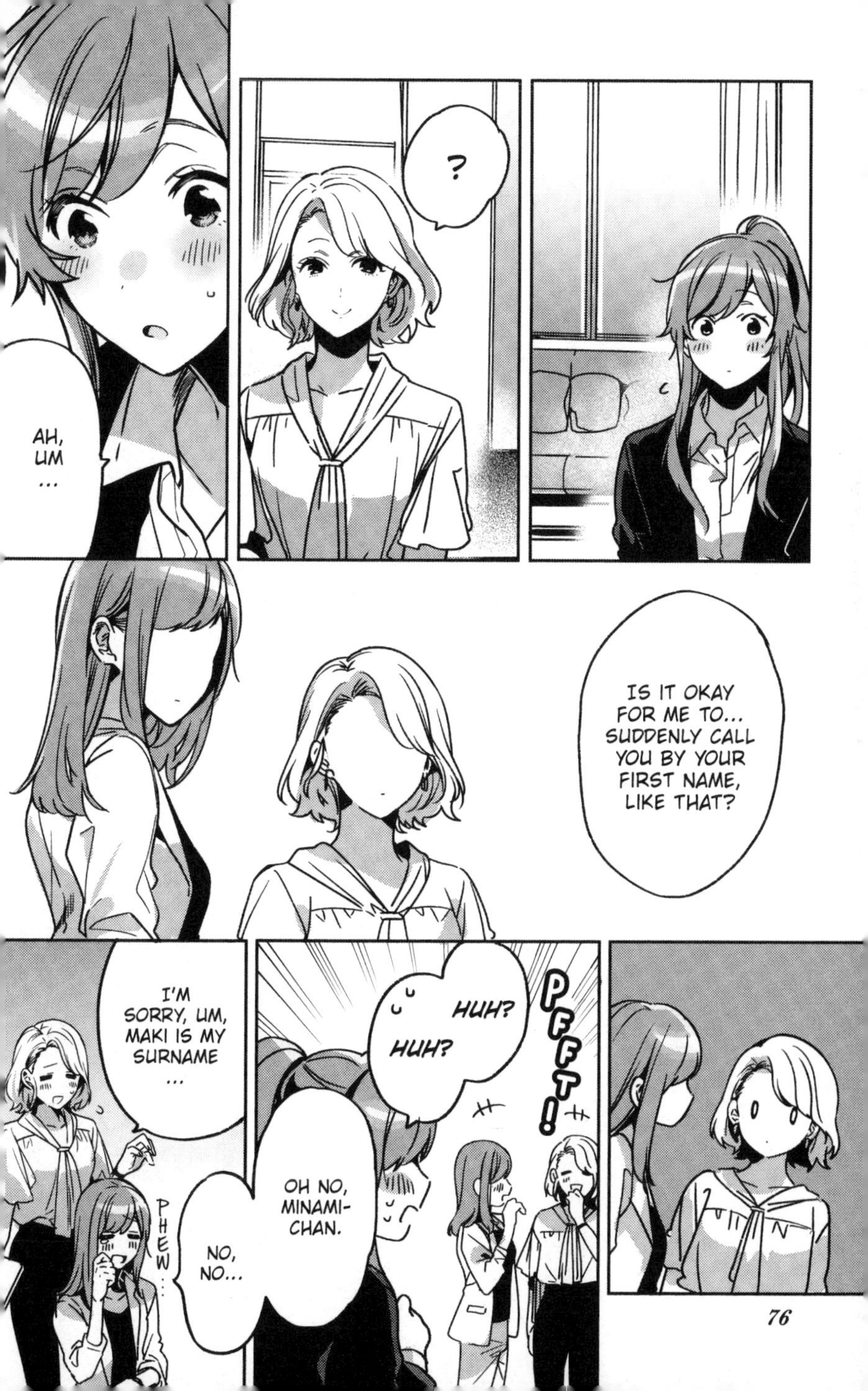
?
AH, UM ...
IS IT OKAY FOR ME TO... SUDDENLY CALL YOU BY YOUR FIRST NAME, LIKE THAT?
PFFT!
HUH? HUH?
OH NO, MINAMI-CHAN.
NO, NO...
I'M SORRY, UM, MAKI IS MY SURNAME ...
PHEW...

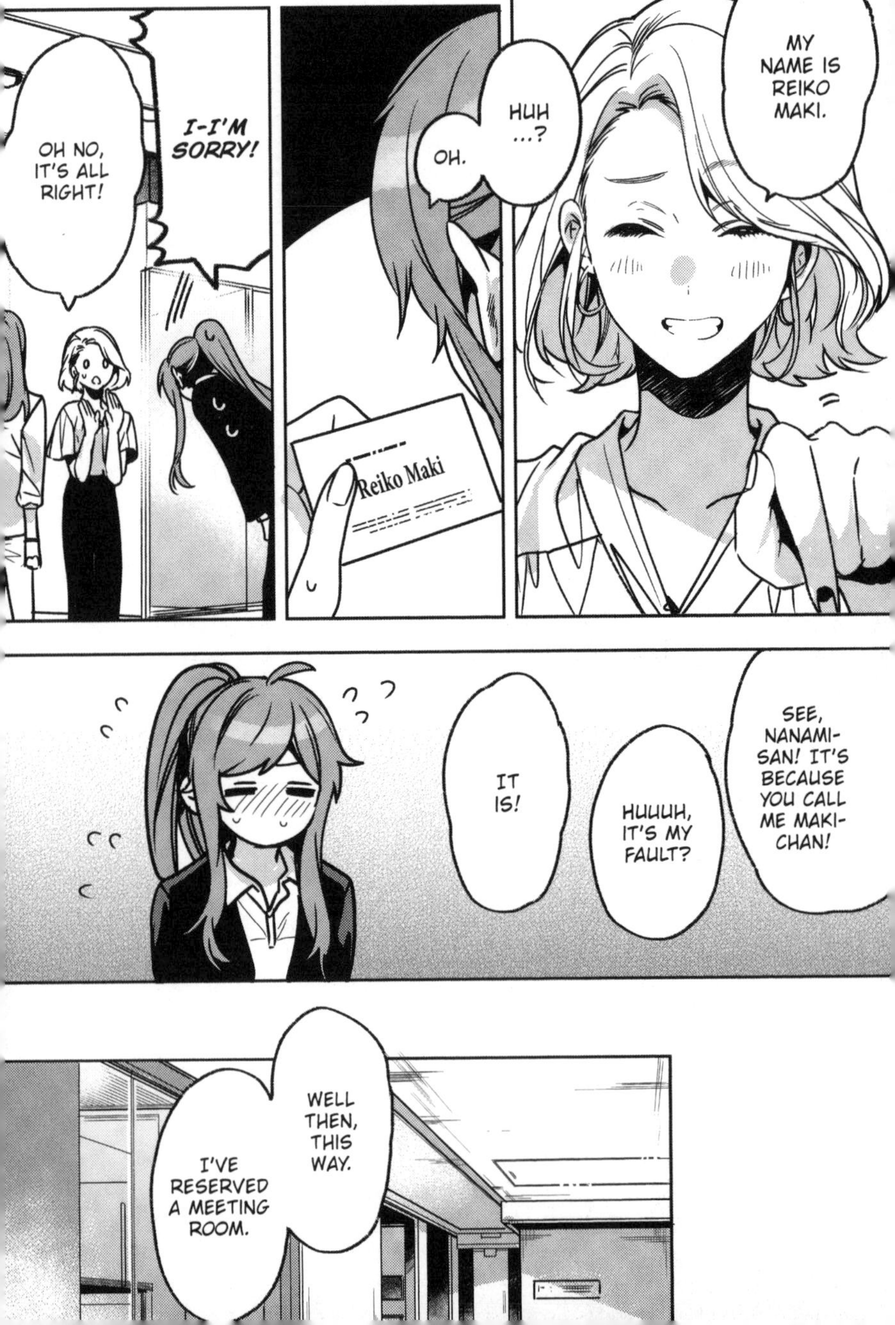
MY NAME IS REIKO MAKI.
HUH ...?
OH.
Reiko Maki
I-I'M SORRY!
OH NO, IT'S ALL RIGHT!
SEE, NANAMI-SAN! IT'S BECAUSE YOU CALL ME MAKI-CHAN!
HUUUH, IT'S MY FAULT?
IT IS!
WELL THEN, THIS WAY.
I'VE RESERVED A MEETING ROOM.

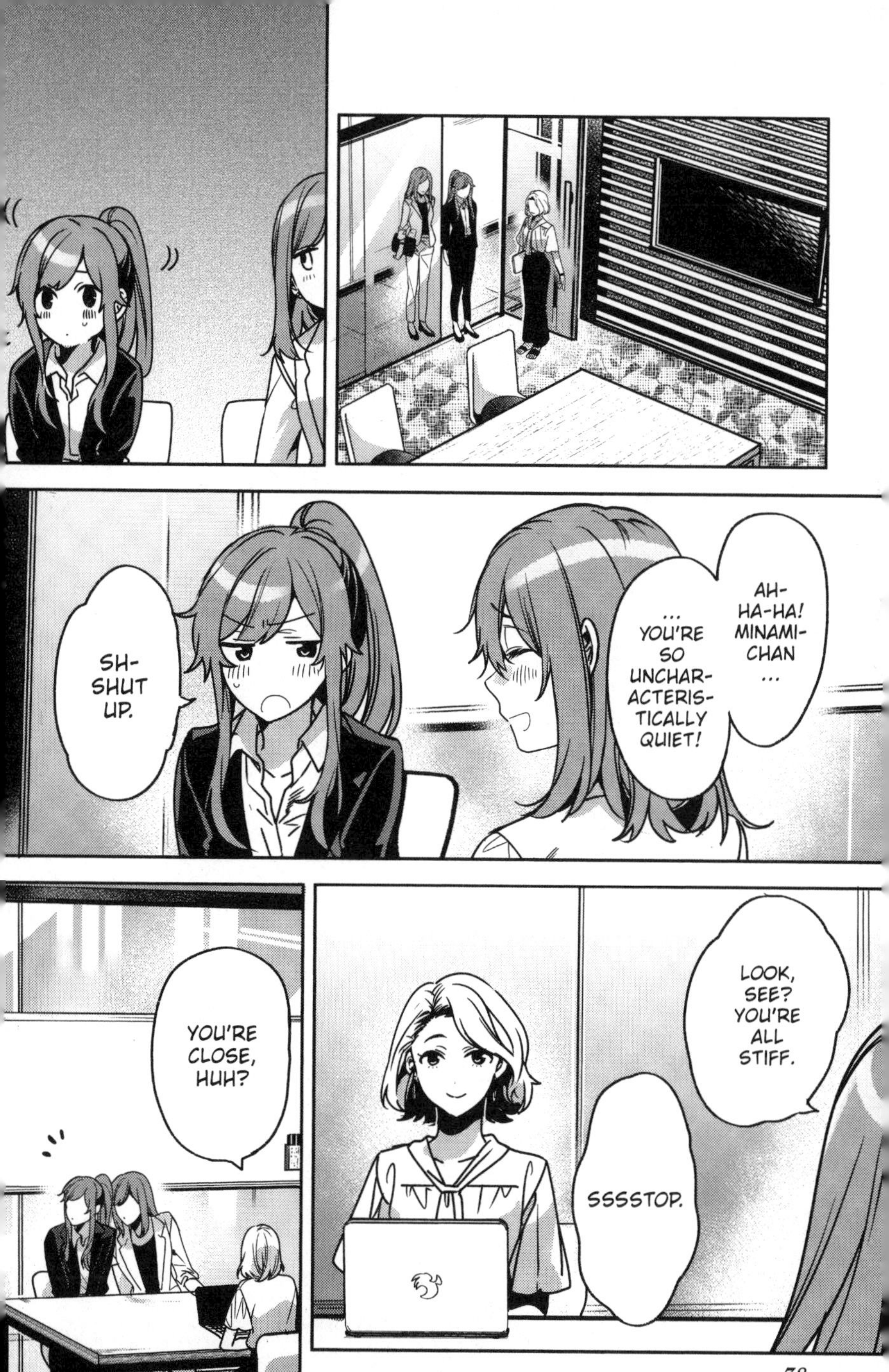
AH-HA-HA! MINAMI-CHAN...
...YOU'RE SO UNCHAR-ACTERIS-TICALLY QUIET!
SH-SHUT UP.
LOOK, SEE? YOU'RE ALL STIFF.
SSSSTOP.
YOU'RE CLOSE, HUH?

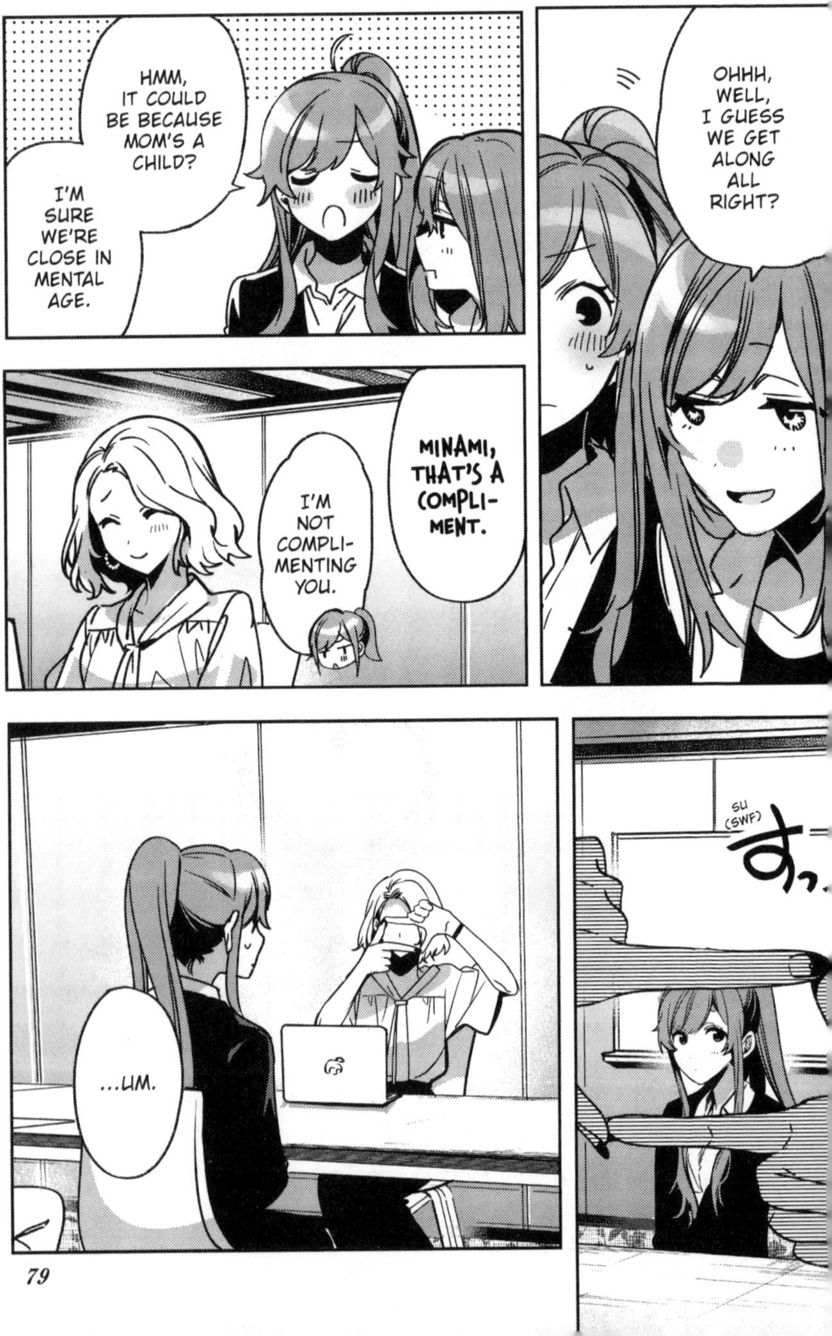
OHHH, WELL, I GUESS WE GET ALONG ALL RIGHT?
HMM, IT COULD BE BECAUSE MOM'S A CHILD?
I'M SURE WE'RE CLOSE IN MENTAL AGE.
MINAMI, THAT'S A COMPLI-MENT.
I'M NOT COMPLI-MENTING YOU.
SU (SWF)
すっ
...UM.

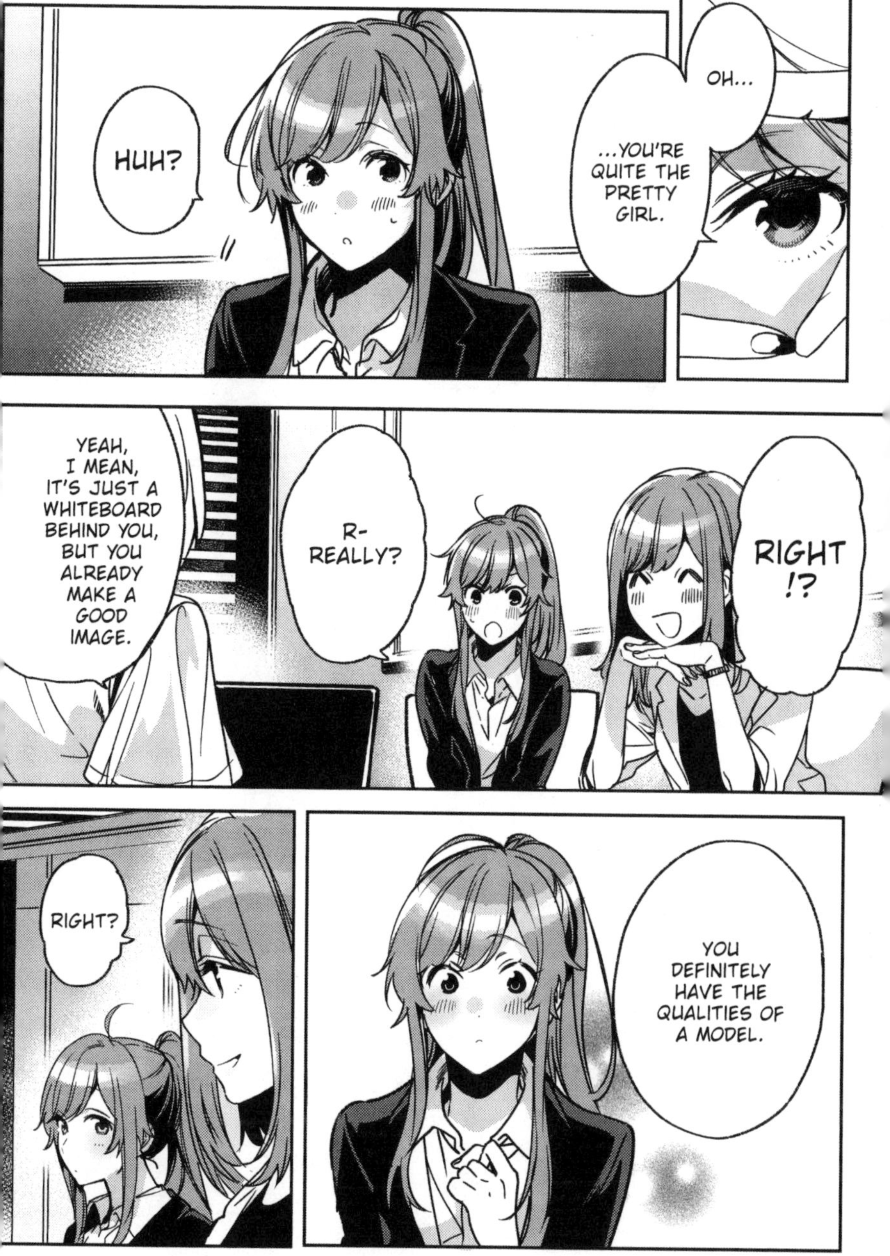
OH...
...YOU'RE QUITE THE PRETTY GIRL.
HUH?
RIGHT!?
R-REALLY?
YEAH, I MEAN, IT'S JUST A WHITEBOARD BEHIND YOU, BUT YOU ALREADY MAKE A GOOD IMAGE.
YOU DEFINITELY HAVE THE QUALITIES OF A MODEL.
RIGHT?

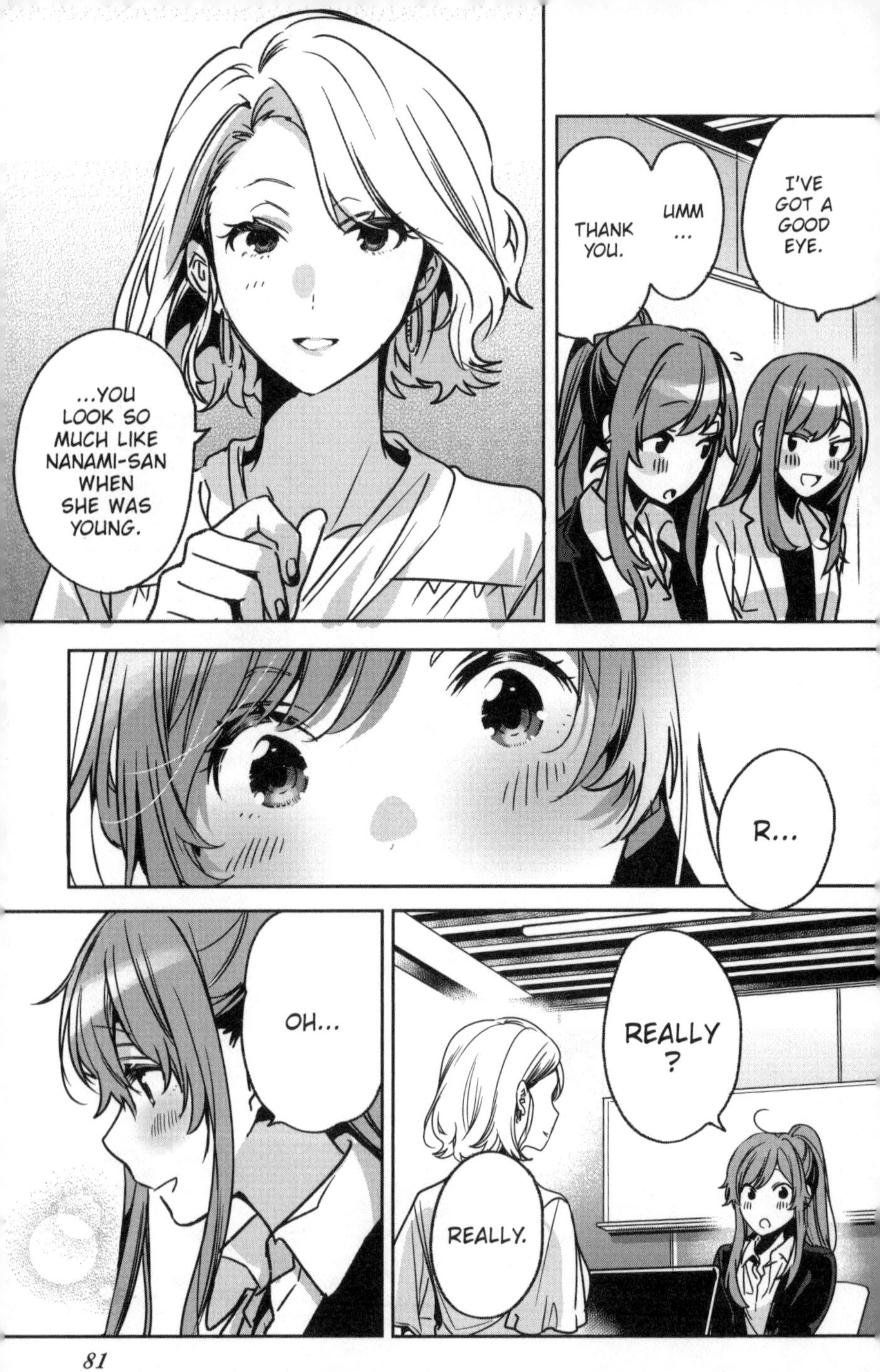
I'VE GOT A GOOD EYE.
UMM...
THANK YOU.
...YOU LOOK SO MUCH LIKE NANAMI-SAN WHEN SHE WAS YOUNG.
R...
REALLY?
REALLY.
OH...

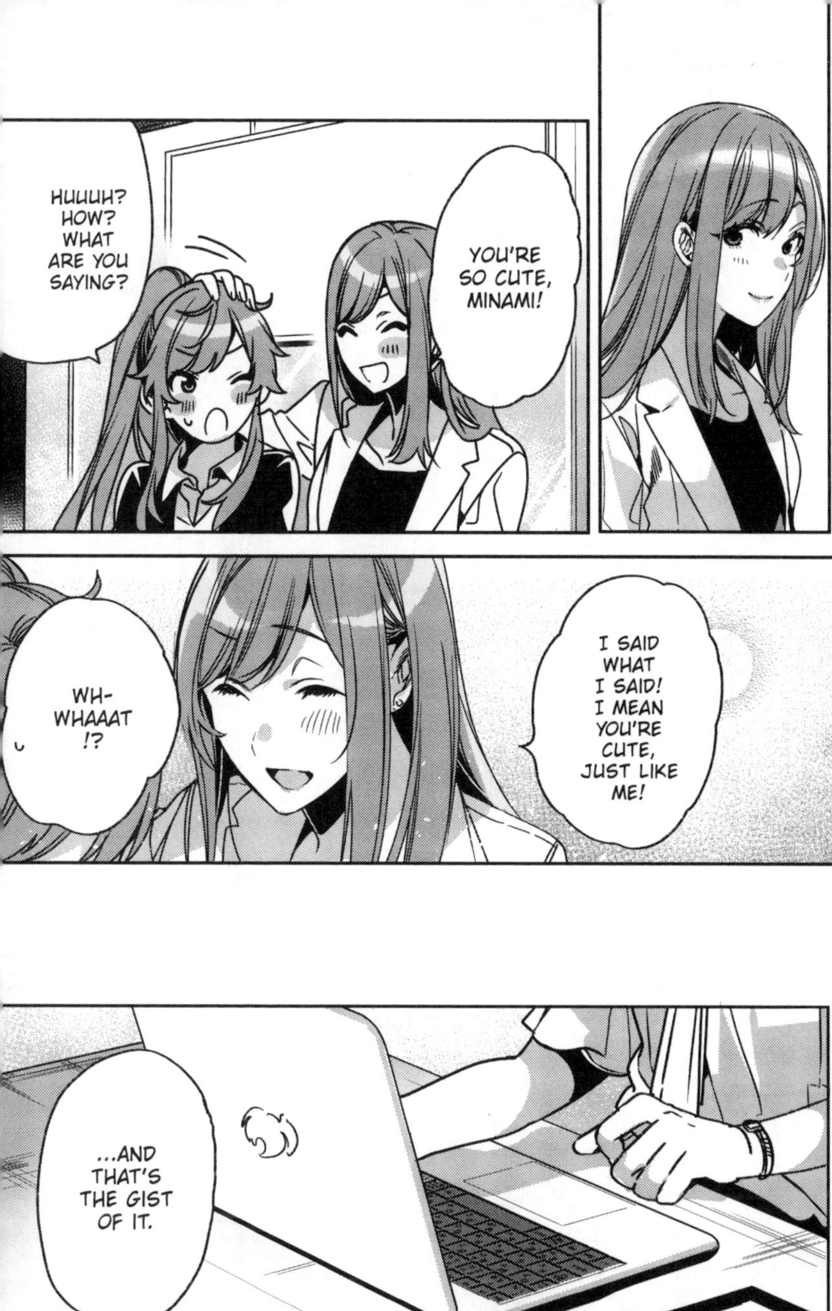
YOU'RE SO CUTE, MINAMI!
HUUUH? HOW? WHAT ARE YOU SAYING?
I SAID WHAT I SAID! I MEAN YOU'RE CUTE, JUST LIKE ME!
WH- WHAAAT !?
...AND THAT'S THE GIST OF IT.

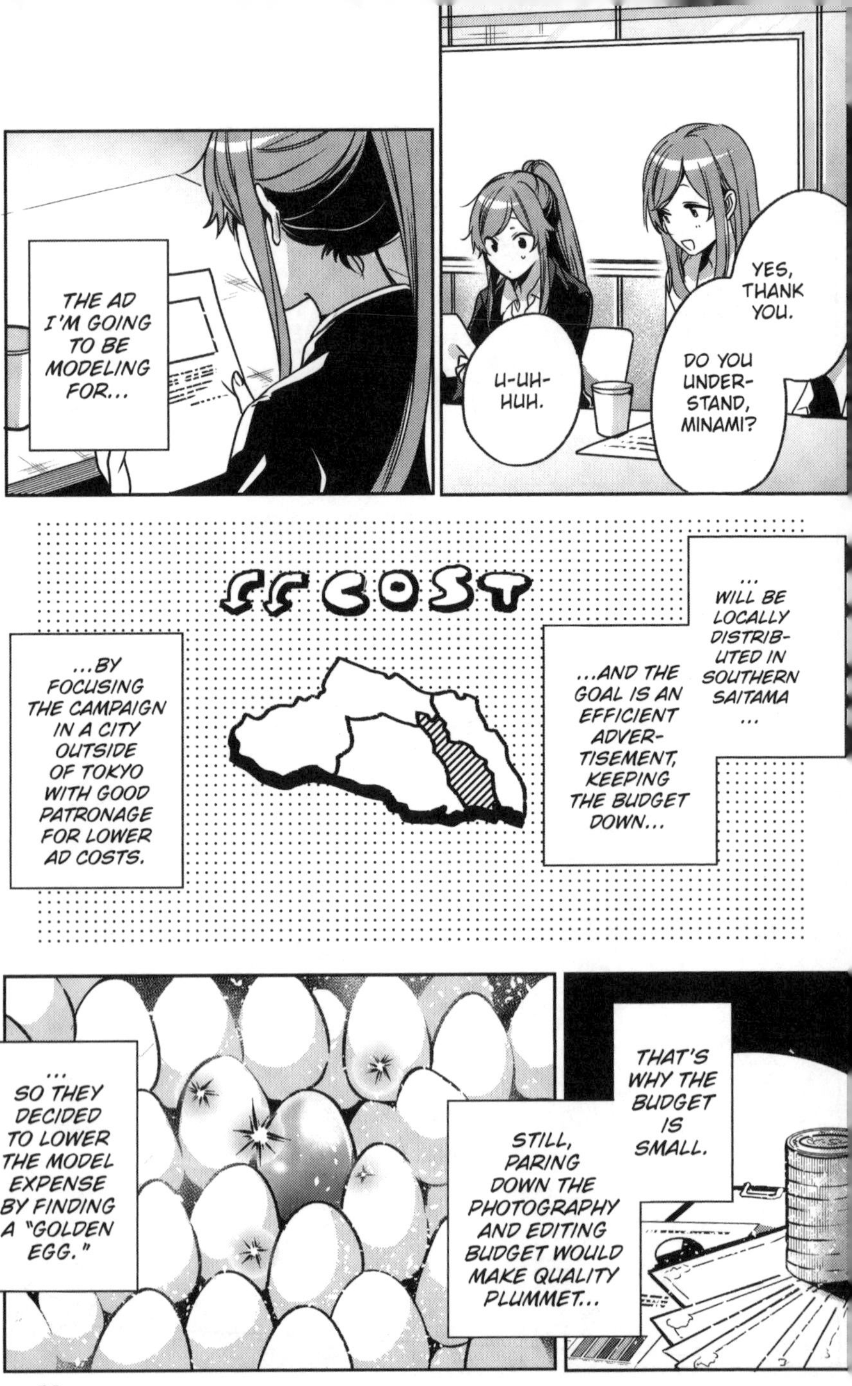
YES, THANK YOU.
DO YOU UNDERSTAND, MINAMI?
U-UH-HUH.
THE AD I'M GOING TO BE MODELING FOR...
...WILL BE LOCALLY DISTRIBUTED IN SOUTHERN SAITAMA...
...AND THE GOAL IS AN EFFICIENT ADVERTISEMENT, KEEPING THE BUDGET DOWN...
COST
...BY FOCUSING THE CAMPAIGN IN A CITY OUTSIDE OF TOKYO WITH GOOD PATRONAGE FOR LOWER AD COSTS.
THAT'S WHY THE BUDGET IS SMALL.
STILL, PARING DOWN THE PHOTOGRAPHY AND EDITING BUDGET WOULD MAKE QUALITY PLUMMET...
...SO THEY DECIDED TO LOWER THE MODEL EXPENSE BY FINDING A "GOLDEN EGG."

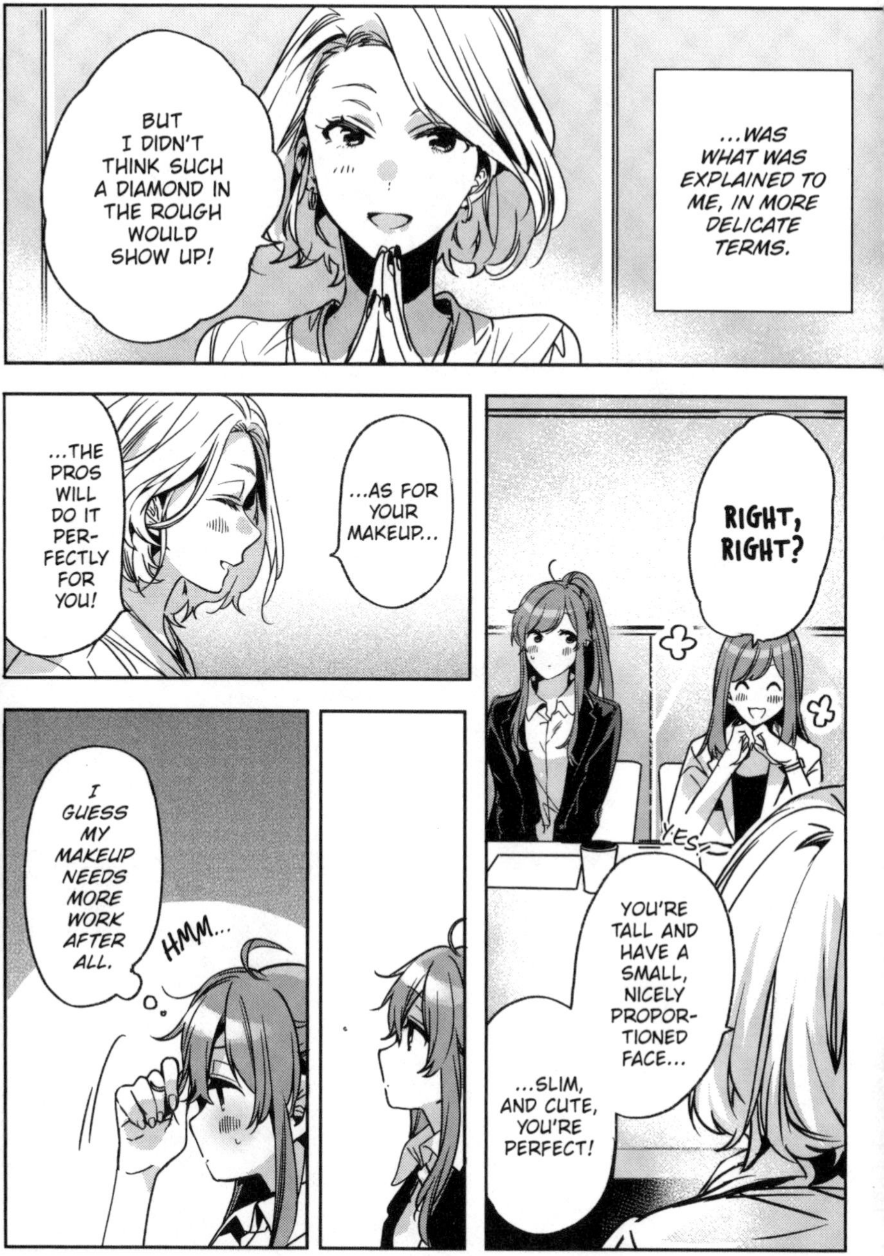
BUT I DIDN'T THINK SUCH A DIAMOND IN THE ROUGH WOULD SHOW UP!
...WAS WHAT WAS EXPLAINED TO ME, IN MORE DELICATE TERMS.
...AS FOR YOUR MAKEUP...
...THE PROS WILL DO IT PERFECTLY FOR YOU!
I GUESS MY MAKEUP NEEDS MORE WORK AFTER ALL.
HMM...
YOU'RE TALL AND HAVE A SMALL, NICELY PROPORTIONED FACE...
...SLIM, AND CUTE, YOU'RE PERFECT!
RIGHT, RIGHT?
YES!

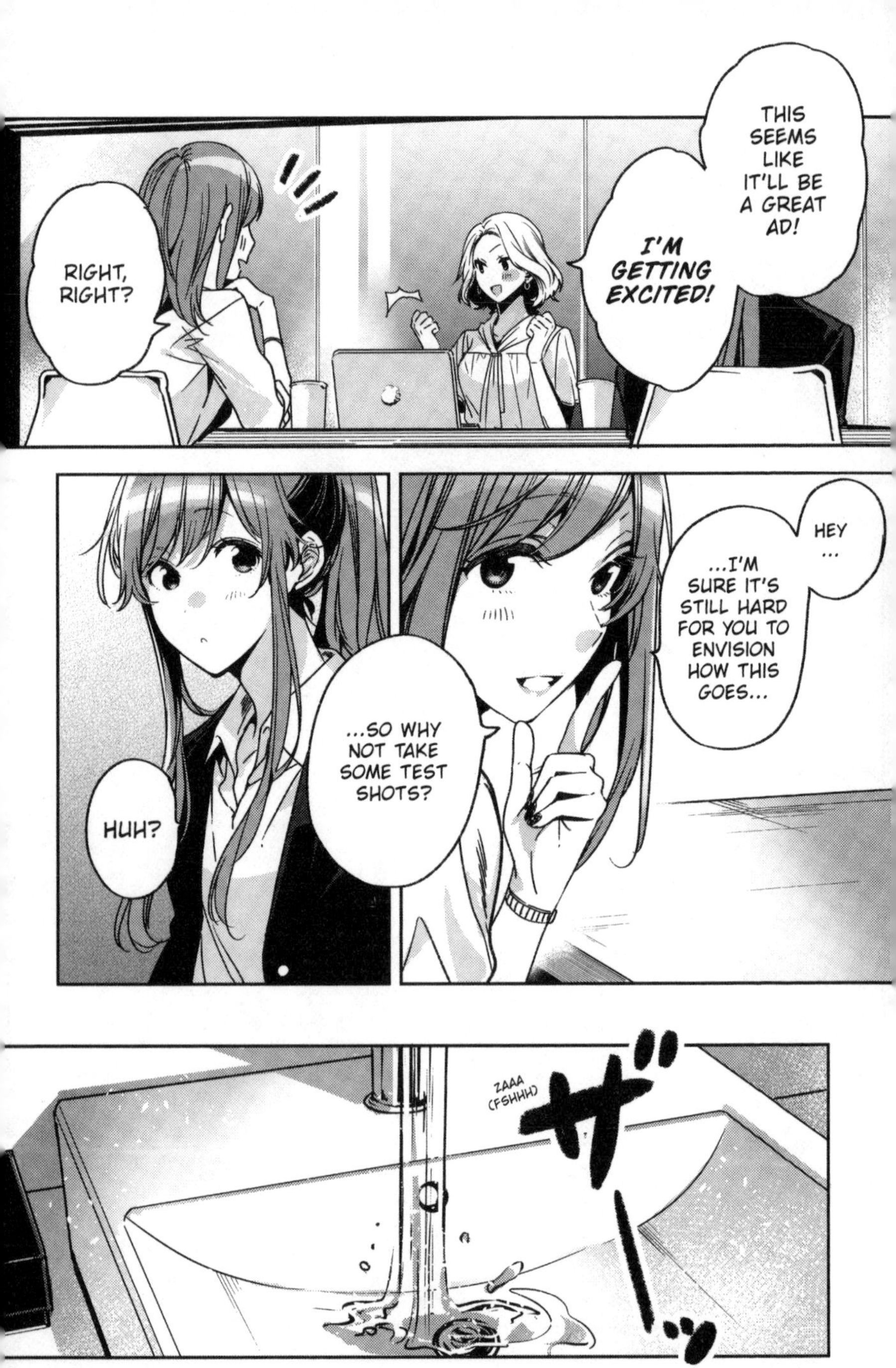
THIS SEEMS LIKE IT'LL BE A GREAT AD!
I'M GETTING EXCITED!
RIGHT, RIGHT?
HEY...
...I'M SURE IT'S STILL HARD FOR YOU TO ENVISION HOW THIS GOES...
...SO WHY NOT TAKE SOME TEST SHOTS?
HUH?
ZAAA (FSHHH)

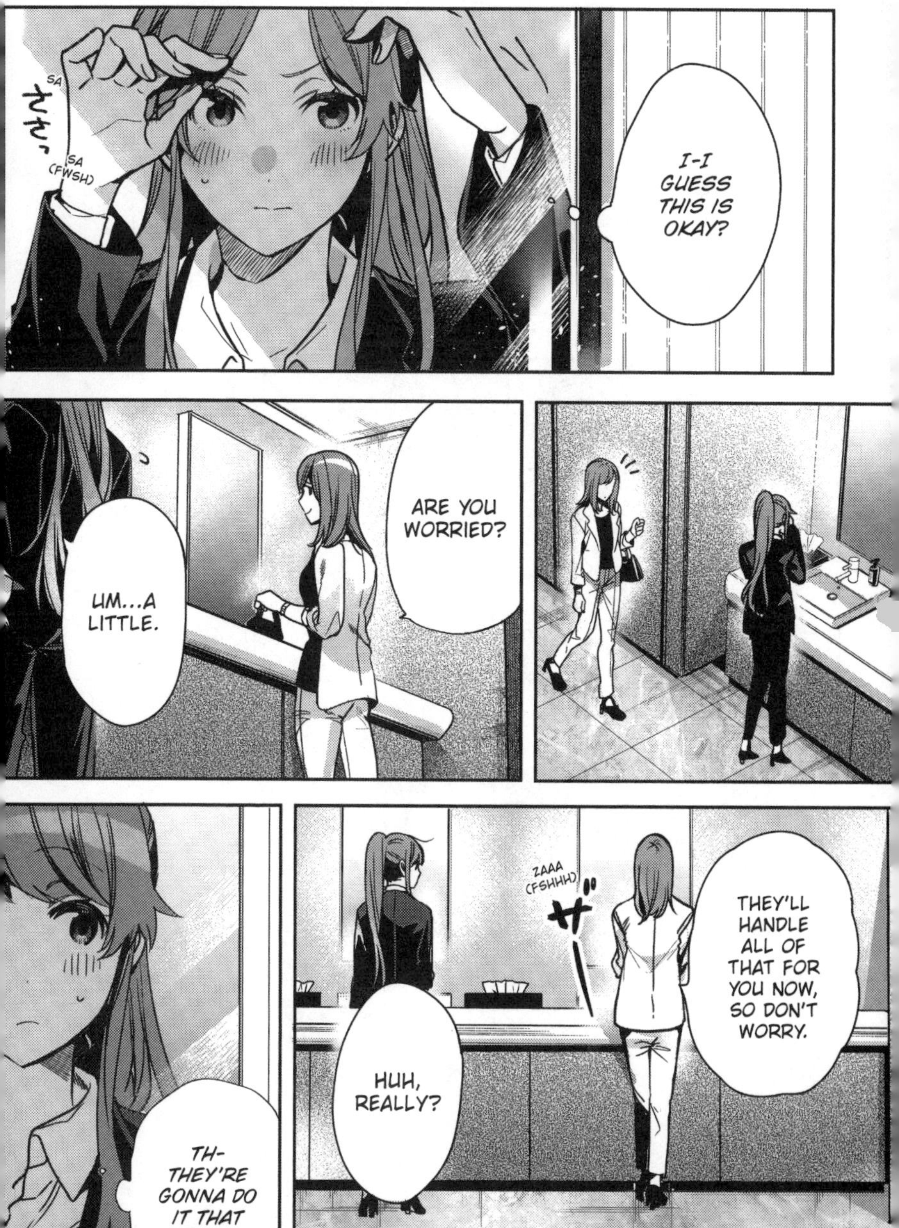
I-I GUESS THIS IS OKAY?
SA SA (FWSH)
ARE YOU WORRIED?
UM...A LITTLE.
THEY'LL HANDLE ALL OF THAT FOR YOU NOW, SO DON'T WORRY.
ZAAA (FSHHH)
HUH, REALLY?
TH- THEY'RE GONNA DO IT THAT LEGIT...

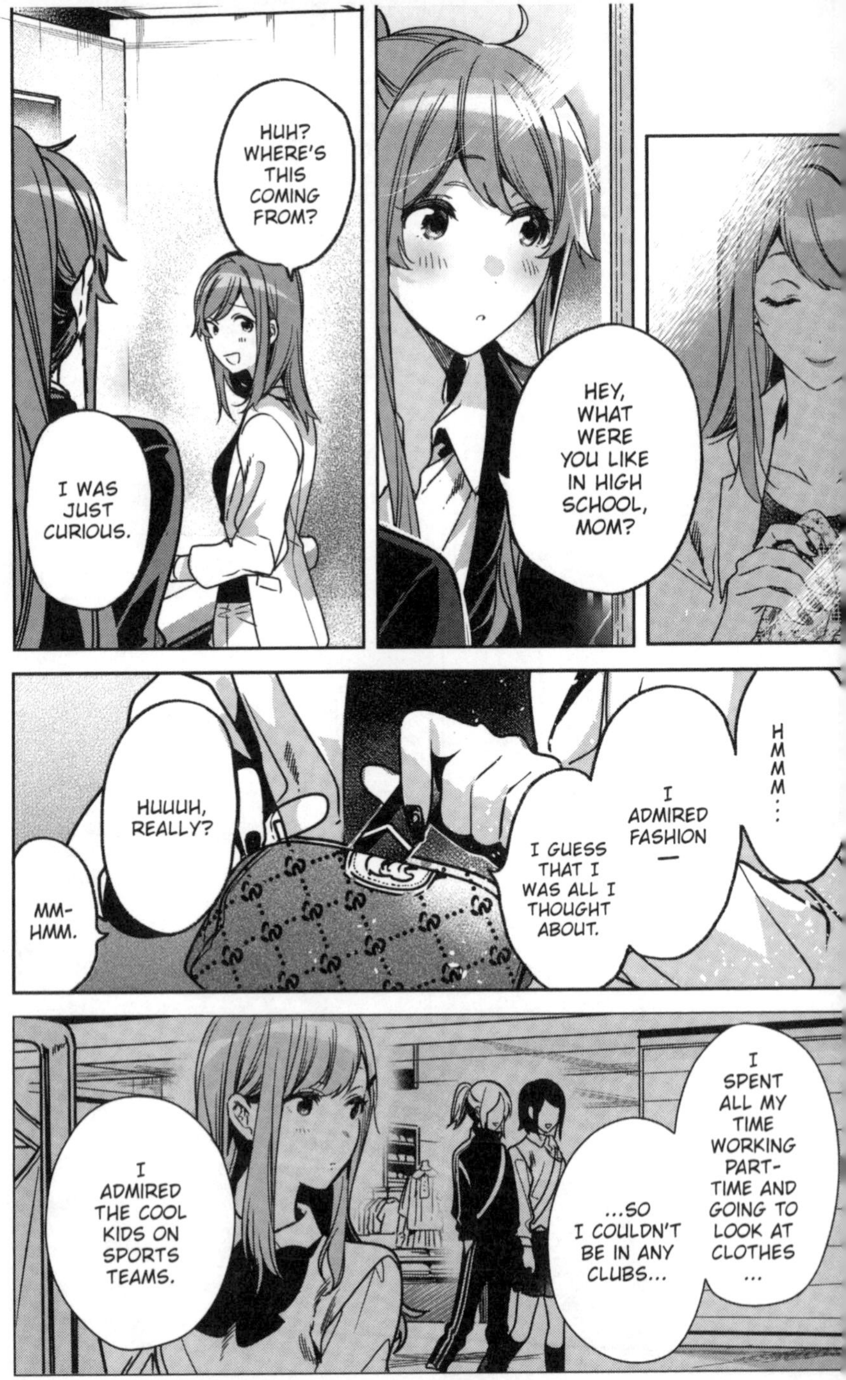
HEY, WHAT WERE YOU LIKE IN HIGH SCHOOL, MOM?
HUH? WHERE'S THIS COMING FROM?
I WAS JUST CURIOUS.
HMMM...
I ADMIRED FASHION—
I GUESS THAT I WAS ALL I THOUGHT ABOUT.
HUUUH, REALLY?
MM-HMM.
I SPENT ALL MY TIME WORKING PART-TIME AND GOING TO LOOK AT CLOTHES...
...SO I COULDN'T BE IN ANY CLUBS...
I ADMIRED THE COOL KIDS ON SPORTS TEAMS.

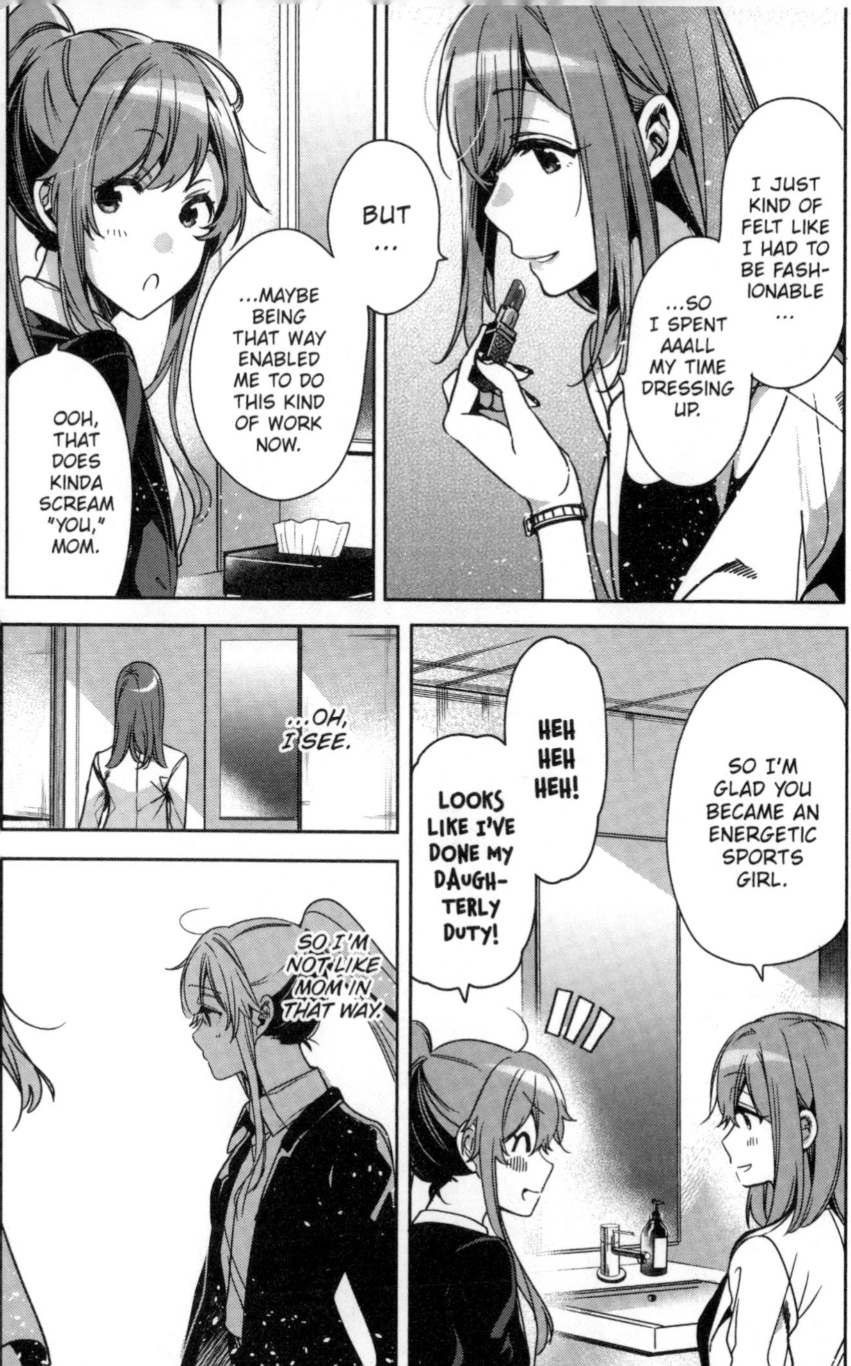
I JUST KIND OF FELT LIKE I HAD TO BE FASHIONABLE...
...SO I SPENT AAALL MY TIME DRESSING UP.
BUT...
...MAYBE BEING THAT WAY ENABLED ME TO DO THIS KIND OF WORK NOW.
OOH, THAT DOES KINDA SCREAM "YOU," MOM.
SO I'M GLAD YOU BECAME AN ENERGETIC SPORTS GIRL.
HEH HEH HEH!
LOOKS LIKE I'VE DONE MY DAUGHTERLY DUTY!
...OH, I SEE.
SO I'M NOT LIKE MOM IN THAT WAY.

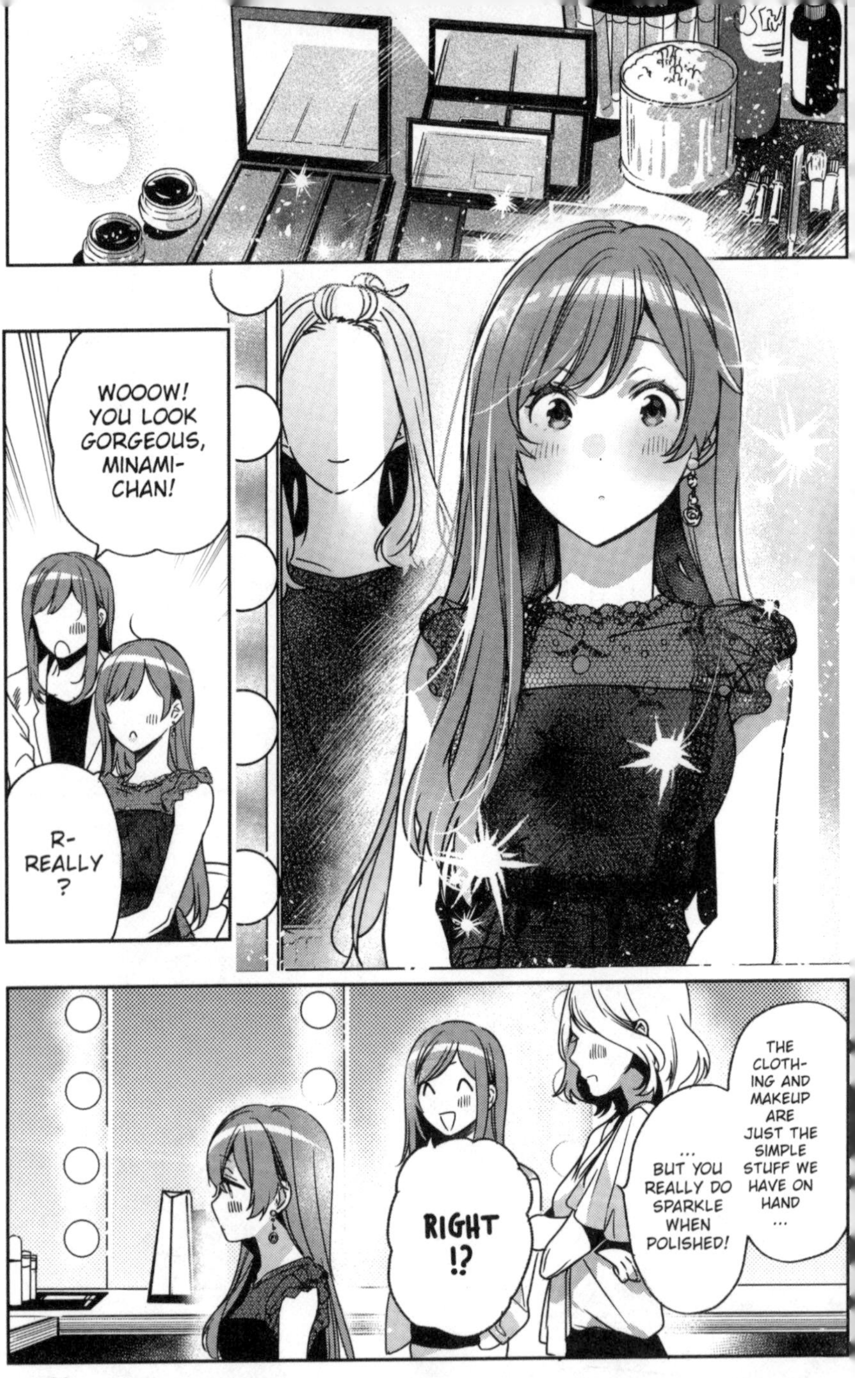
WOOOW! YOU LOOK GORGEOUS, MINAMI-CHAN!
R-REALLY?
THE CLOTHING AND MAKEUP ARE JUST THE SIMPLE STUFF WE HAVE ON HAND...
...BUT YOU REALLY DO SPARKLE WHEN POLISHED!
RIGHT!?

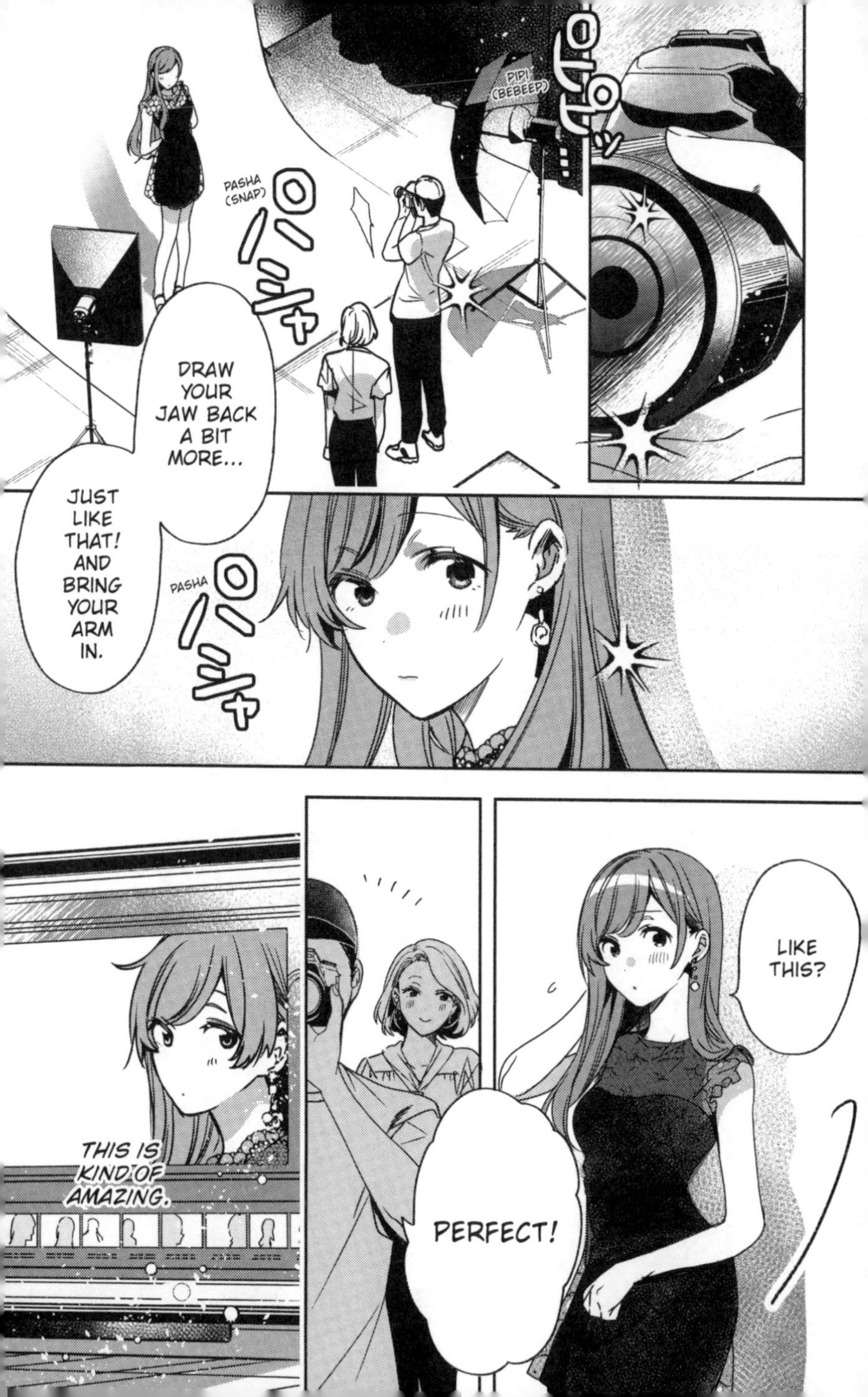
ピピッ
PIPI (BEBEEP)
パシャ
PASHA (SNAP)
DRAW YOUR JAW BACK A BIT MORE...
JUST LIKE THAT! AND BRING YOUR ARM IN.
パシャ
PASHA
LIKE THIS?
PERFECT!
THIS IS KIND OF AMAZING.

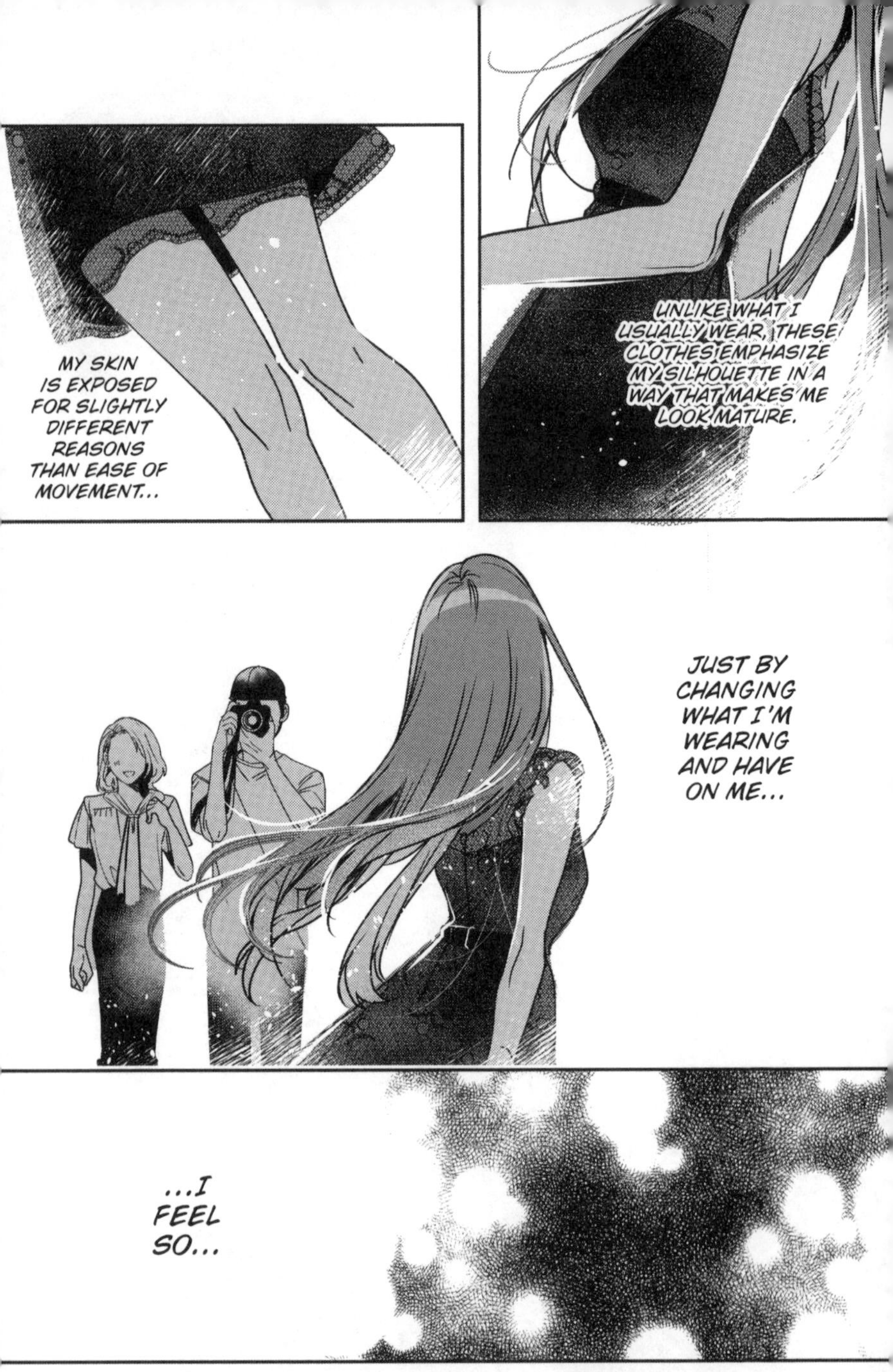
UNLIKE WHAT I USUALLY WEAR, THESE CLOTHES EMPHASIZE MY SILHOUETTE IN A WAY THAT MAKES ME LOOK MATURE.
MY SKIN IS EXPOSED FOR SLIGHTLY DIFFERENT REASONS THAN EASE OF MOVEMENT...
JUST BY CHANGING WHAT I'M WEARING AND HAVE ON ME...
...I FEEL SO...

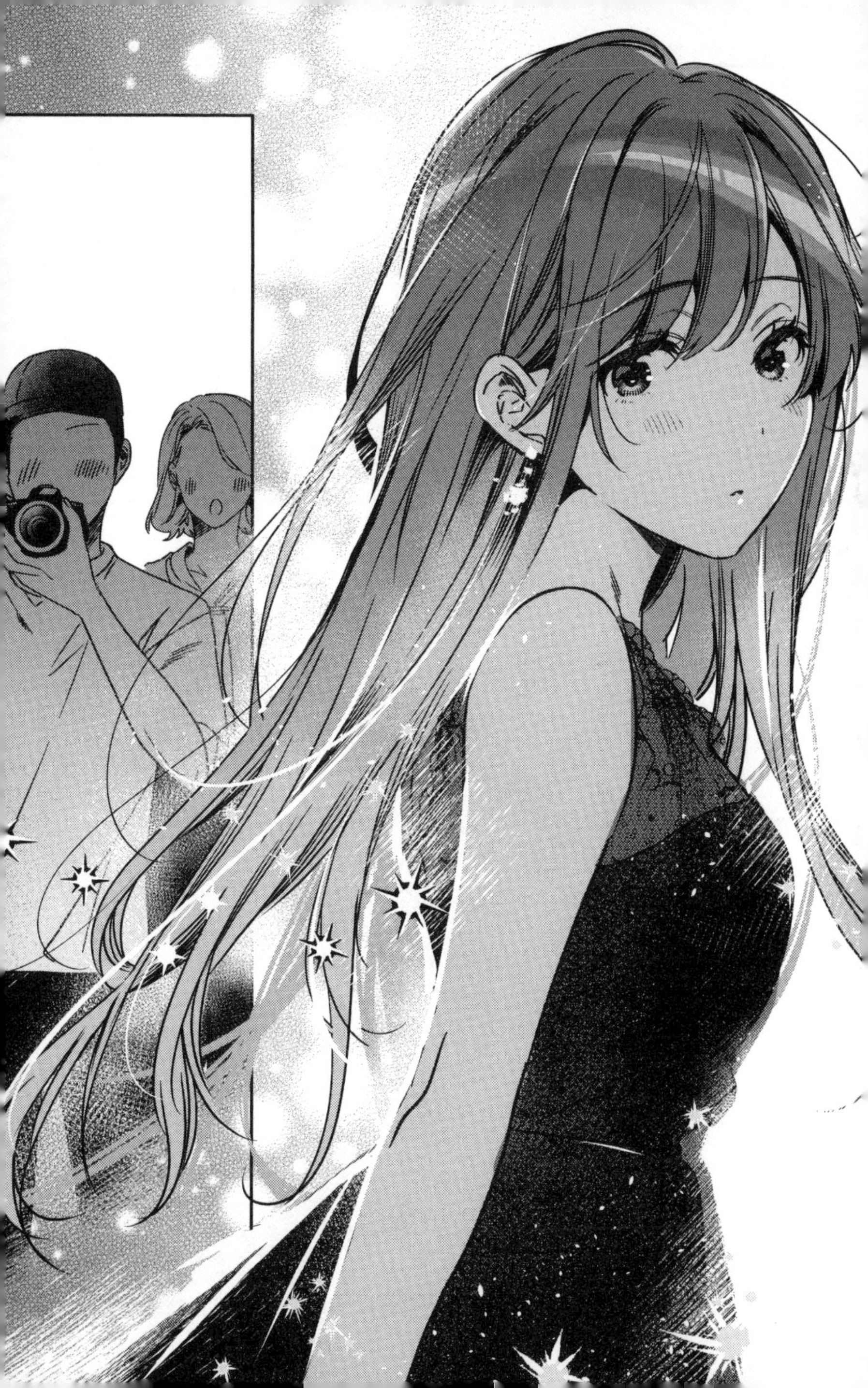

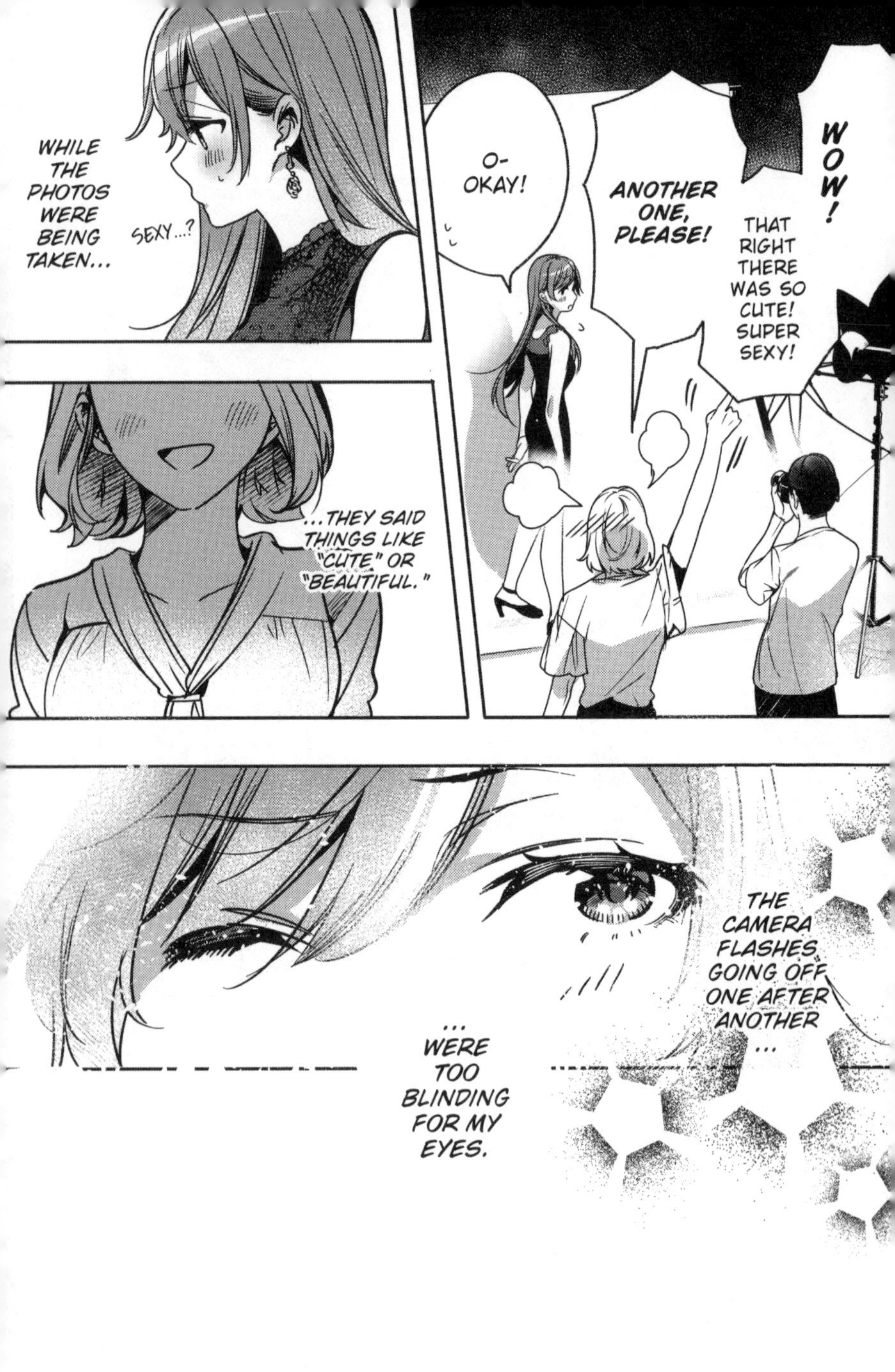
WOW!
THAT RIGHT THERE WAS SO CUTE! SUPER SEXY!
ANOTHER ONE, PLEASE!
O-OKAY!
WHILE THE PHOTOS WERE BEING TAKEN...
SEXY...?
...THEY SAID THINGS LIKE "CUTE" OR "BEAUTIFUL."
THE CAMERA FLASHES GOING OFF ONE AFTER ANOTHER...
...WERE TOO BLINDING FOR MY EYES.

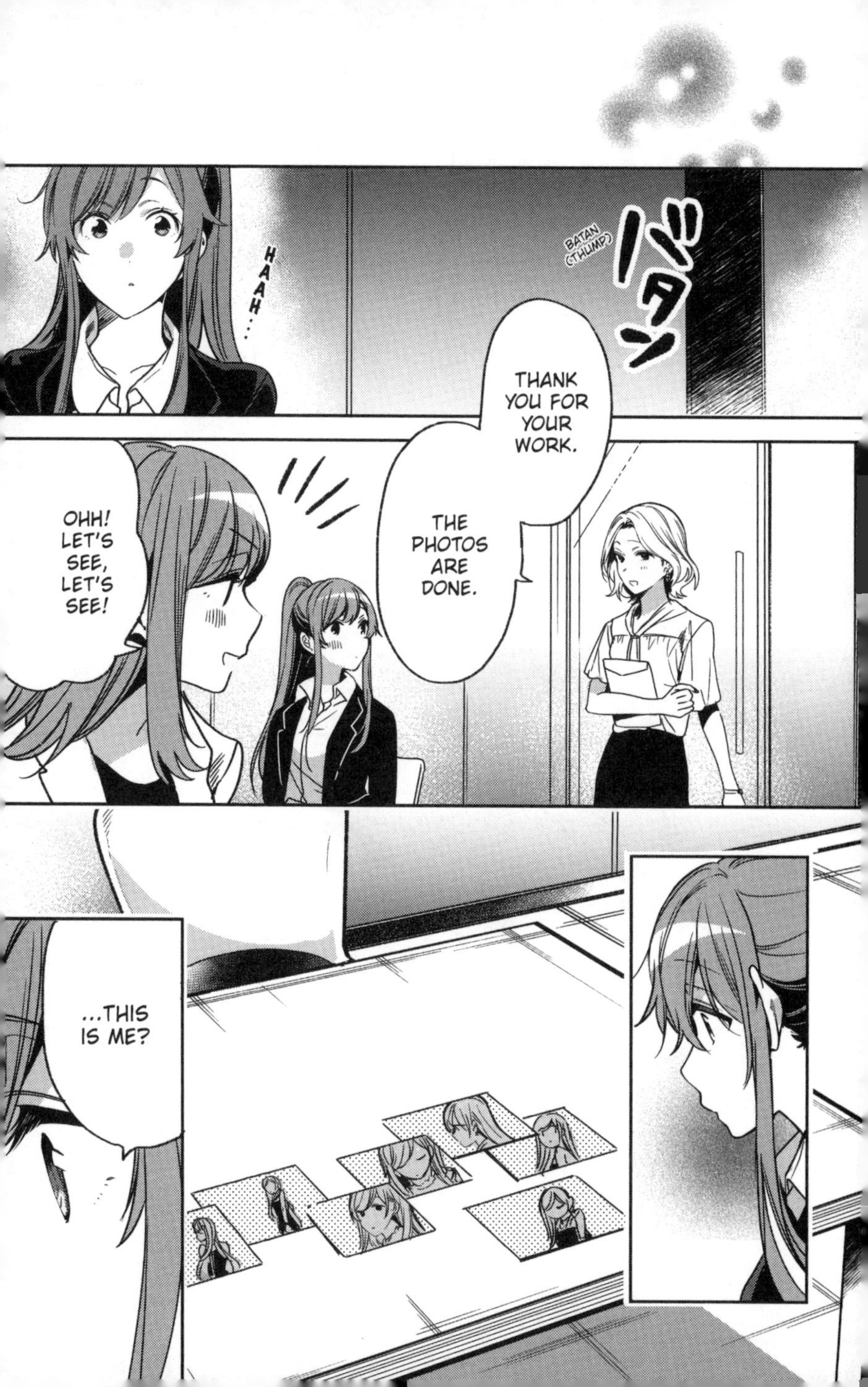
バタン
BATAN (THUMP)
HAAH...
THANK YOU FOR YOUR WORK.
THE PHOTOS ARE DONE.
OHH! LET'S SEE, LET'S SEE!
...THIS IS ME?

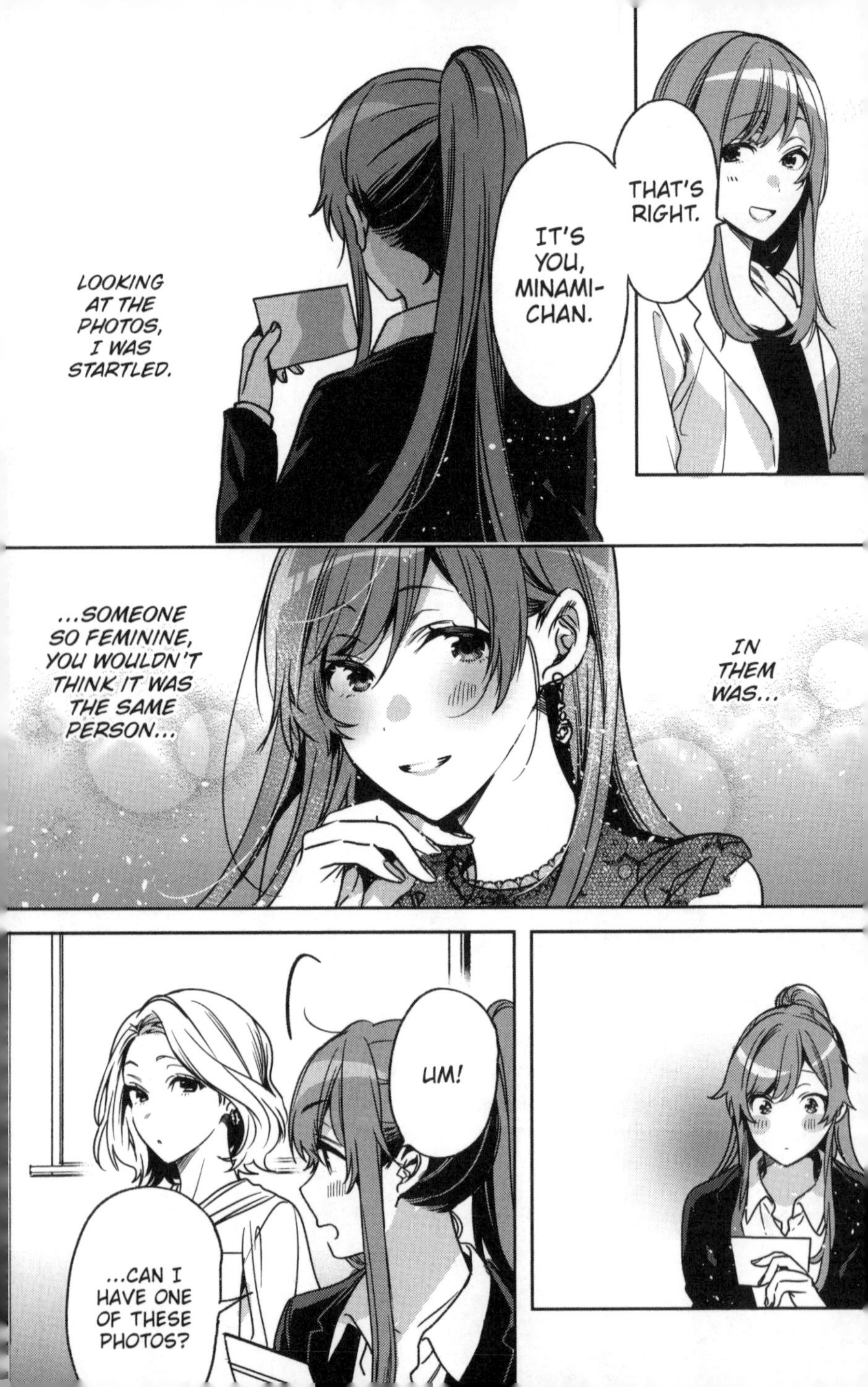
THAT'S RIGHT.
IT'S YOU, MINAMI-CHAN.
LOOKING AT THE PHOTOS, I WAS STARTLED.
IN THEM WAS...
...SOMEONE SO FEMININE, YOU WOULDN'T THINK IT WAS THE SAME PERSON...
UM!
...CAN I HAVE ONE OF THESE PHOTOS?

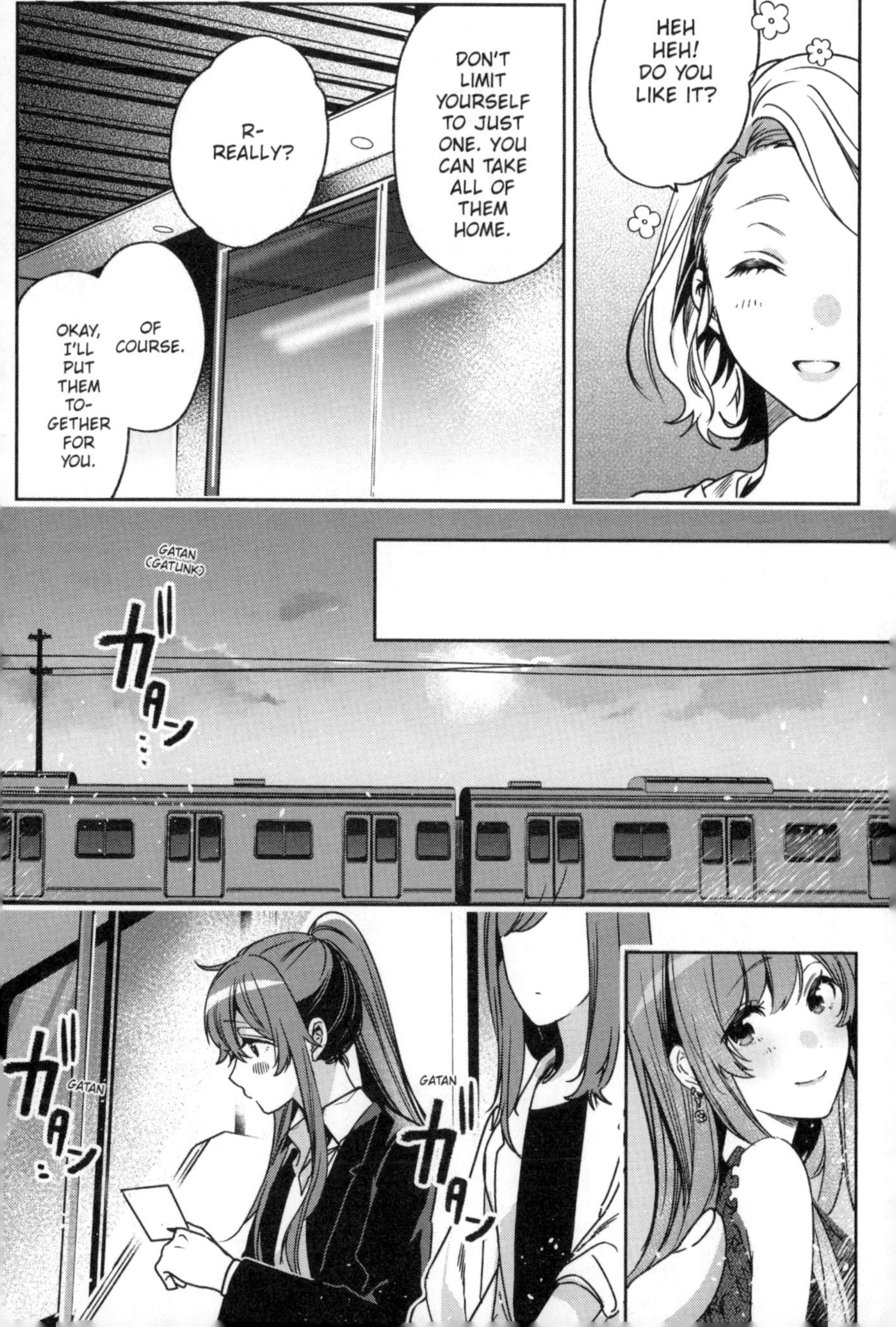
HEH HEH! DO YOU LIKE IT?
DON'T LIMIT YOURSELF TO JUST ONE. YOU CAN TAKE ALL OF THEM HOME.
R-REALLY?
OF COURSE.
OKAY, I'LL PUT THEM TO-GETHER FOR YOU.
GATAN (GATUNK)
ガタン…
GATAN
ガタン
GATAN
ガタン…

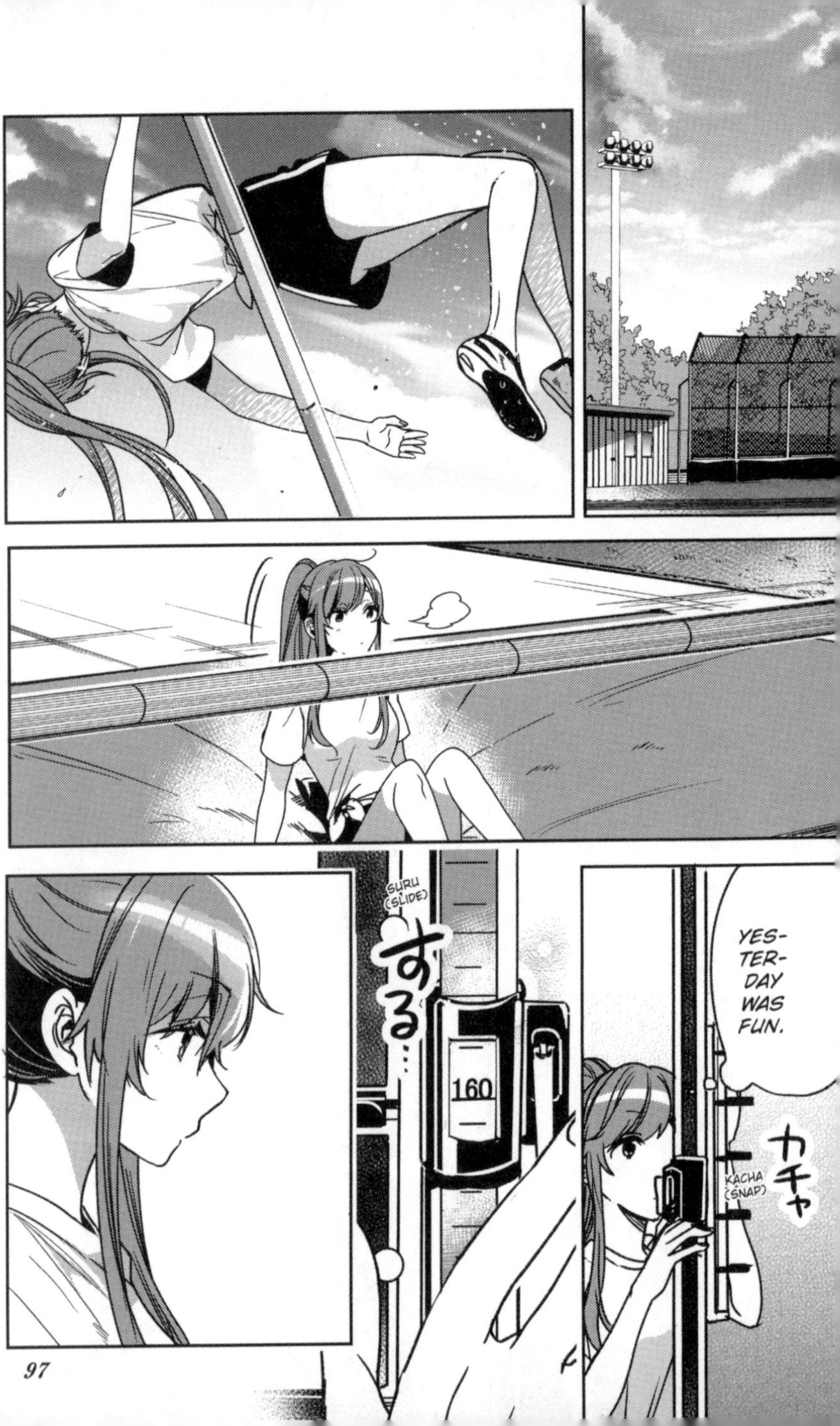
YES-TER-DAY WAS FUN.
カチャ
KACHA (SNAP)
する…
SURU (SLIDE)
160

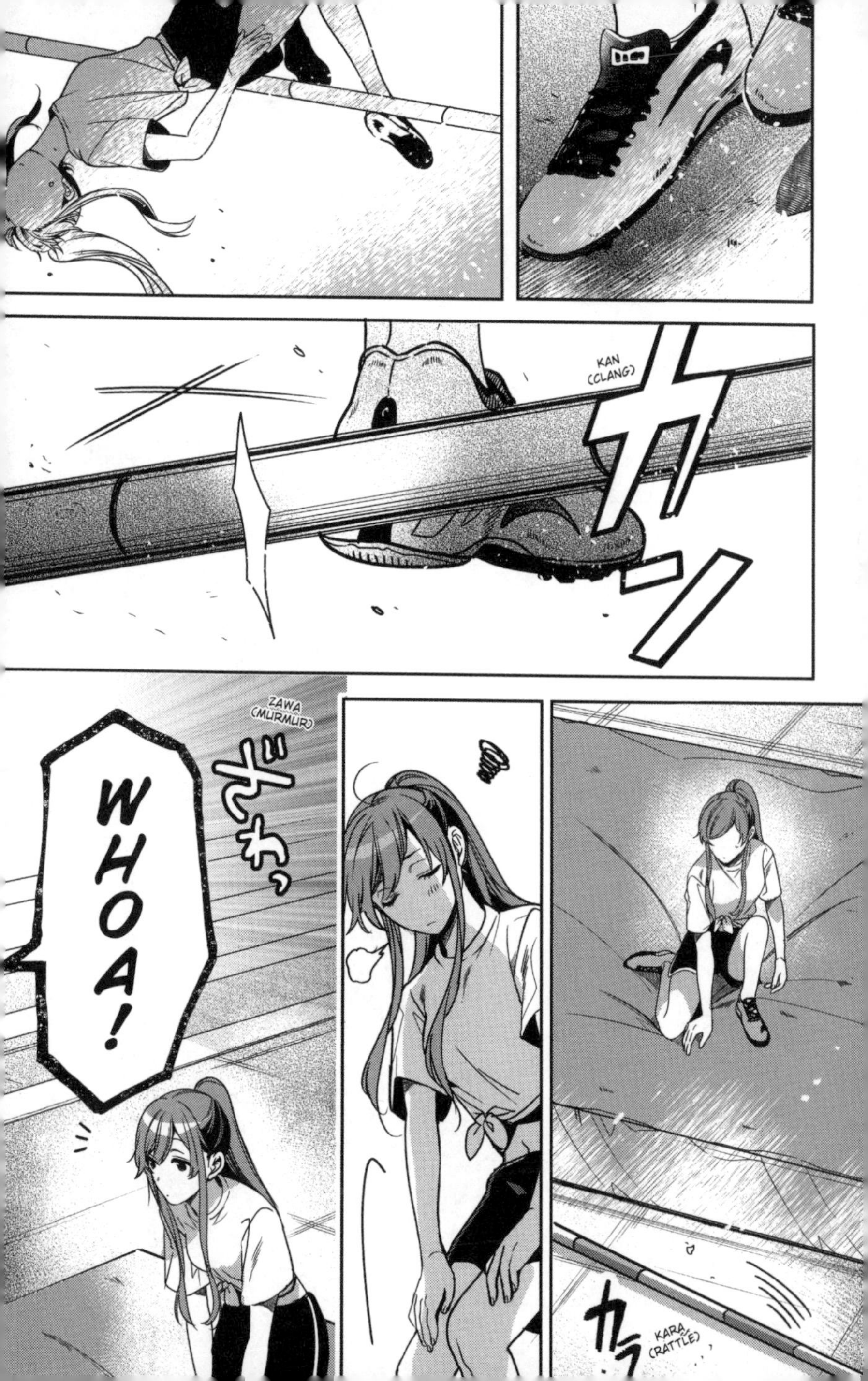
KAN (CLANG)
KARA (RATTLE)
ZAWA (MURMUR)
WHOA!

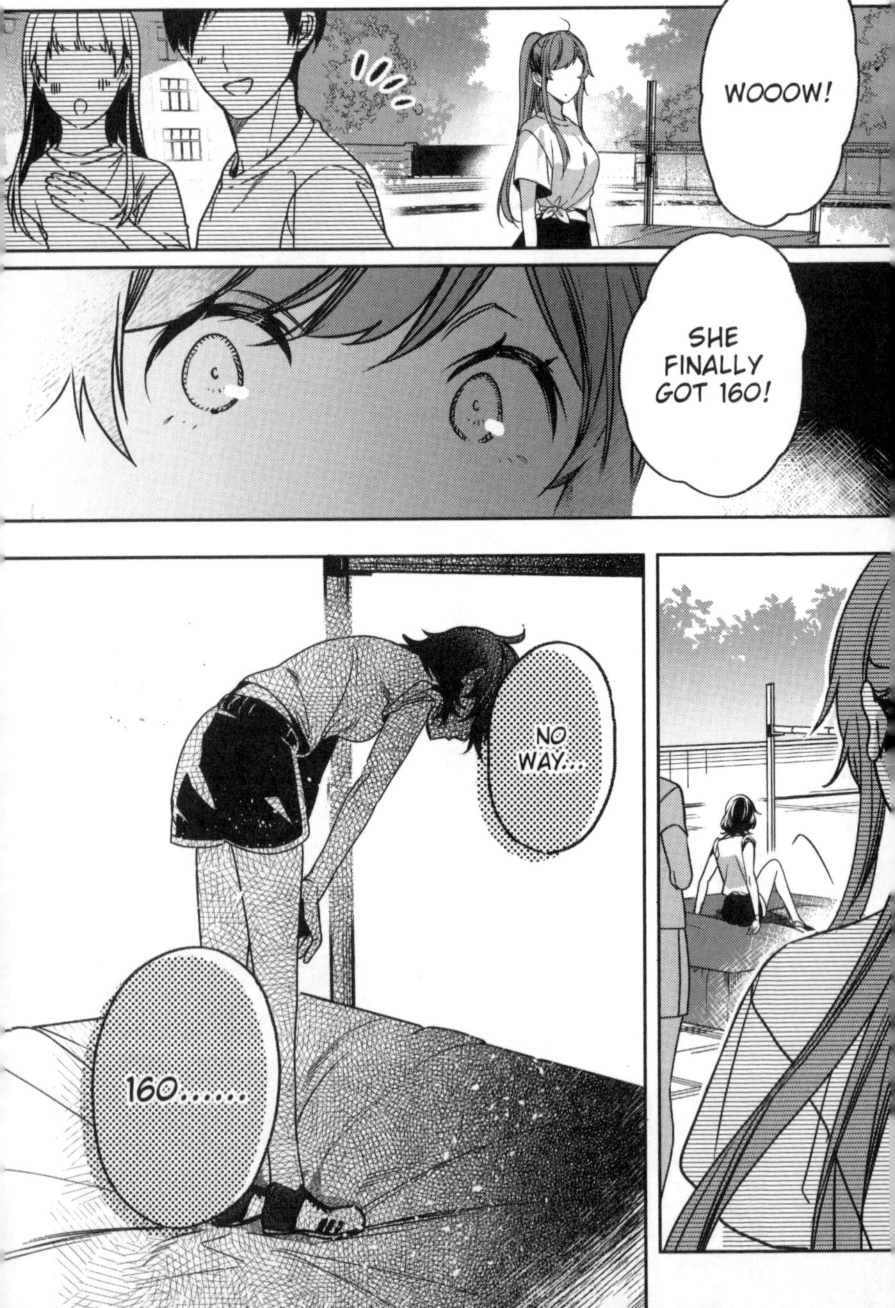
WOOOW!
OOOO
SHE FINALLY GOT 160!
NO WAY...
160......

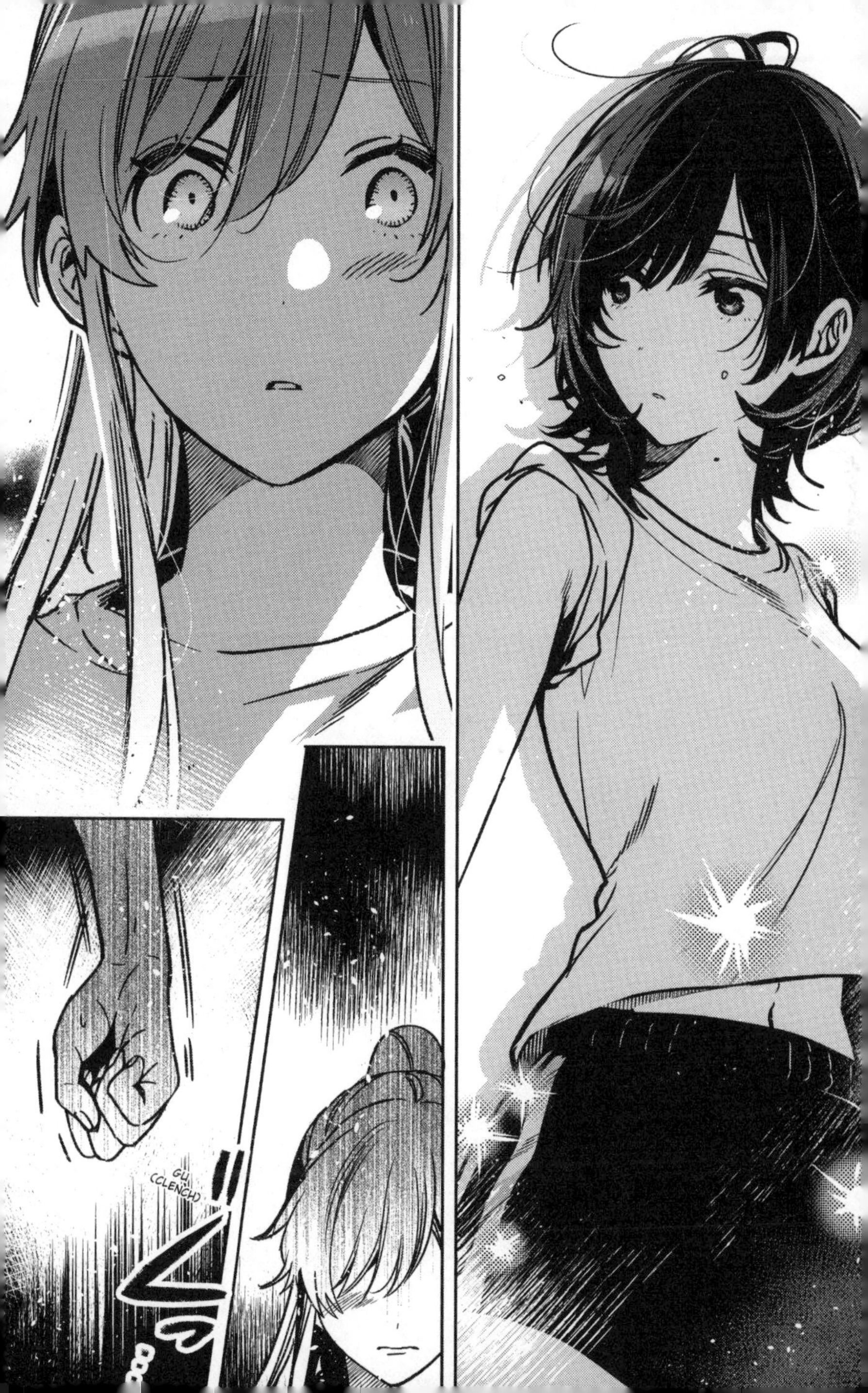
GU (CLENCH)

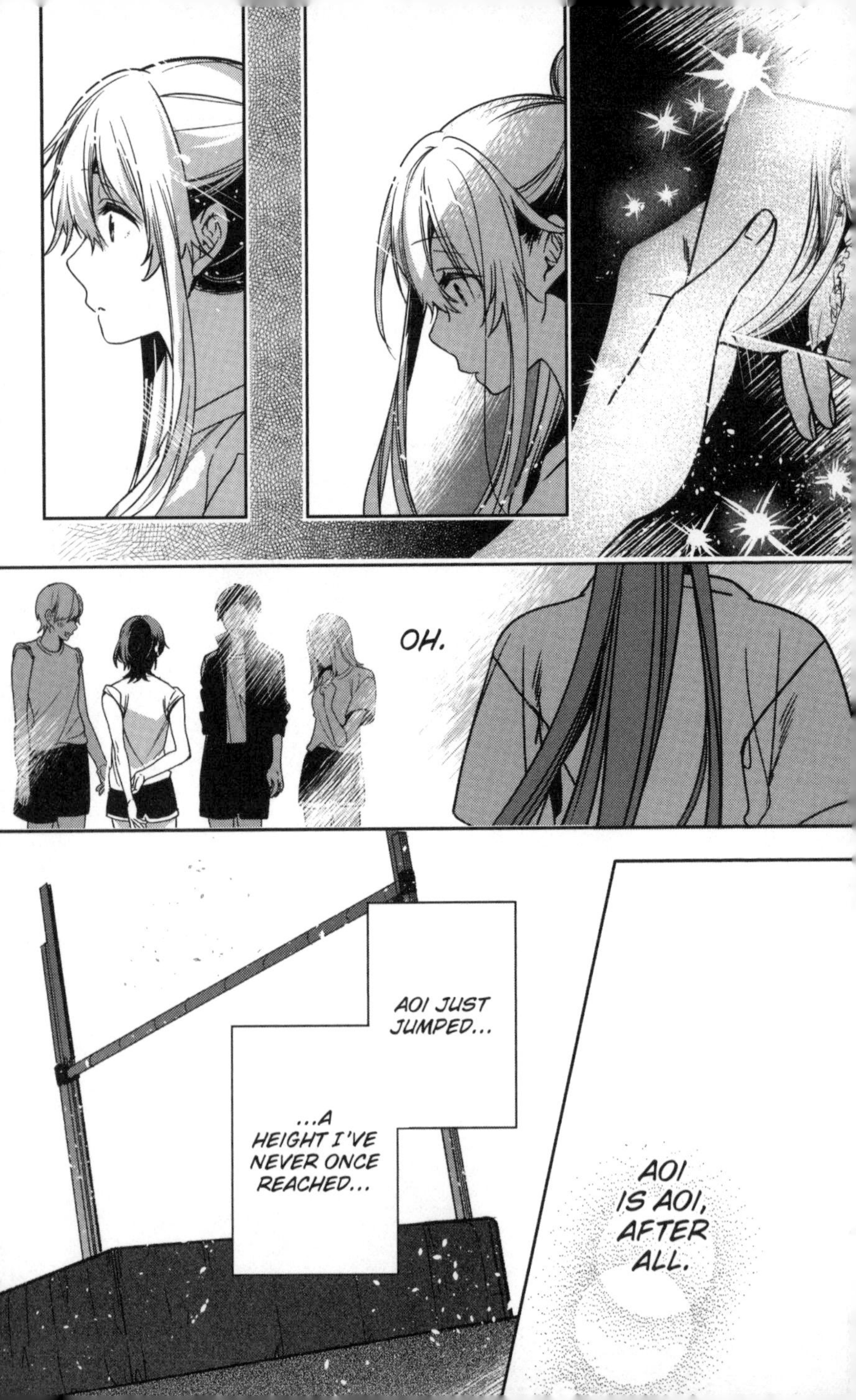
OH.
AOI IS AOI, AFTER ALL.
AOI JUST JUMPED...
...A HEIGHT I'VE NEVER ONCE REACHED...

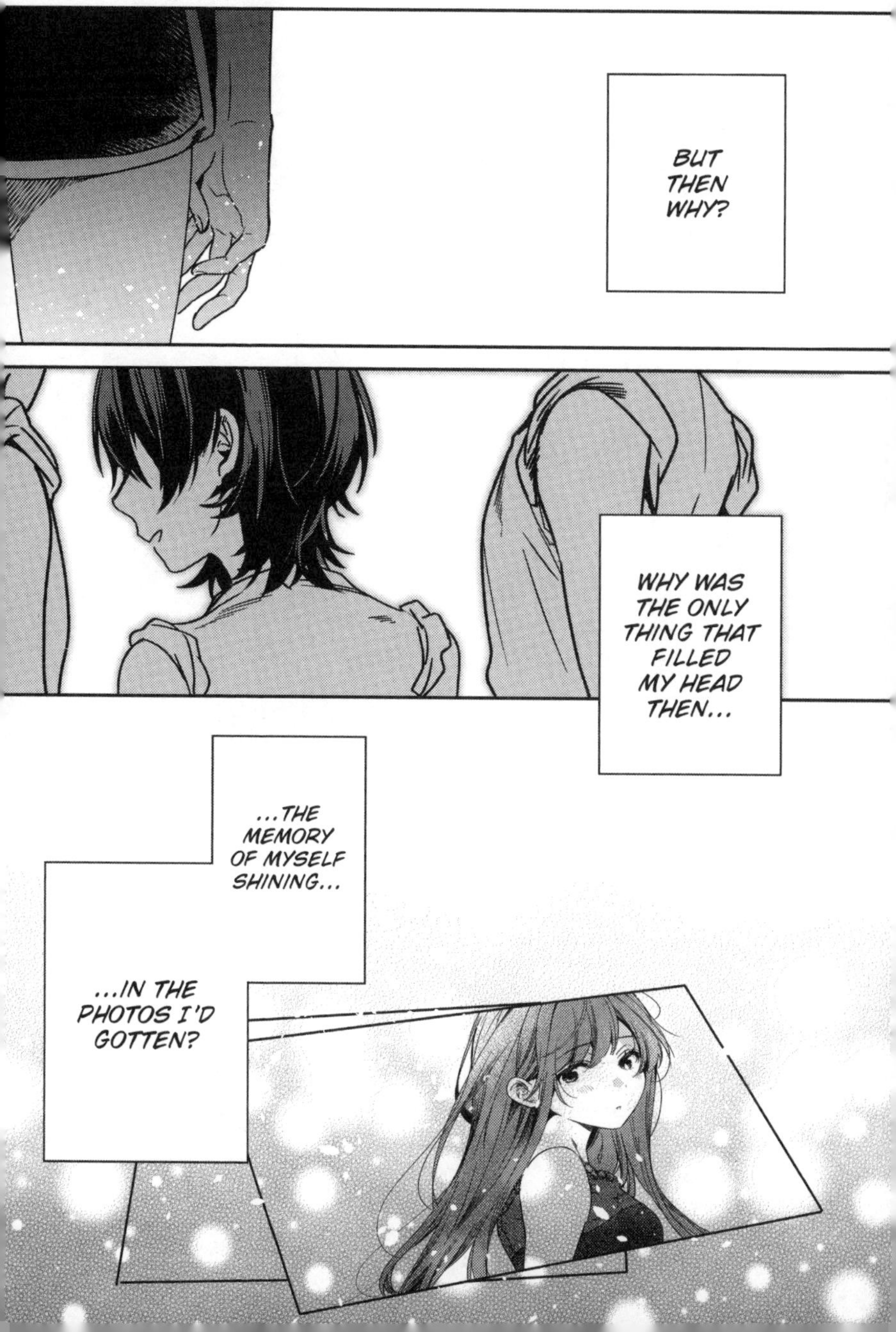
BUT THEN WHY?
WHY WAS THE ONLY THING THAT FILLED MY HEAD THEN...
...THE MEMORY OF MYSELF SHINING...
...IN THE PHOTOS I'D GOTTEN?

Chapter 4 EFFORT AND TALENT

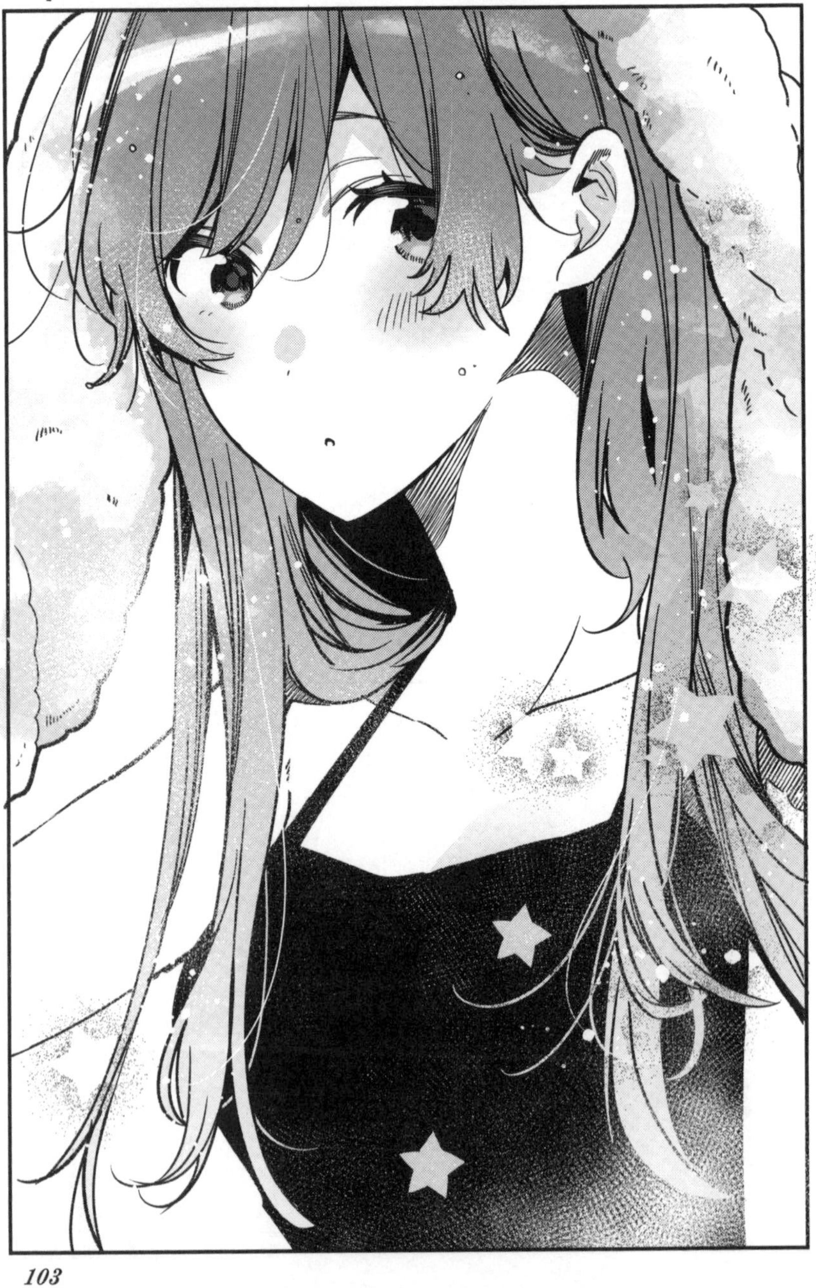

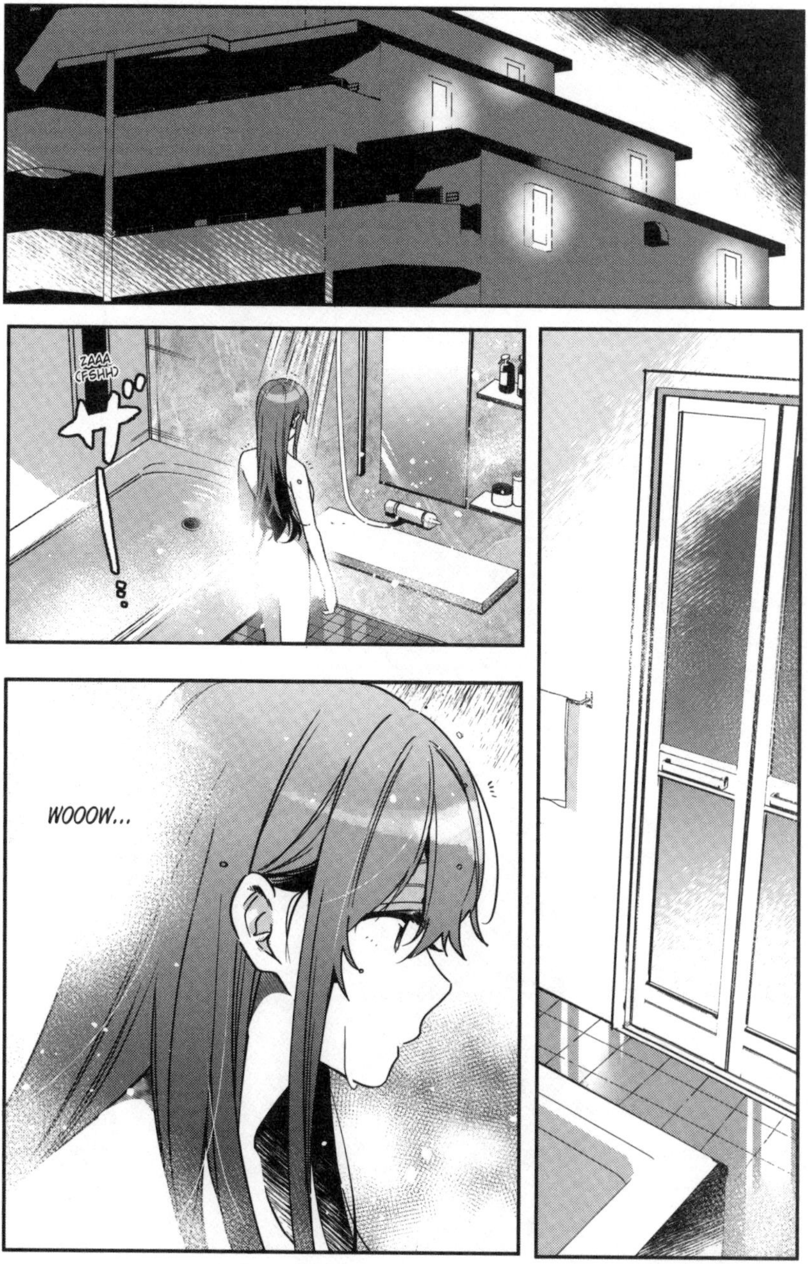
ZAAA (FSHH)
WOOOW...

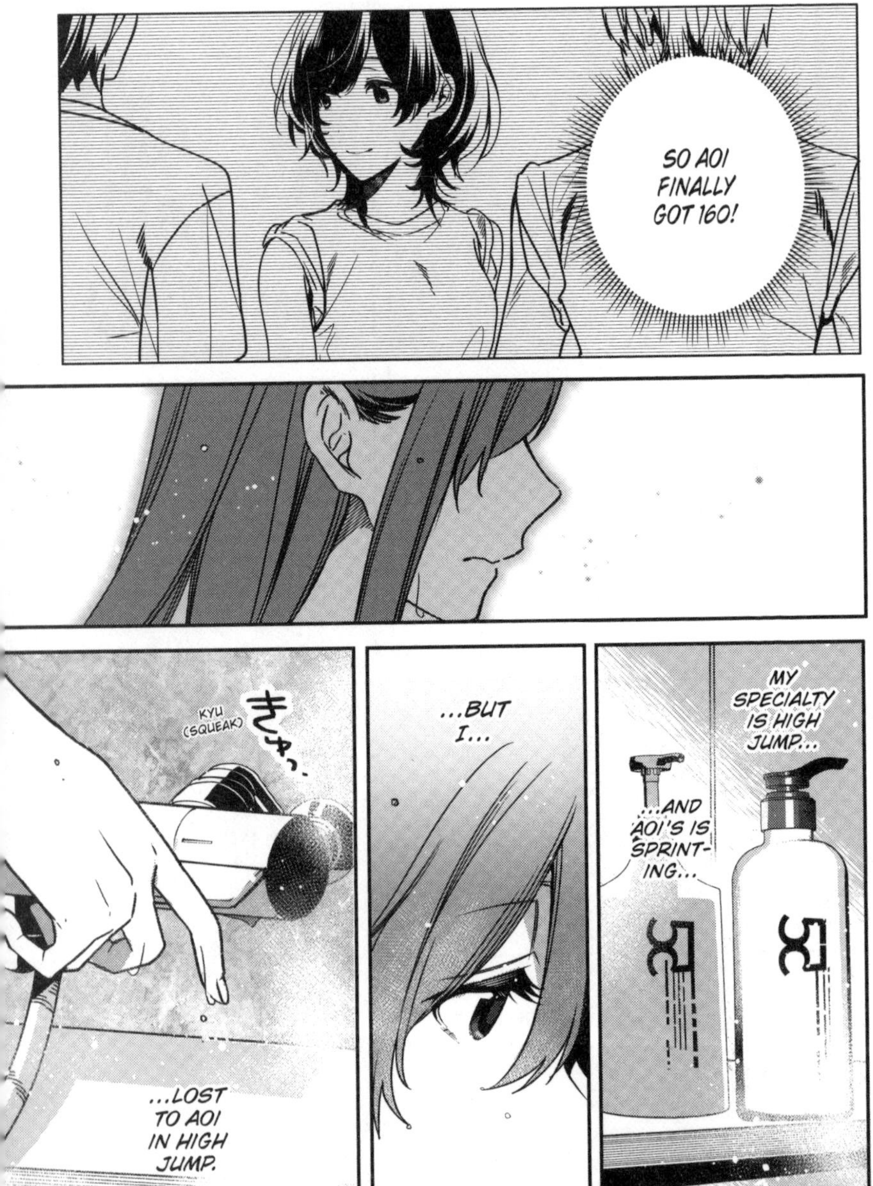
SO AOI FINALLY GOT 160!
MY SPECIALTY IS HIGH JUMP...
...AND AOI'S IS SPRINT-ING...
...BUT I...
きゅっ
KYU (SQUEAK)
...LOST TO AOI IN HIGH JUMP.

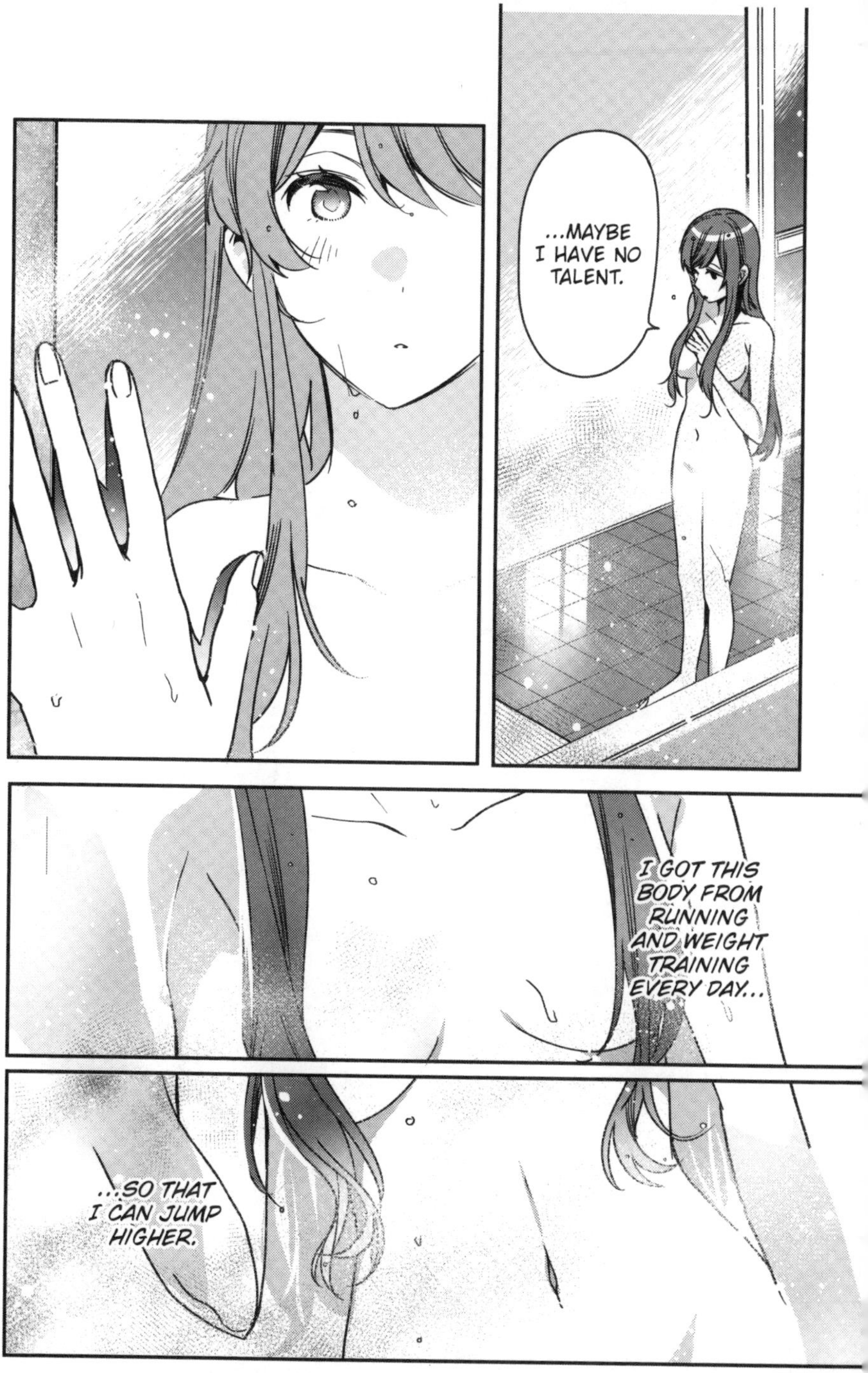
...MAYBE I HAVE NO TALENT.
I GOT THIS BODY FROM RUNNING AND WEIGHT TRAINING EVERY DAY...
...SO THAT I CAN JUMP HIGHER.

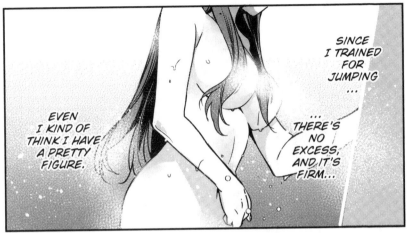

SINCE I TRAINED FOR JUMPING...
...THERE'S NO EXCESS, AND IT'S FIRM...
EVEN I KIND OF THINK I HAVE A PRETTY FIGURE.
BUT...
WOW! YOUR FIGURE'S AS GOOD AS A PINUP IDOL!
THAT WASN'T WHAT I WAS GOING FOR...

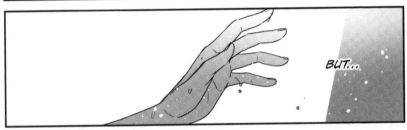

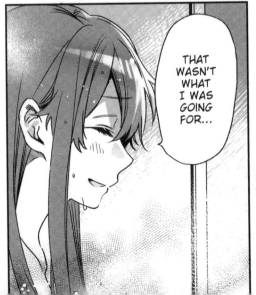

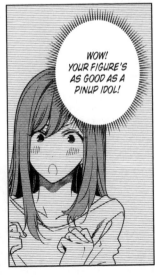

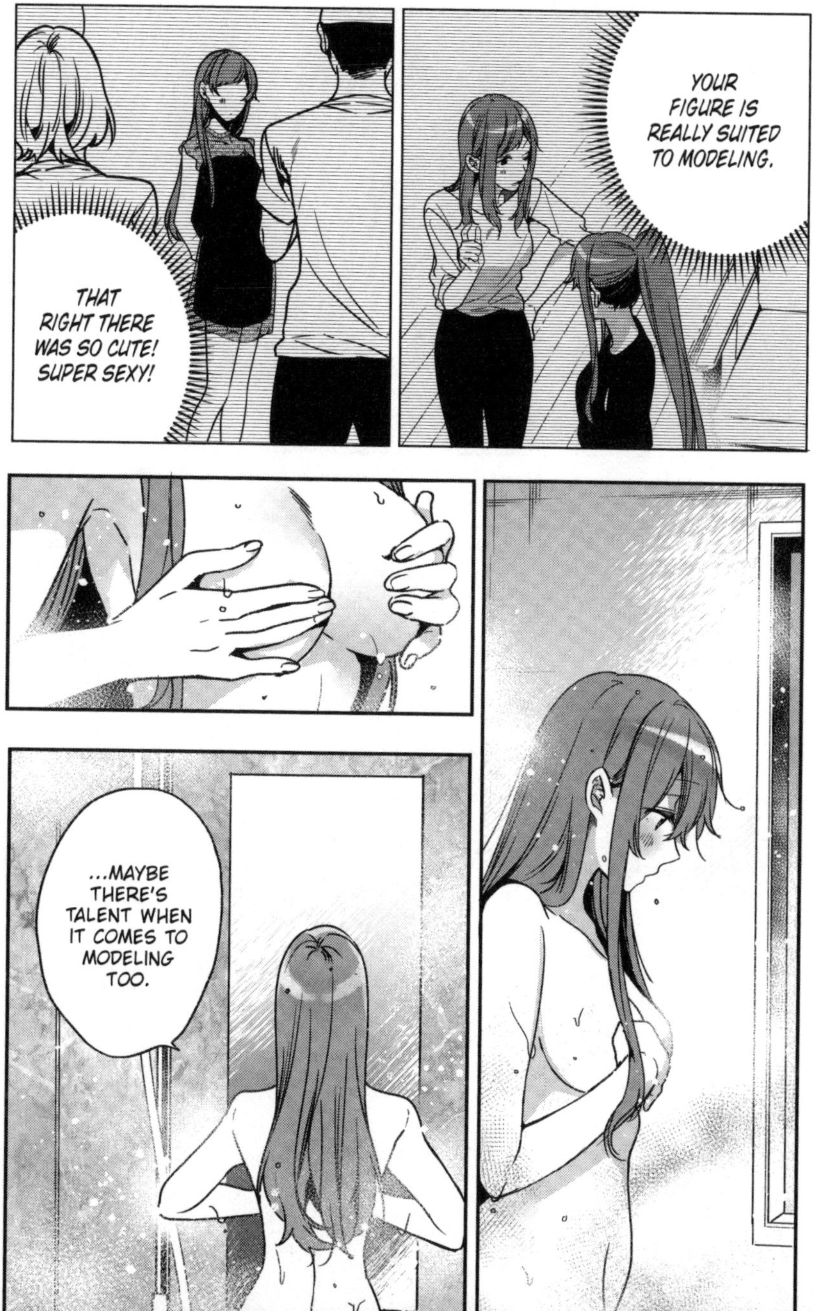
YOUR FIGURE IS REALLY SUITED TO MODELING.
THAT RIGHT THERE WAS SO CUTE! SUPER SEXY!
...MAYBE THERE'S TALENT WHEN IT COMES TO MODELING TOO.

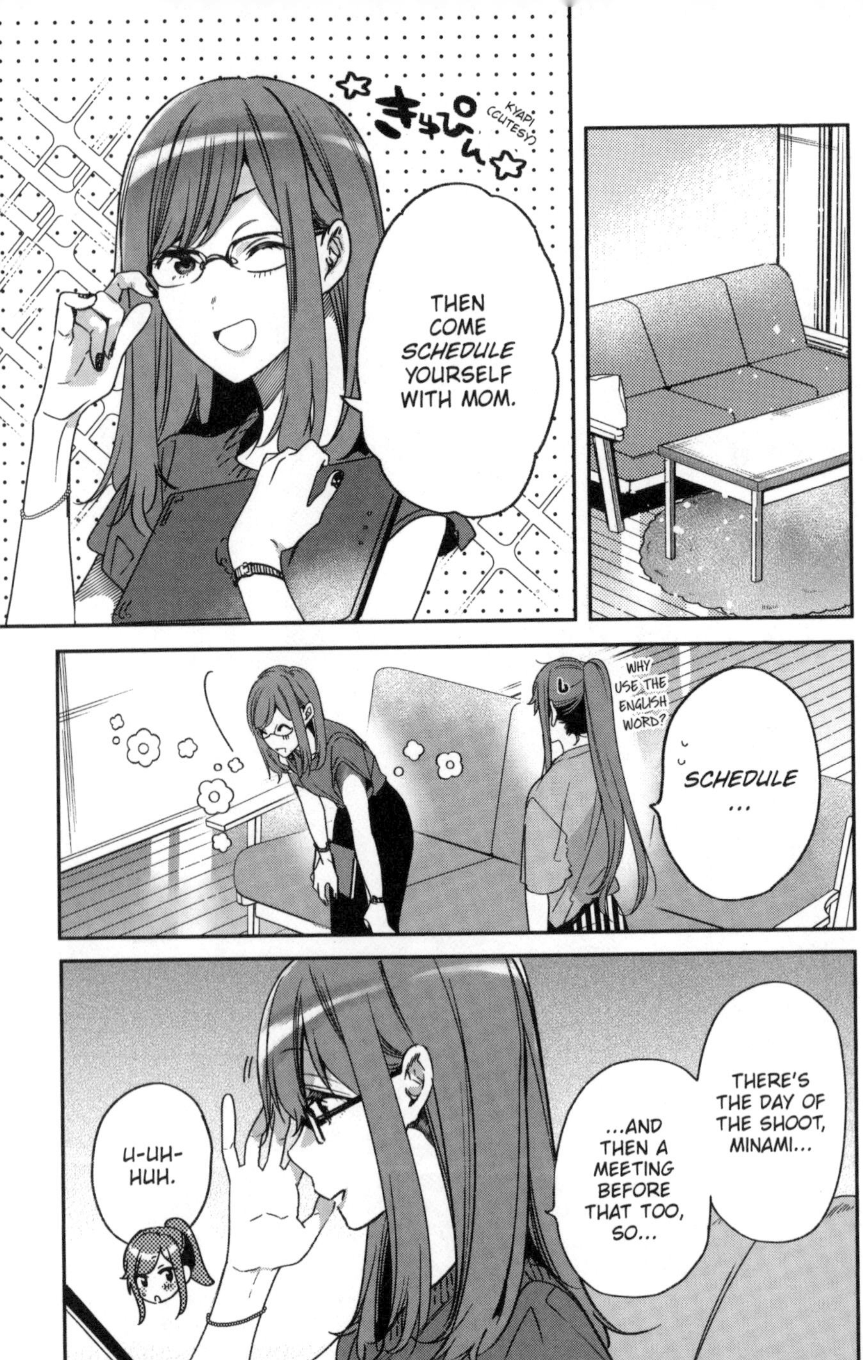
きゃぴん
KYAPI (CUTESY)
THEN COME SCHEDULE YOURSELF WITH MOM.
WHY USE THE ENGLISH WORD?
SCHEDULE ...
THERE'S THE DAY OF THE SHOOT, MINAMI...
...AND THEN A MEETING BEFORE THAT TOO, SO...
U-UH-HUH.

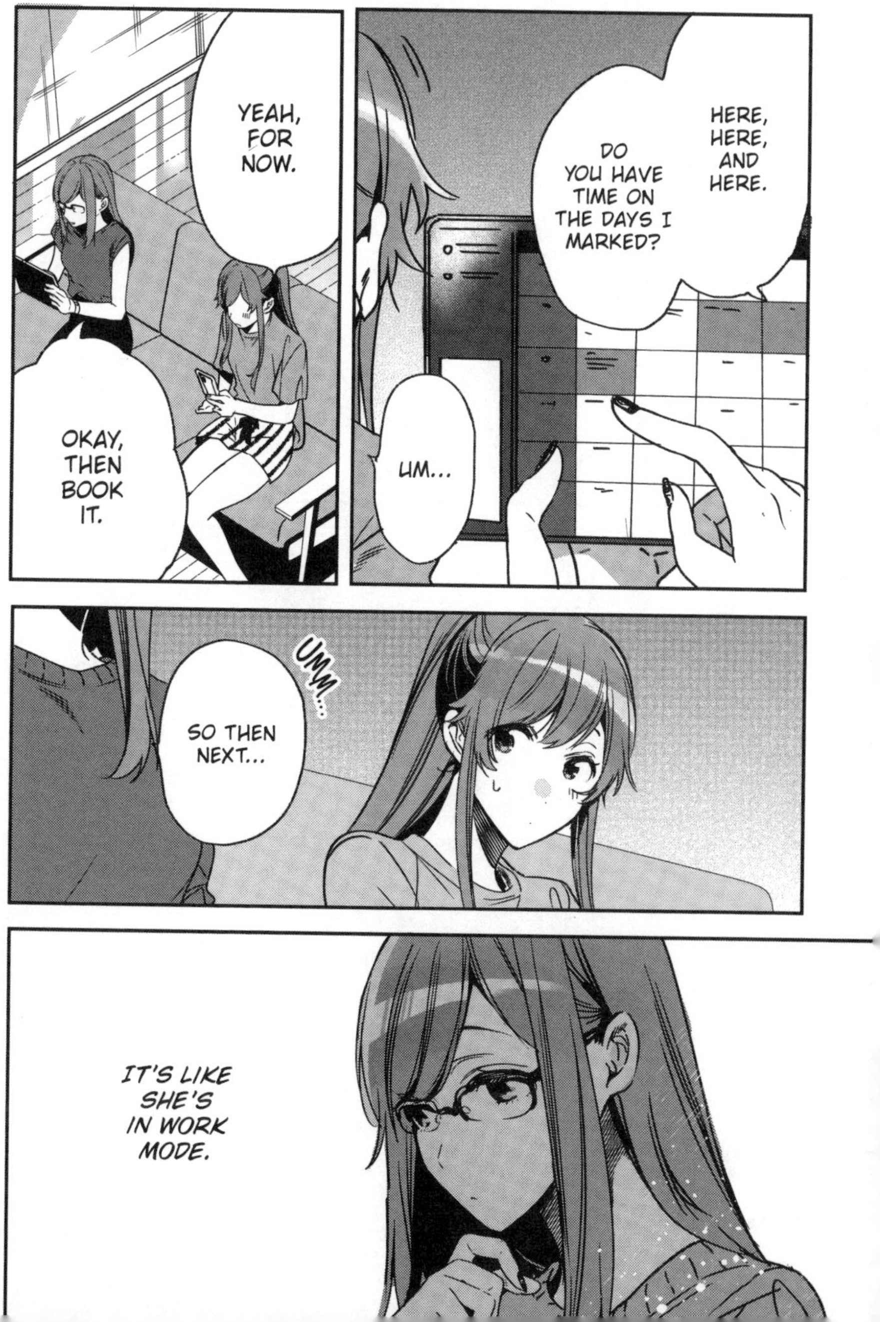
HERE, HERE, AND HERE.
DO YOU HAVE TIME ON THE DAYS I MARKED?
UM...
YEAH, FOR NOW.
OKAY, THEN BOOK IT.
UMM...
SO THEN NEXT...
IT'S LIKE SHE'S IN WORK MODE.

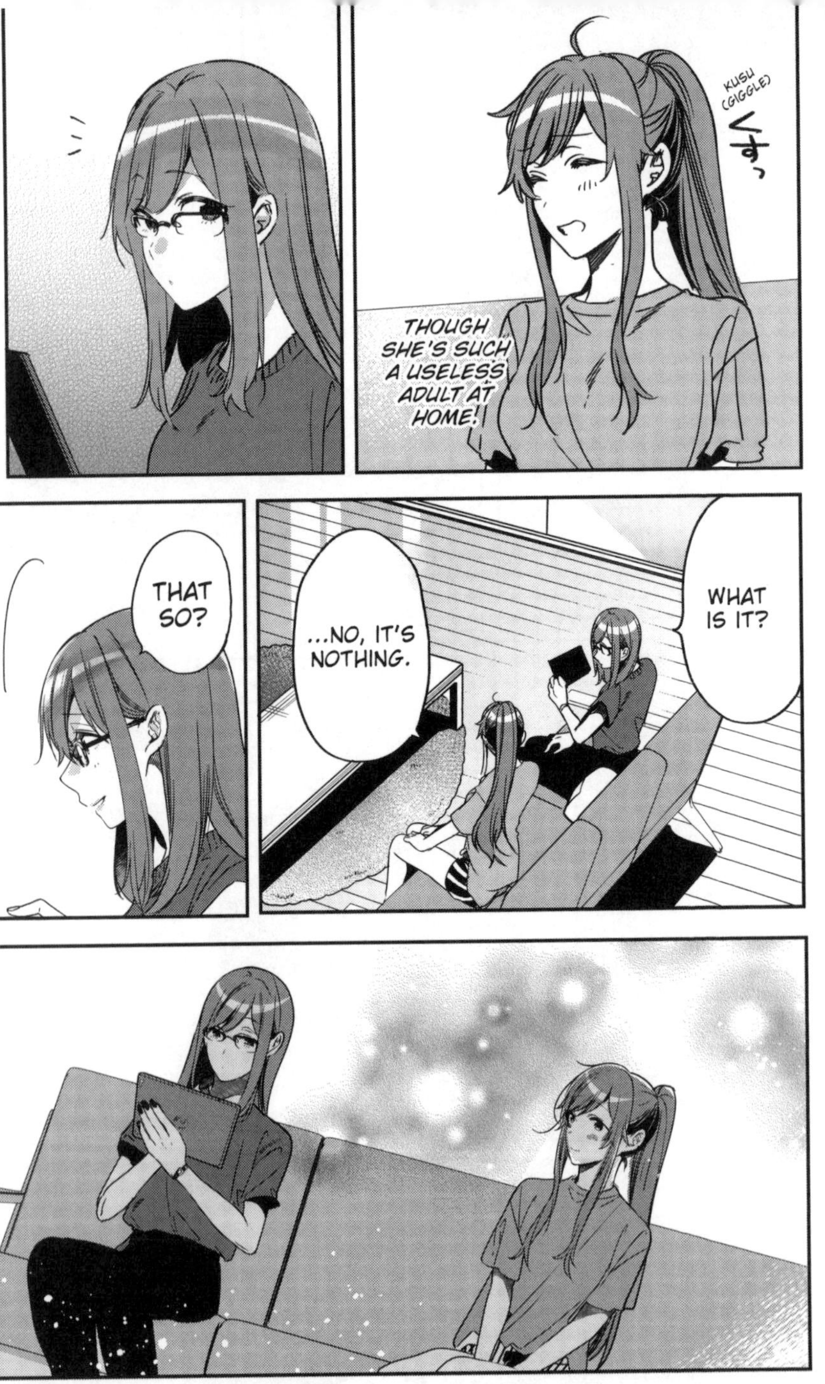
KUSU (GIGGLE)
くすっ
THOUGH SHE'S SUCH A USELESS ADULT AT HOME!
WHAT IS IT?
...NO, IT'S NOTHING.
THAT SO?

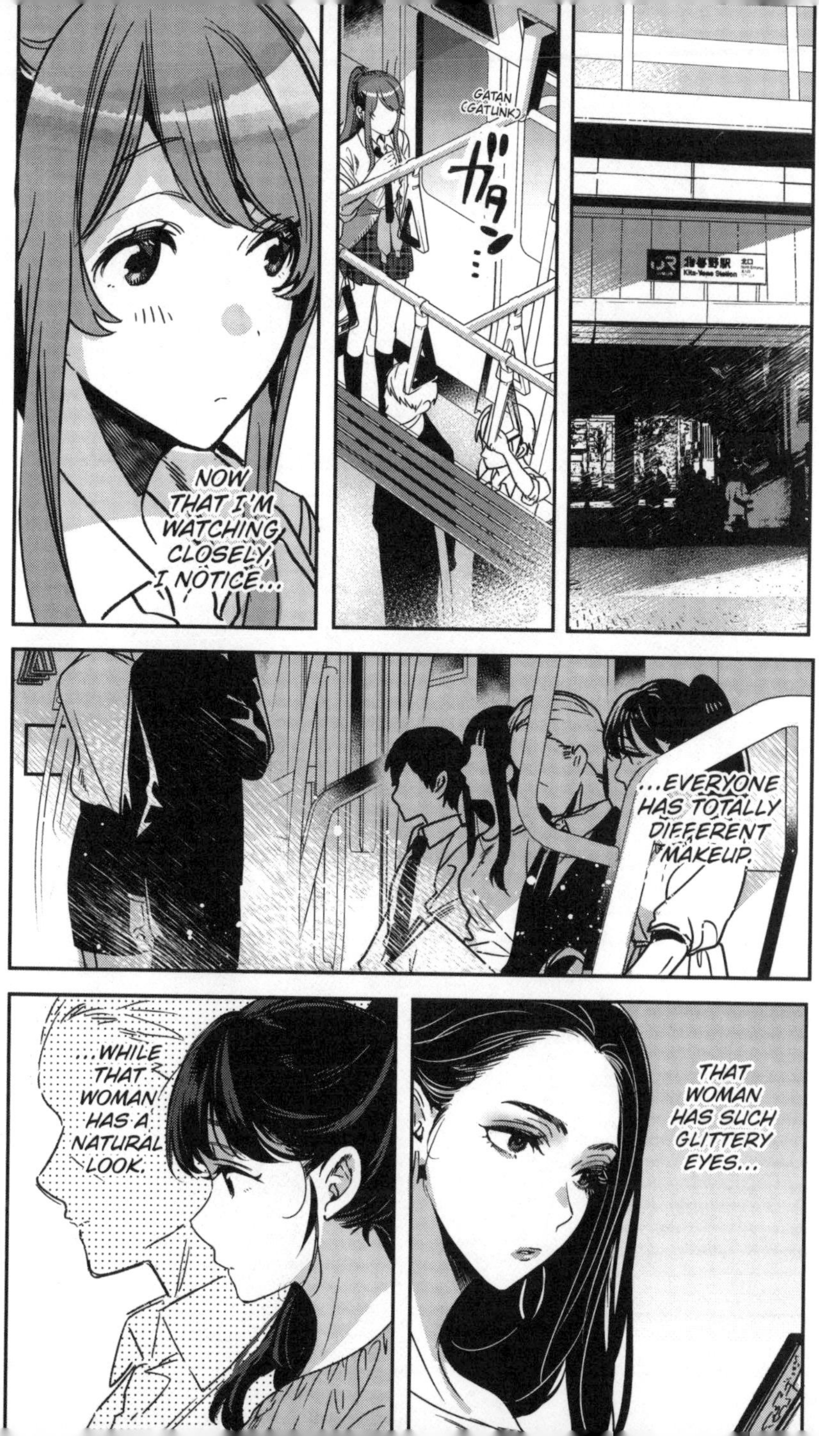
GATAN (GATUNK)
ガタン…
NOW THAT I'M WATCHING CLOSELY, I NOTICE...
...EVERYONE HAS TOTALLY DIFFERENT MAKEUP.
THAT WOMAN HAS SUCH GLITTERY EYES...
...WHILE THAT WOMAN HAS A NATURAL LOOK.

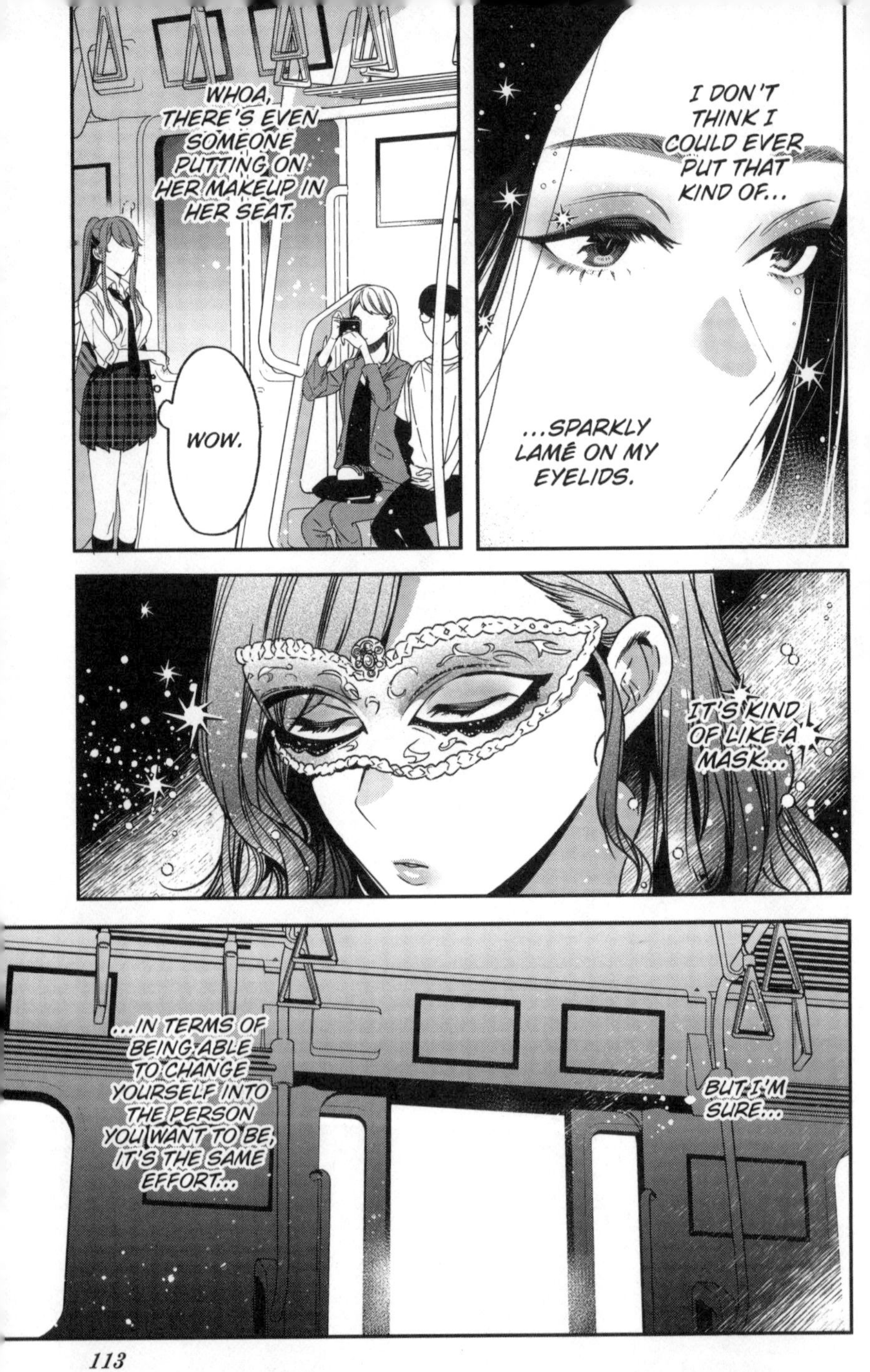
I DON'T THINK I COULD EVER PUT THAT KIND OF...
...SPARKLY LAMÉ ON MY EYELIDS.
WHOA, THERE'S EVEN SOMEONE PUTTING ON HER MAKEUP IN HER SEAT.
WOW.
IT'S KIND OF LIKE A MASK...
BUT I'M SURE...
...IN TERMS OF BEING ABLE TO CHANGE YOURSELF INTO THE PERSON YOU WANT TO BE, IT'S THE SAME EFFORT...

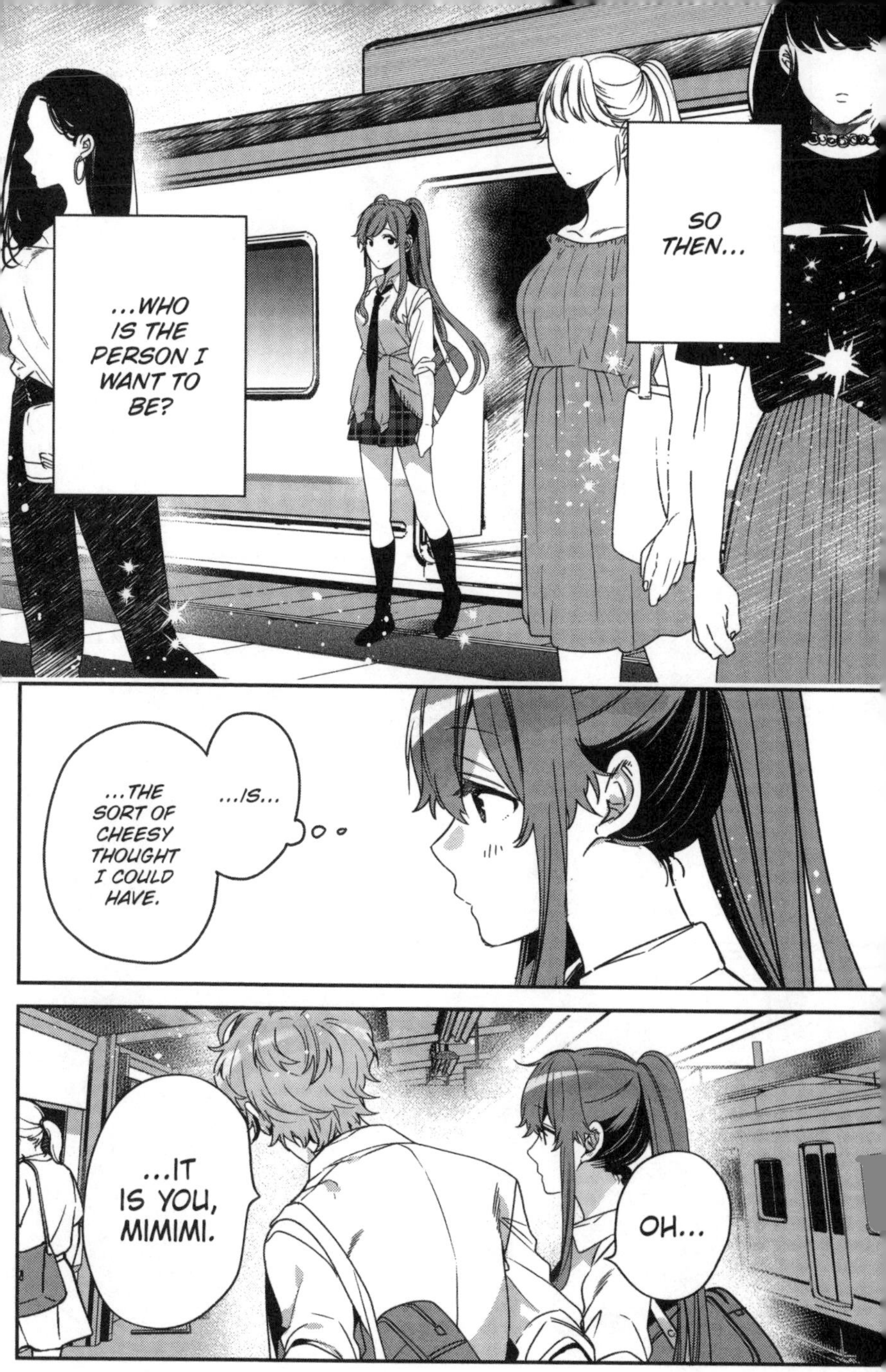
SO THEN…
…WHO IS THE PERSON I WANT TO BE?
…IS…
…THE SORT OF CHEESY THOUGHT I COULD HAVE.
OH…
…IT IS YOU, MIMIMI.

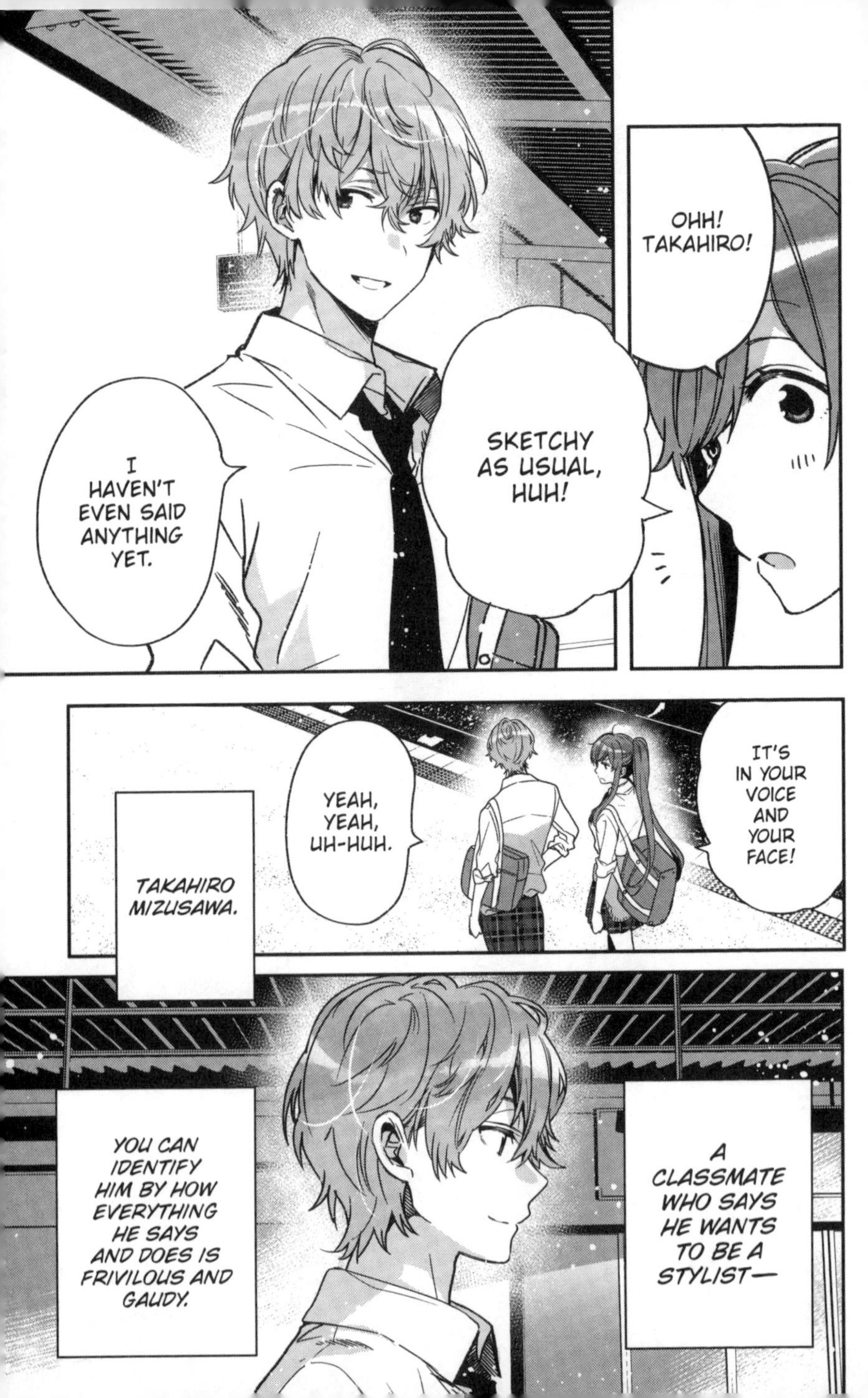
OHH! TAKAHIRO!
SKETCHY AS USUAL, HUH!
I HAVEN'T EVEN SAID ANYTHING YET.
IT'S IN YOUR VOICE AND YOUR FACE!
YEAH, YEAH, UH-HUH.
TAKAHIRO MIZUSAWA.
A CLASSMATE WHO SAYS HE WANTS TO BE A STYLIST—
YOU CAN IDENTIFY HIM BY HOW EVERYTHING HE SAYS AND DOES IS FRIVILOUS AND GAUDY.

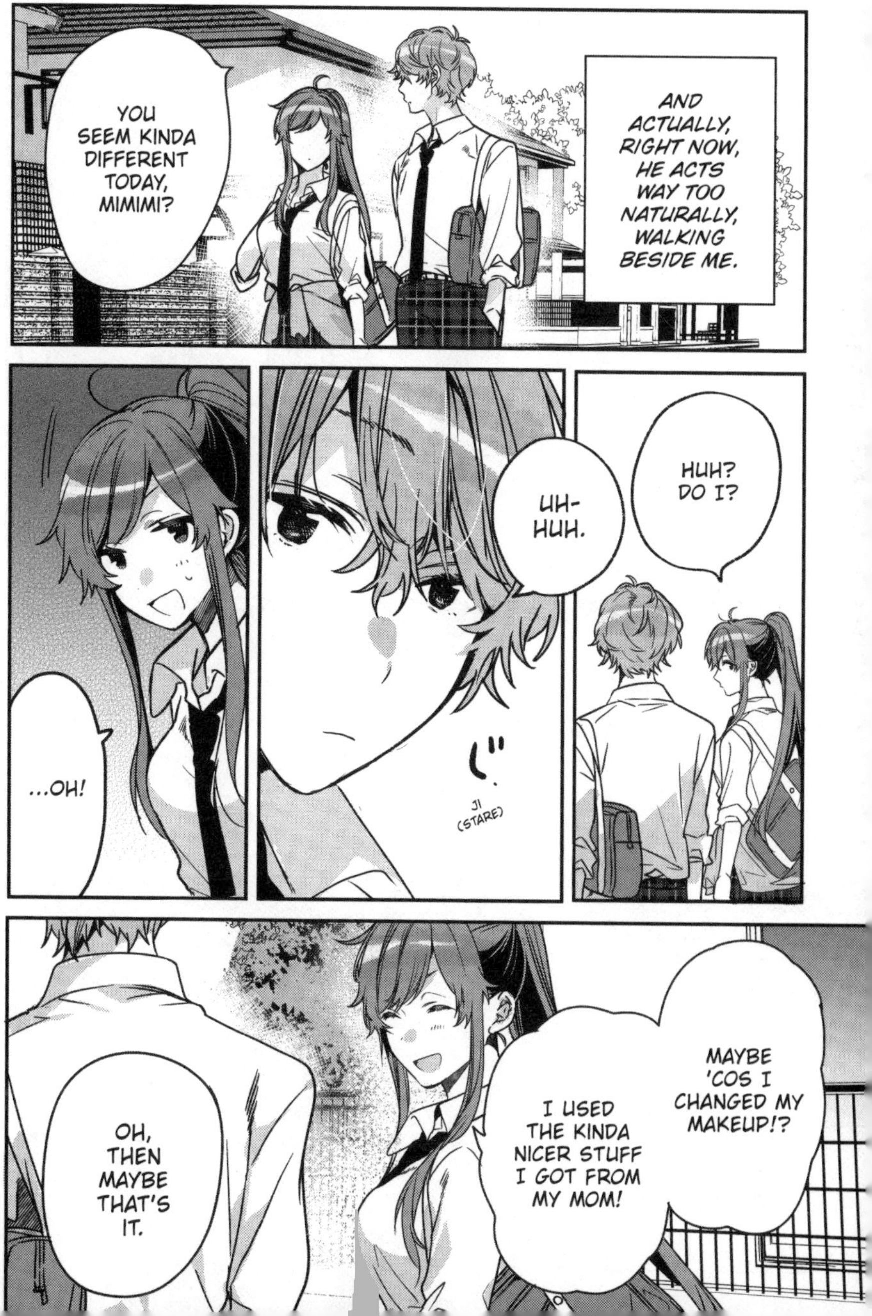
AND ACTUALLY, RIGHT NOW, HE ACTS WAY TOO NATURALLY, WALKING BESIDE ME.
YOU SEEM KINDA DIFFERENT TODAY, MIMIMI?
HUH? DO I?
UH-HUH.
じ
JI (STARE)
...OH!
MAYBE 'COS I CHANGED MY MAKEUP!?
I USED THE KINDA NICER STUFF I GOT FROM MY MOM!
OH, THEN MAYBE THAT'S IT.

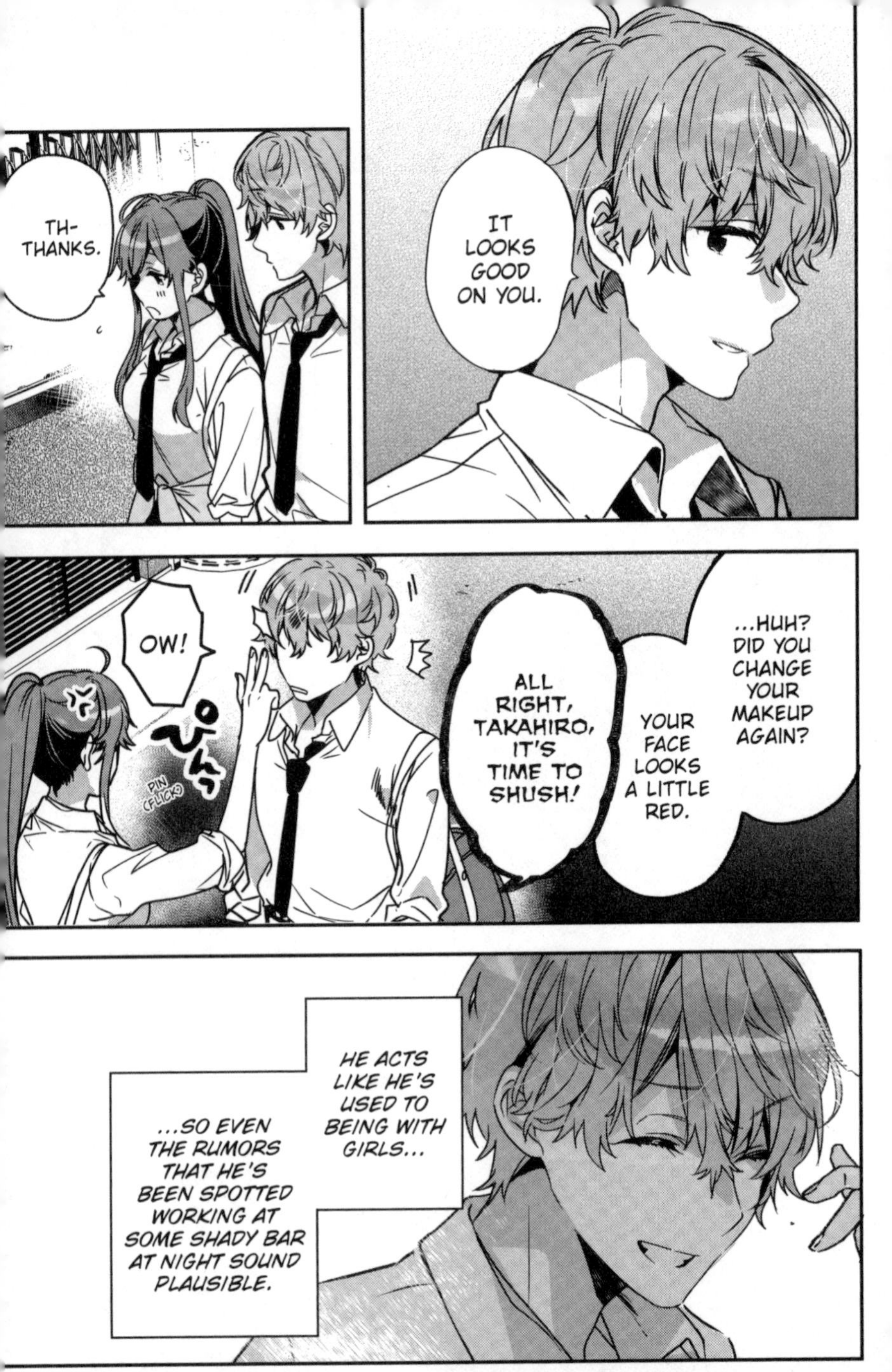
IT LOOKS GOOD ON YOU.
TH- THANKS.
...HUH? DID YOU CHANGE YOUR MAKEUP AGAIN?
YOUR FACE LOOKS A LITTLE RED.
ALL RIGHT, TAKAHIRO, IT'S TIME TO SHUSH!
OW!
PIN (FLICK)
HE ACTS LIKE HE'S USED TO BEING WITH GIRLS...
...SO EVEN THE RUMORS THAT HE'S BEEN SPOTTED WORKING AT SOME SHADY BAR AT NIGHT SOUND PLAUSIBLE.

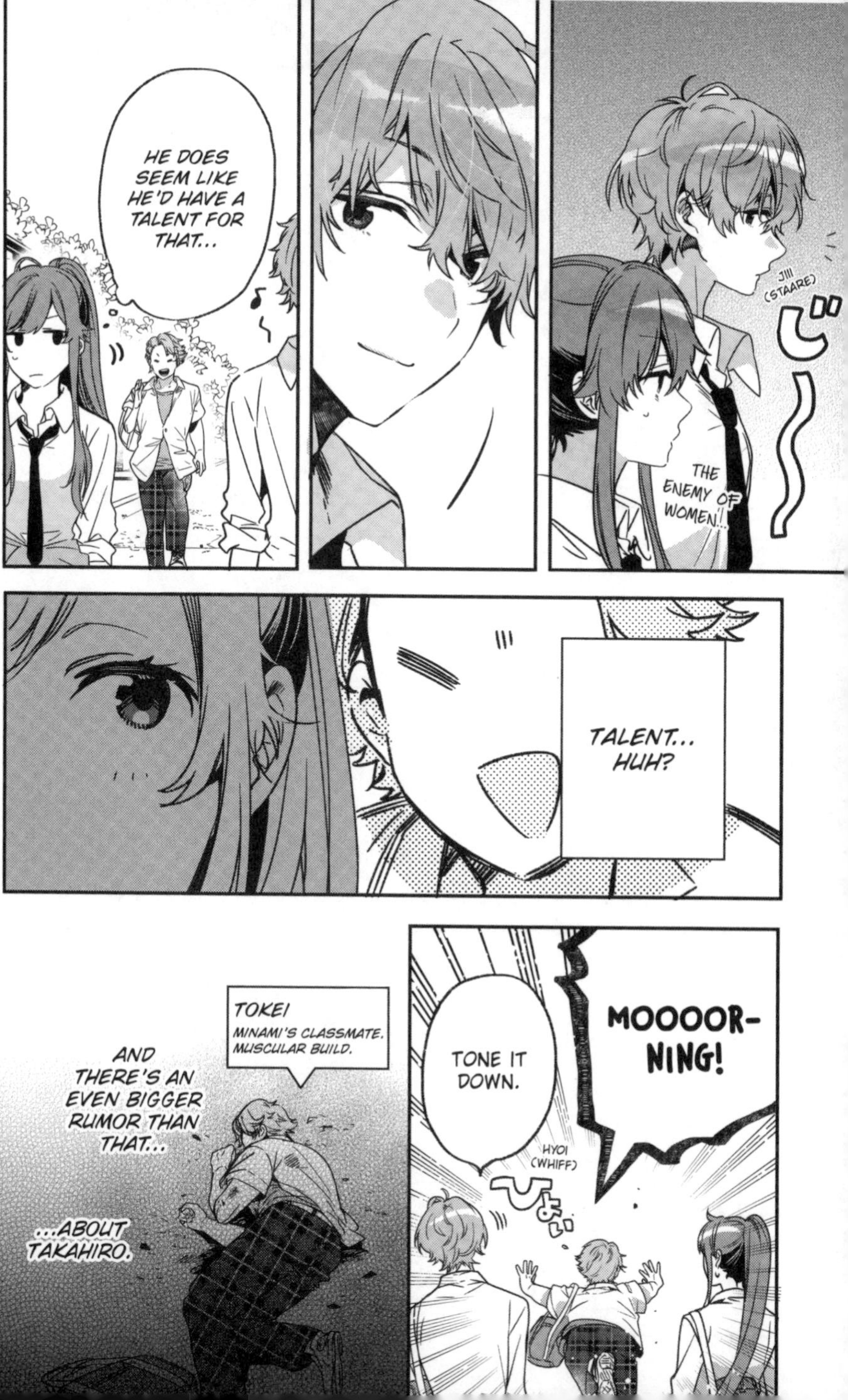
JIII (STAARE)
じー
THE ENEMY OF WOMEN...
HE DOES SEEM LIKE HE'D HAVE A TALENT FOR THAT...
TALENT... HUH?
MOOOOR-NING!
TONE IT DOWN.
HYOI (WHIFF)
ひょい
TOKEI
MINAMI'S CLASSMATE. MUSCULAR BUILD.
AND THERE'S AN EVEN BIGGER RUMOR THAN THAT...
...ABOUT TAKAHIRO.

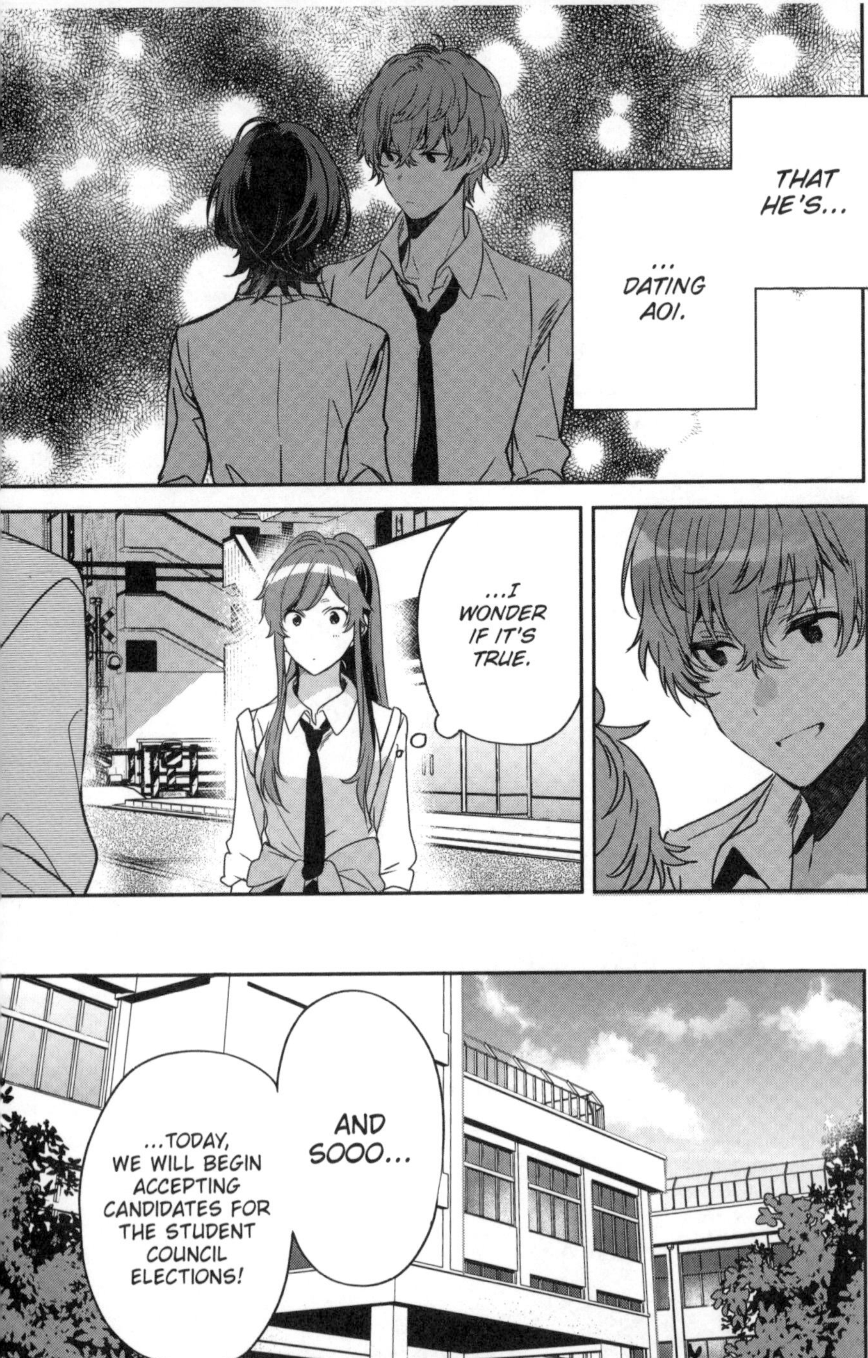
THAT HE'S...
...DATING AOI.
...I WONDER IF IT'S TRUE.
AND SOOO...
...TODAY, WE WILL BEGIN ACCEPTING CANDIDATES FOR THE STUDENT COUNCIL ELECTIONS!

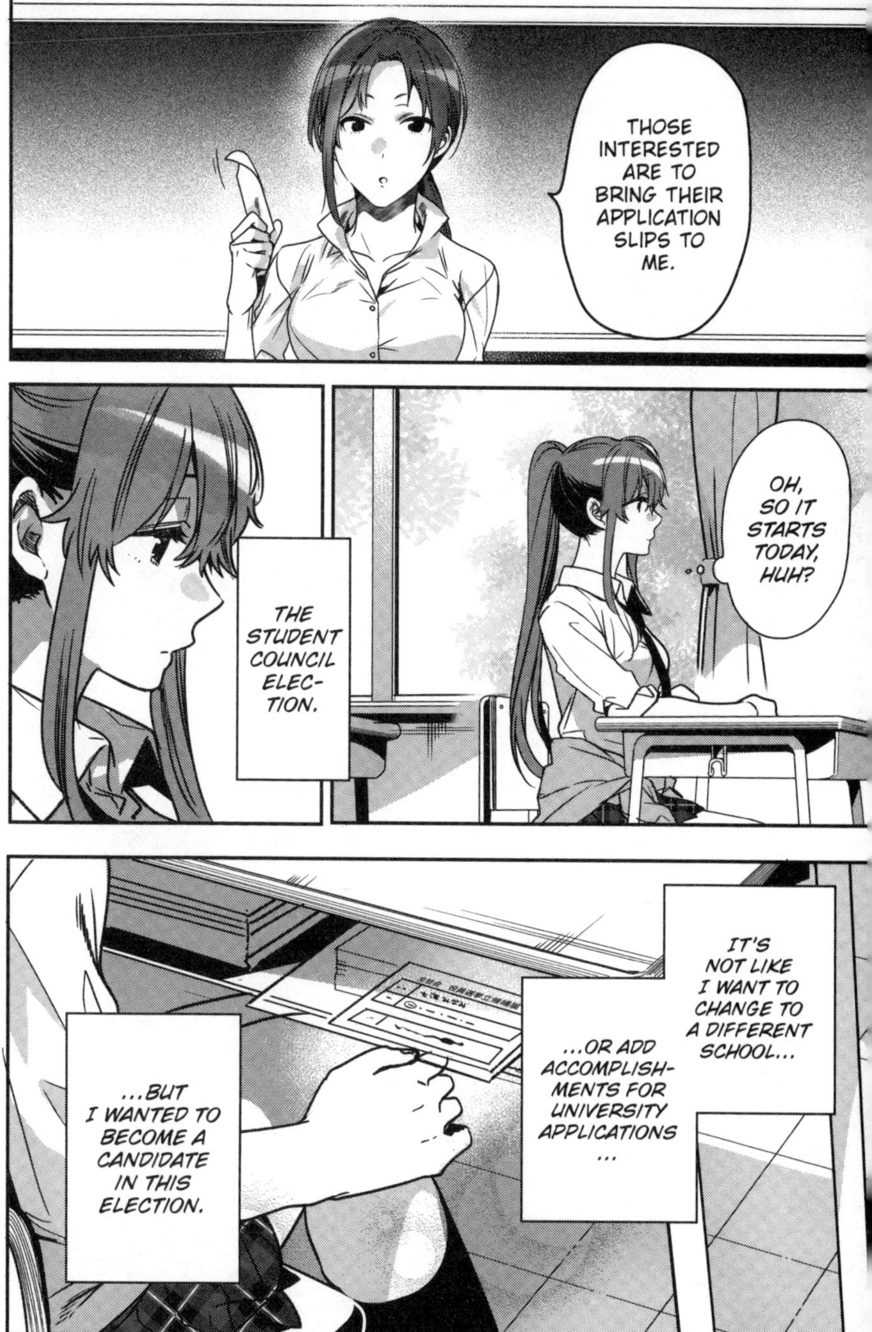
THOSE INTERESTED ARE TO BRING THEIR APPLICATION SLIPS TO ME.
OH, SO IT STARTS TODAY, HUH?
THE STUDENT COUNCIL ELEC-TION.
IT'S NOT LIKE I WANT TO CHANGE TO A DIFFERENT SCHOOL...
...OR ADD ACCOMPLISH-MENTS FOR UNIVERSITY APPLICATIONS...
...BUT I WANTED TO BECOME A CANDIDATE IN THIS ELECTION.

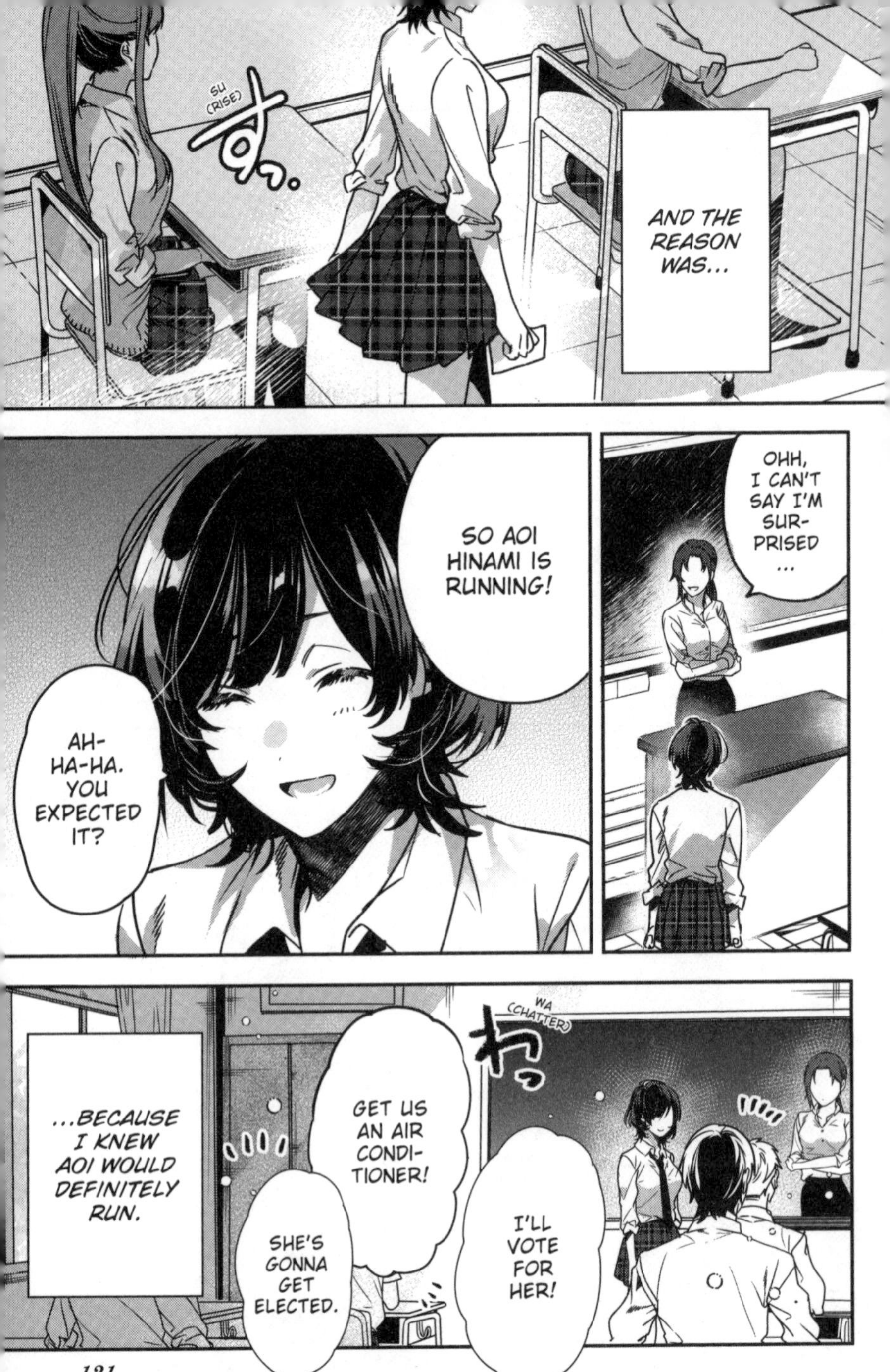
AND THE REASON WAS...
SU (RISE)
OHH, I CAN'T SAY I'M SUR-PRISED...
SO AOI HINAMI IS RUNNING!
AH-HA-HA. YOU EXPECTED IT?
WA (CHATTER)
I'LL VOTE FOR HER!
GET US AN AIR CONDI-TIONER!
SHE'S GONNA GET ELECTED.
...BECAUSE I KNEW AOI WOULD DEFINITELY RUN.

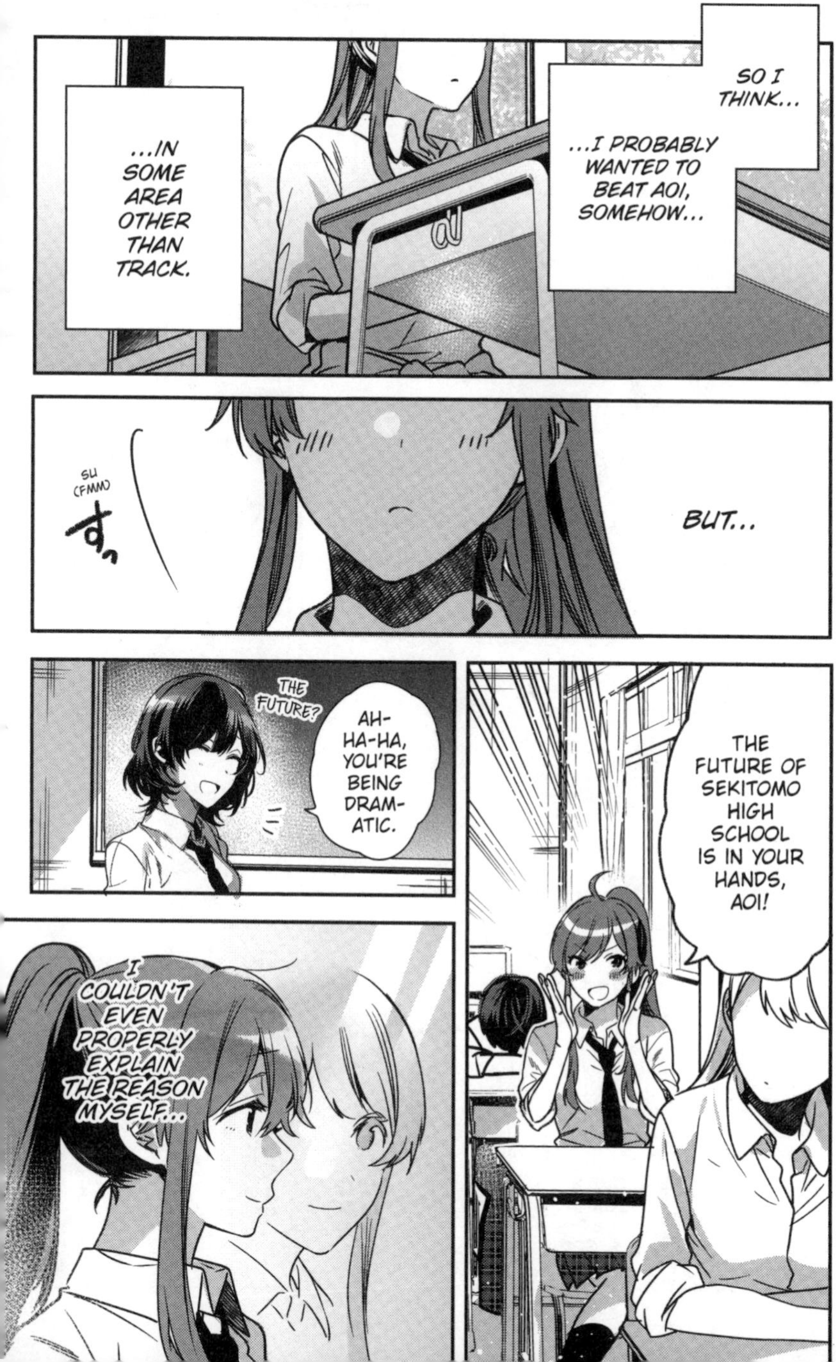
SO I THINK...
...I PROBABLY WANTED TO BEAT AOI, SOMEHOW...
...IN SOME AREA OTHER THAN TRACK.
BUT...
SU (FMM)
すっ
THE FUTURE OF SEKITOMO HIGH SCHOOL IS IN YOUR HANDS, AOI!
THE FUTURE?
AH-HA-HA, YOU'RE BEING DRAMATIC.
I COULDN'T EVEN PROPERLY EXPLAIN THE REASON MYSELF...

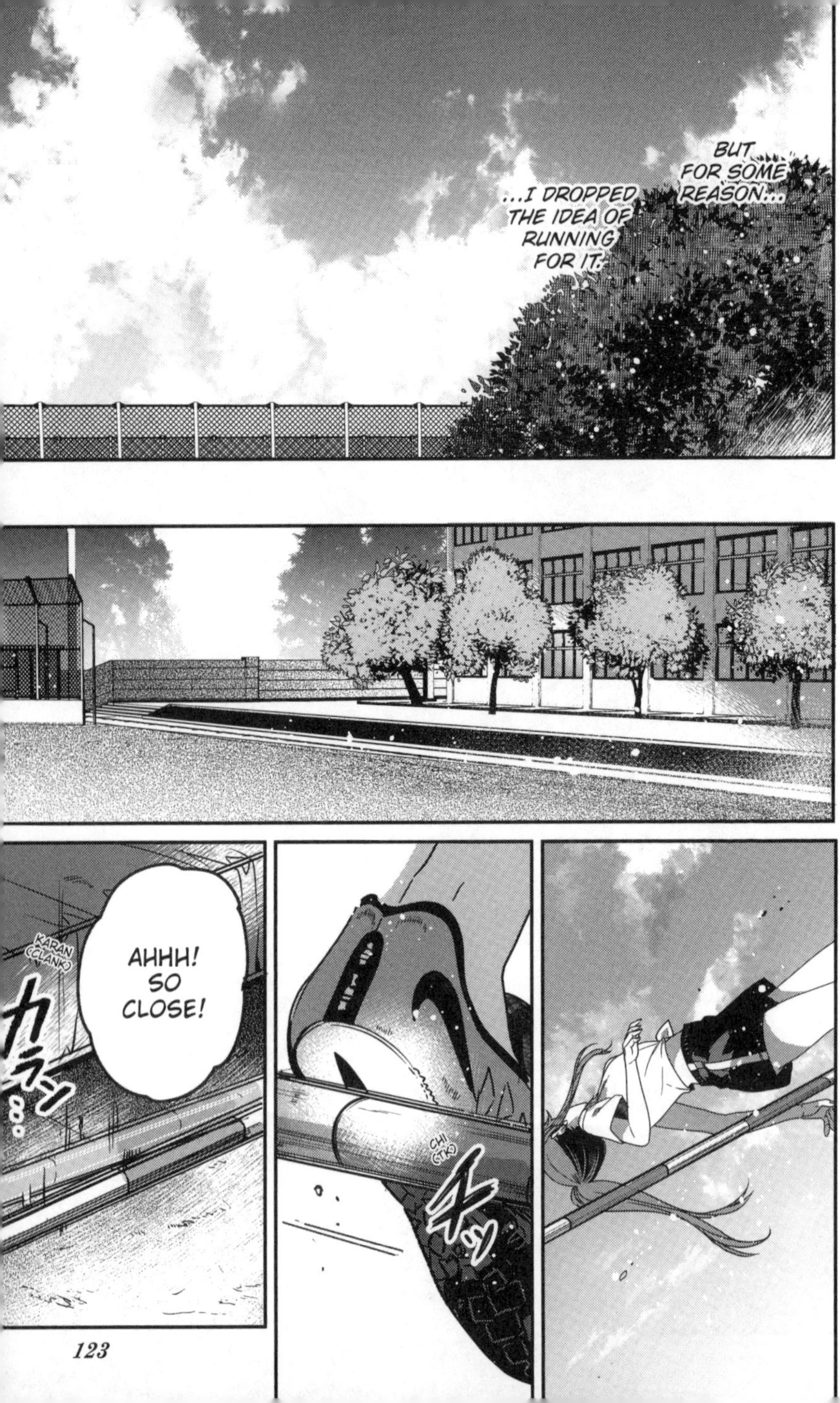
BUT FOR SOME REASON...
...I DROPPED THE IDEA OF RUNNING FOR IT.
CHI (TK)
KARAN (CLANK)
AHHH! SO CLOSE!

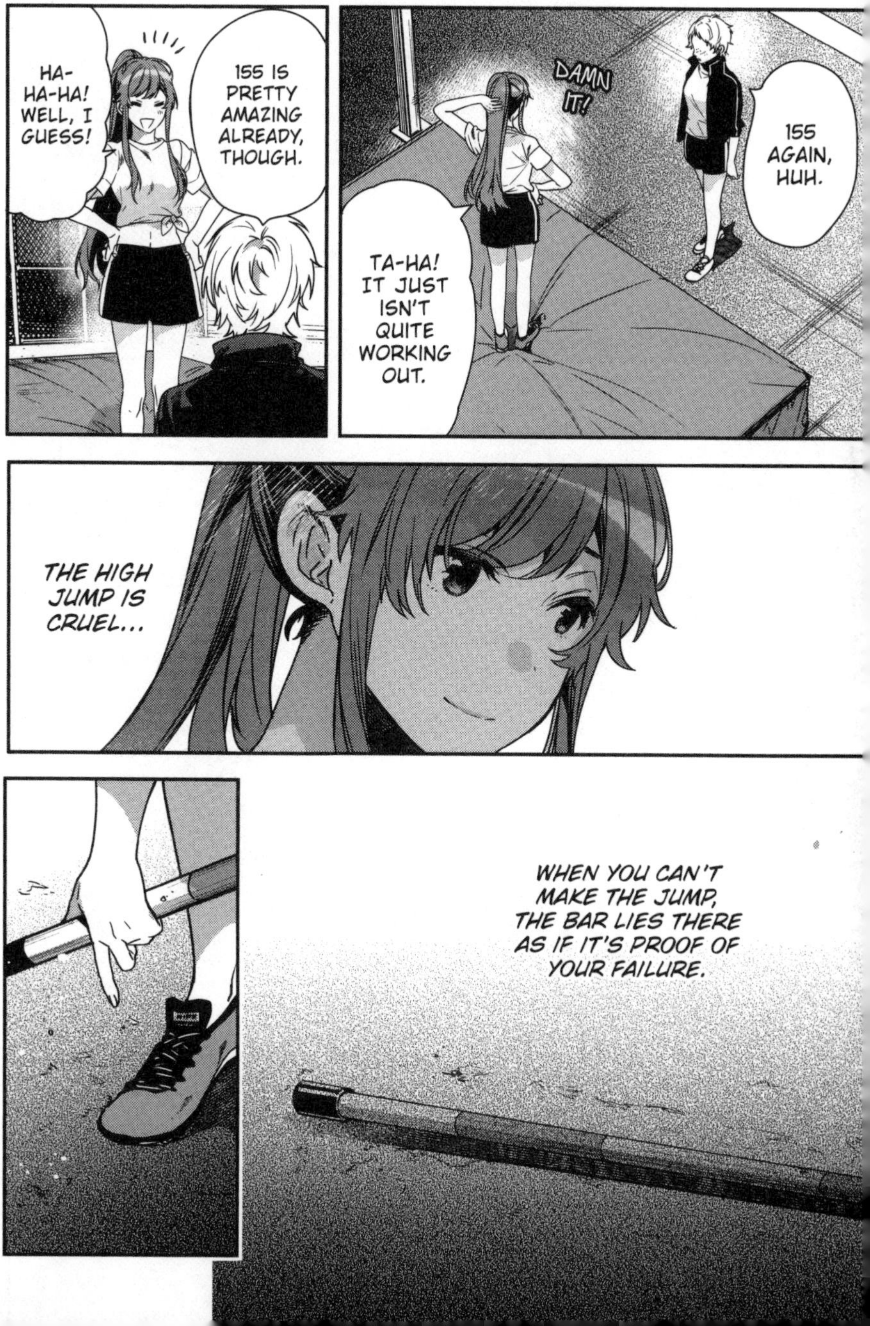
155 AGAIN, HUH.
DAMN IT!
TA-HA! IT JUST ISN'T QUITE WORKING OUT.
155 IS PRETTY AMAZING ALREADY, THOUGH.
HA-HA-HA! WELL, I GUESS!
THE HIGH JUMP IS CRUEL...
WHEN YOU CAN'T MAKE THE JUMP, THE BAR LIES THERE AS IF IT'S PROOF OF YOUR FAILURE.

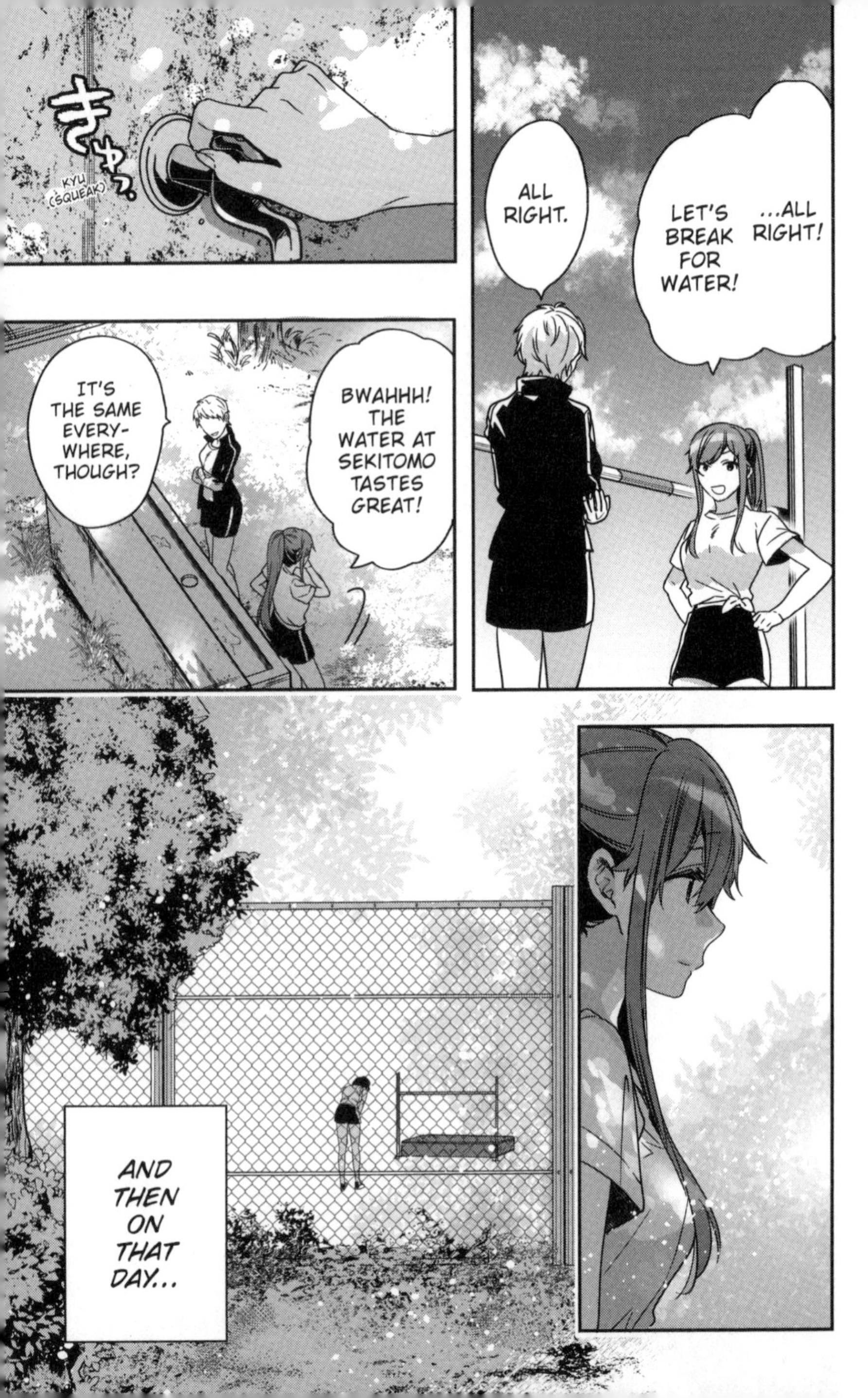
LET'S BREAK FOR WATER! ...ALL RIGHT!
ALL RIGHT.
きゅっ
KYU (SQUEAK)
BWAHHH! THE WATER AT SEKITOMO TASTES GREAT!
IT'S THE SAME EVERY-WHERE, THOUGH?
AND THEN ON THAT DAY...

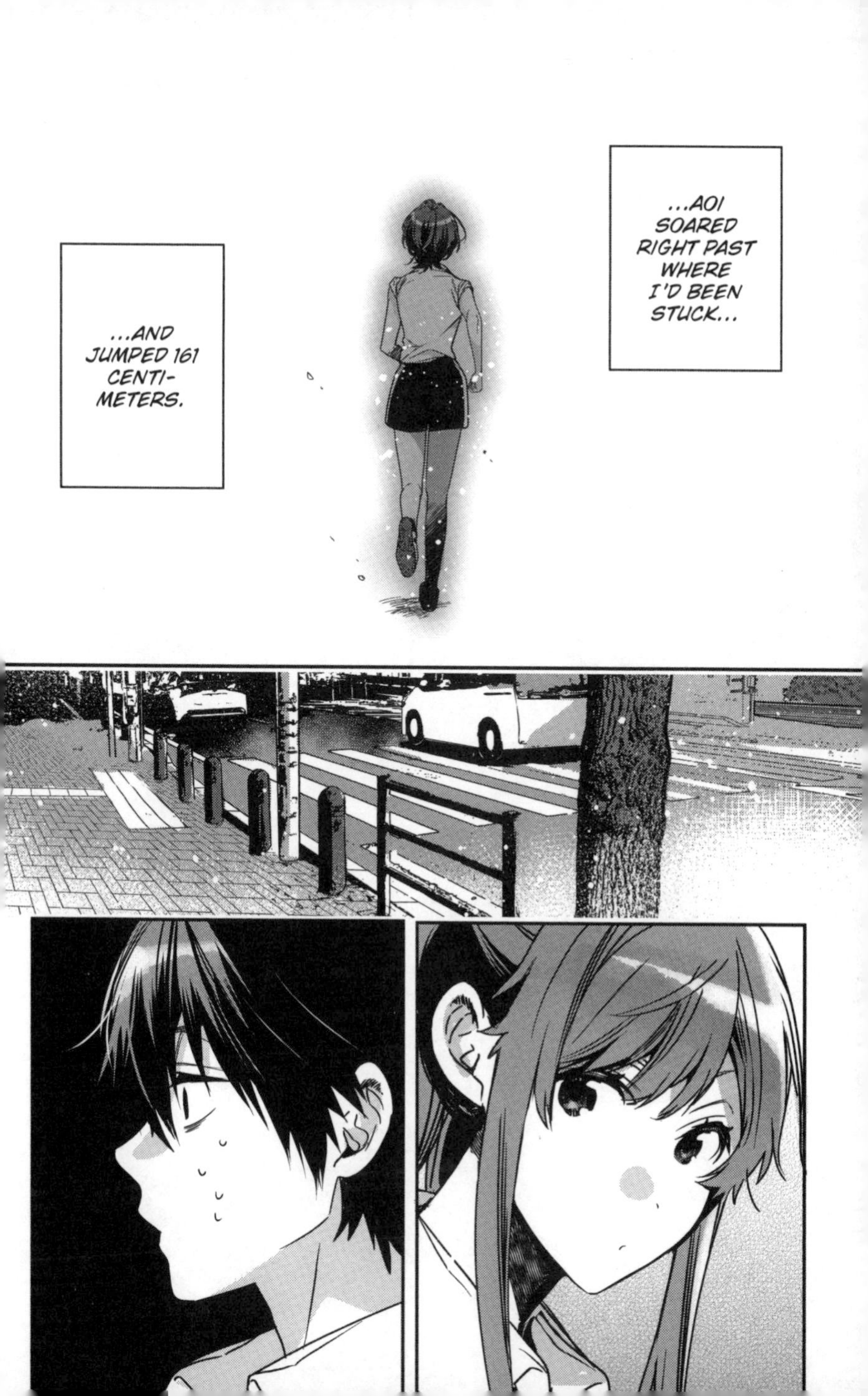
...AOI SOARED RIGHT PAST WHERE I'D BEEN STUCK...
...AND JUMPED 161 CENTI-METERS.

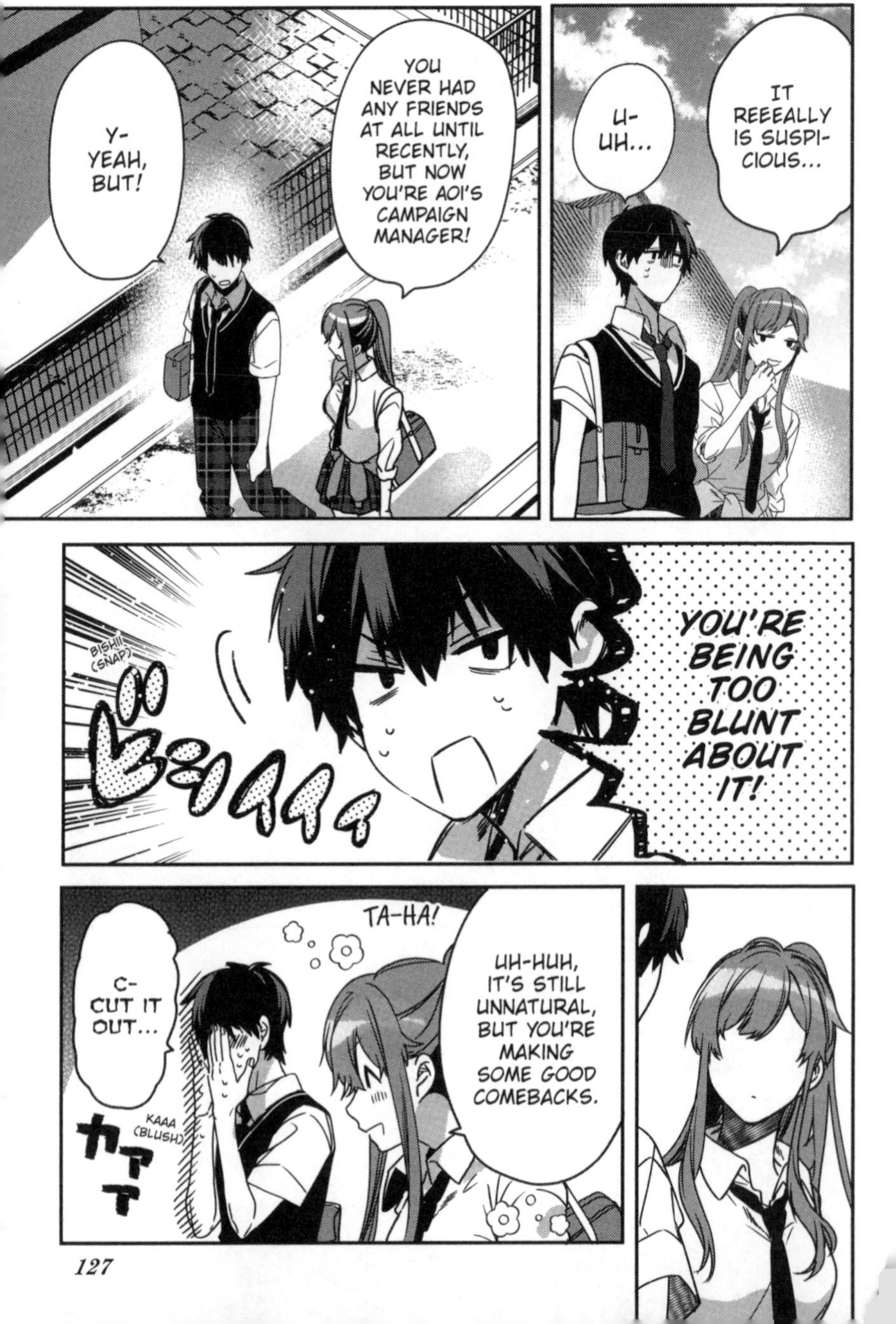
IT REEEALLY IS SUSPICIOUS...
U-UH...
YOU NEVER HAD ANY FRIENDS AT ALL UNTIL RECENTLY, BUT NOW YOU'RE AOI'S CAMPAIGN MANAGER!
Y-YEAH, BUT!
YOU'RE BEING TOO BLUNT ABOUT IT!
BISHII (SNAP)
TA-HA!
UH-HUH, IT'S STILL UNNATURAL, BUT YOU'RE MAKING SOME GOOD COMEBACKS.
C-CUT IT OUT...
KAAA (BLUSH)

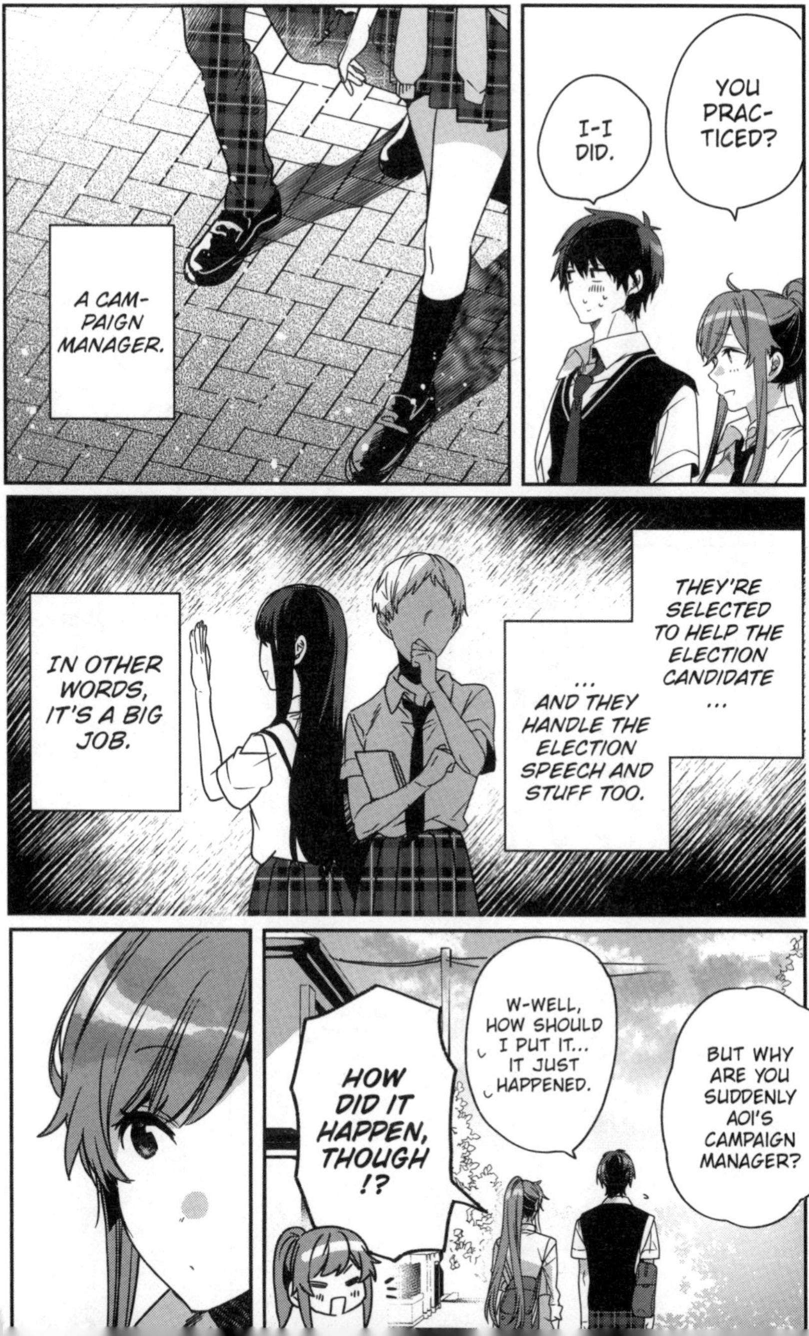
YOU PRAC-TICED?
I-I DID.
A CAM-PAIGN MANAGER.
THEY'RE SELECTED TO HELP THE ELECTION CANDIDATE ...
... AND THEY HANDLE THE ELECTION SPEECH AND STUFF TOO.
IN OTHER WORDS, IT'S A BIG JOB.
BUT WHY ARE YOU SUDDENLY AOI'S CAMPAIGN MANAGER?
W-WELL, HOW SHOULD I PUT IT... IT JUST HAPPENED.
HOW DID IT HAPPEN, THOUGH !?

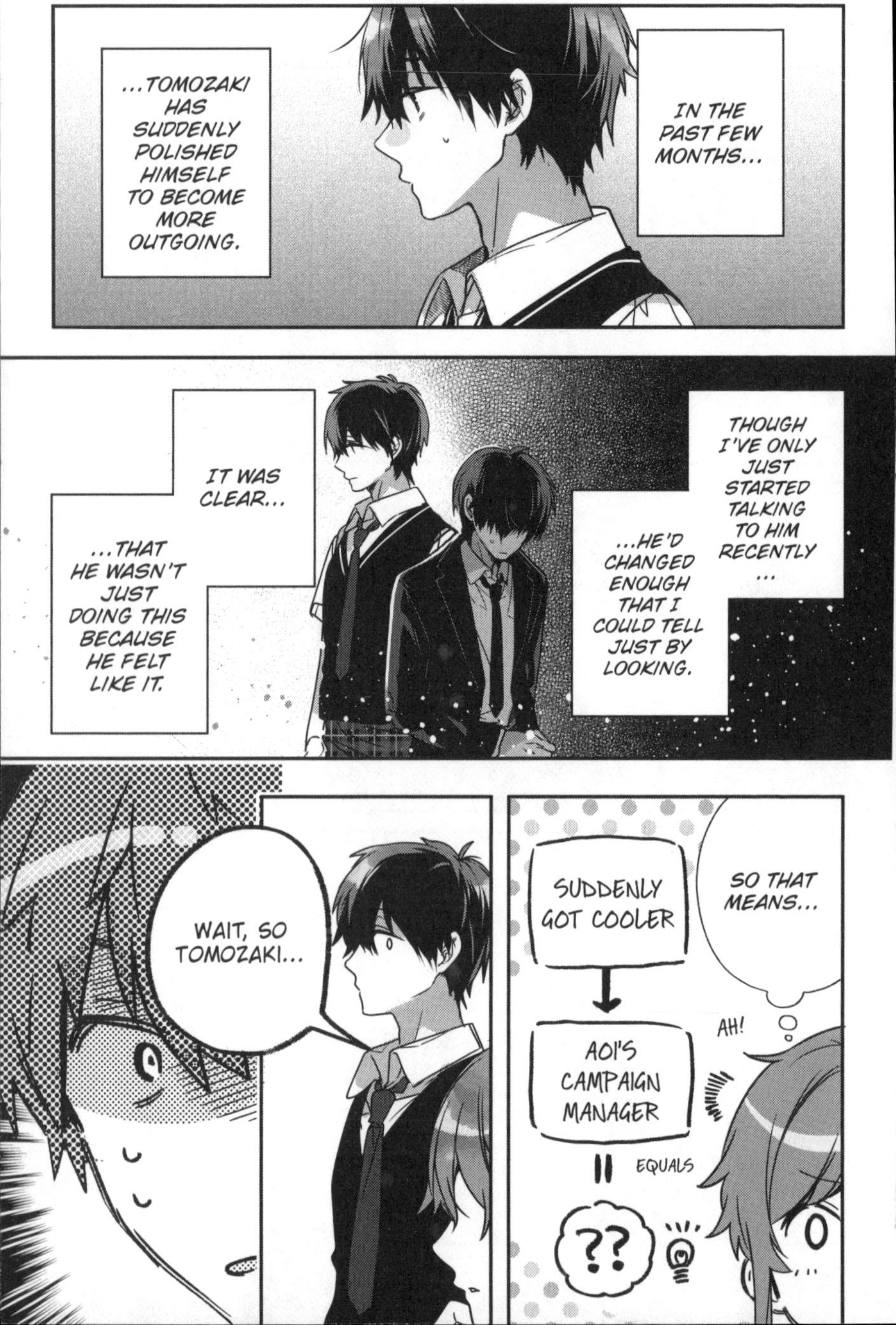
IN THE PAST FEW MONTHS...
...TOMOZAKI HAS SUDDENLY POLISHED HIMSELF TO BECOME MORE OUTGOING.
THOUGH I'VE ONLY JUST STARTED TALKING TO HIM RECENTLY...
...HE'D CHANGED ENOUGH THAT I COULD TELL JUST BY LOOKING.
IT WAS CLEAR...
...THAT HE WASN'T JUST DOING THIS BECAUSE HE FELT LIKE IT.
SO THAT MEANS...
SUDDENLY GOT COOLER
AOI'S CAMPAIGN MANAGER
EQUALS
??
AH!
WAIT, SO TOMOZAKI...

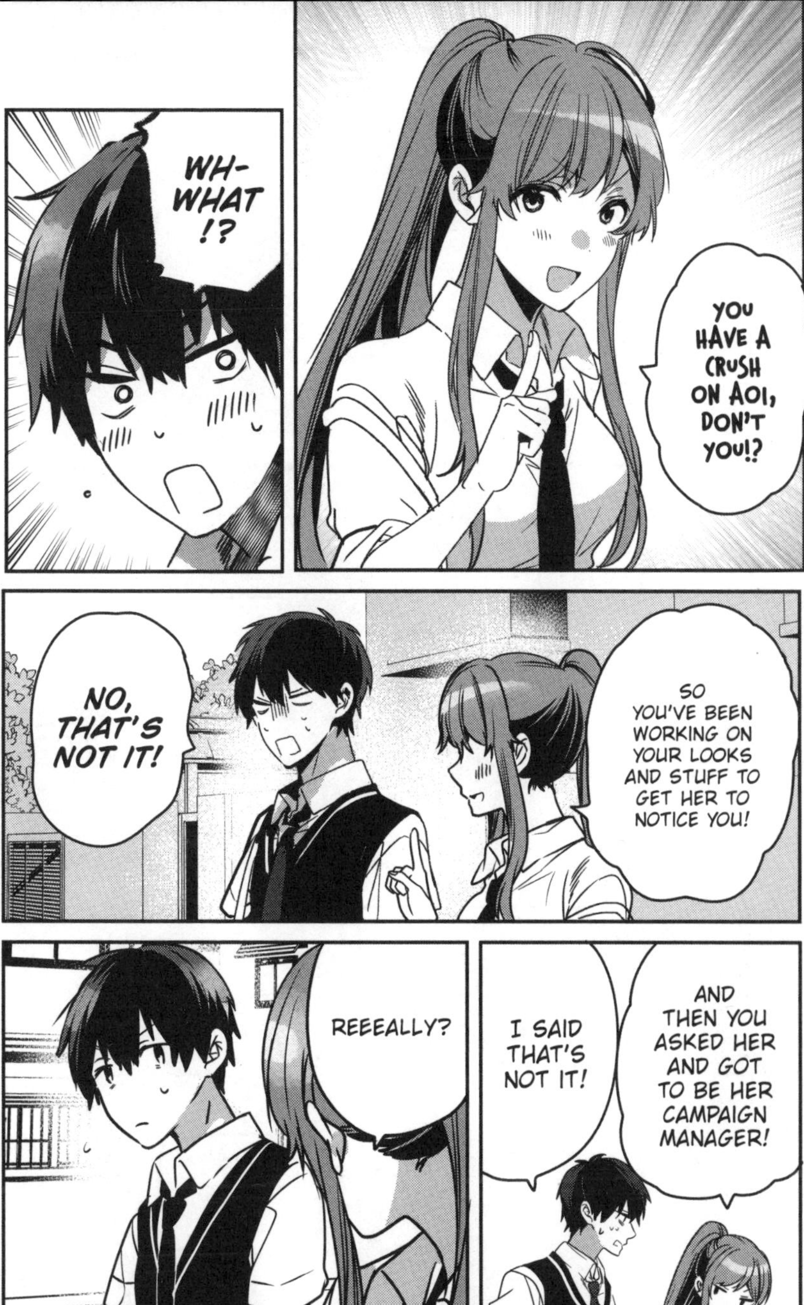
YOU HAVE A CRUSH ON AOI, DON'T YOU!?
WH-WHAT!?
SO YOU'VE BEEN WORKING ON YOUR LOOKS AND STUFF TO GET HER TO NOTICE YOU!
NO, THAT'S NOT IT!
AND THEN YOU ASKED HER AND GOT TO BE HER CAMPAIGN MANAGER!
I SAID THAT'S NOT IT!
REEEALLY?

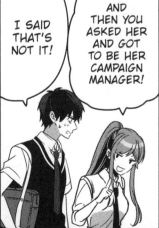

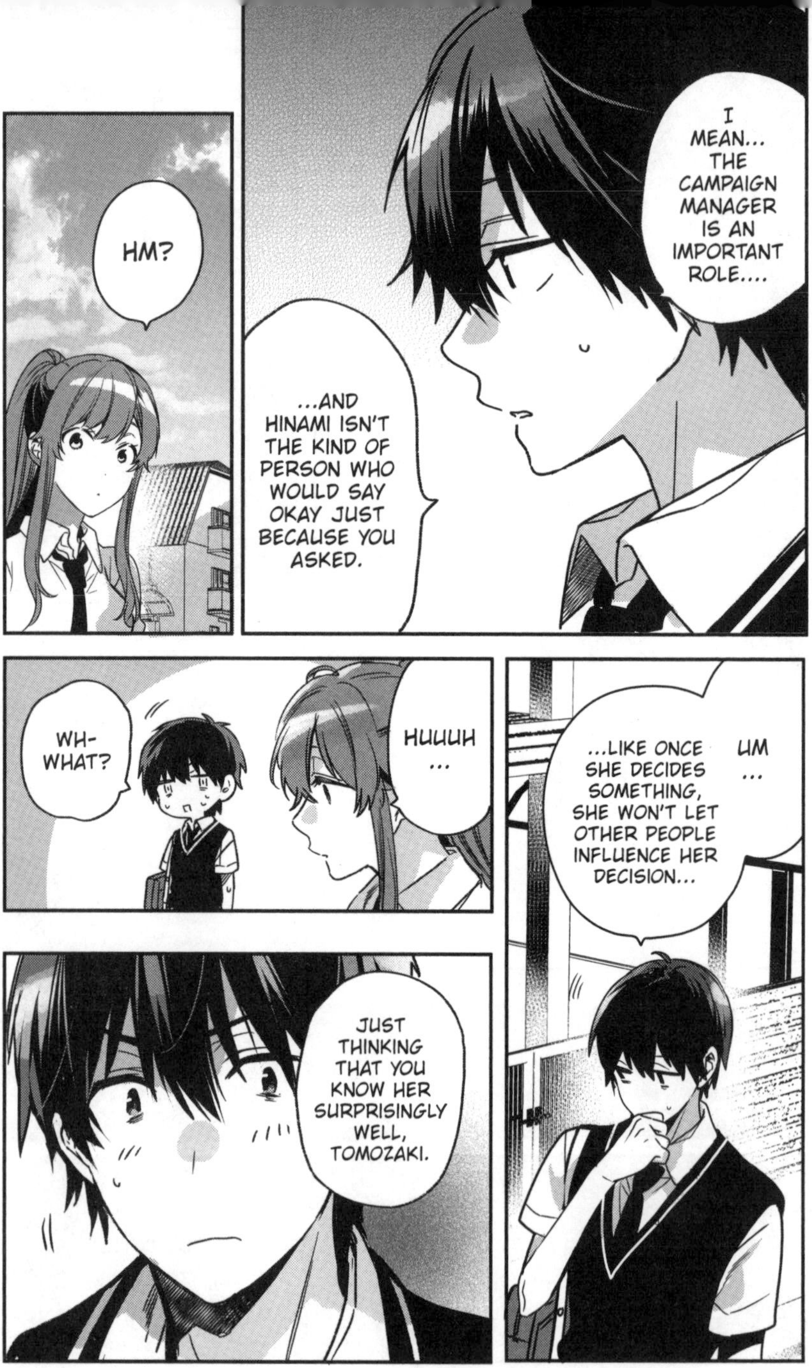
I MEAN... THE CAMPAIGN MANAGER IS AN IMPORTANT ROLE....
...AND HINAMI ISN'T THE KIND OF PERSON WHO WOULD SAY OKAY JUST BECAUSE YOU ASKED.
HM?
UM ...
...LIKE ONCE SHE DECIDES SOMETHING, SHE WON'T LET OTHER PEOPLE INFLUENCE HER DECISION...
HUUUH ...
WH- WHAT?
JUST THINKING THAT YOU KNOW HER SURPRISINGLY WELL, TOMOZAKI.

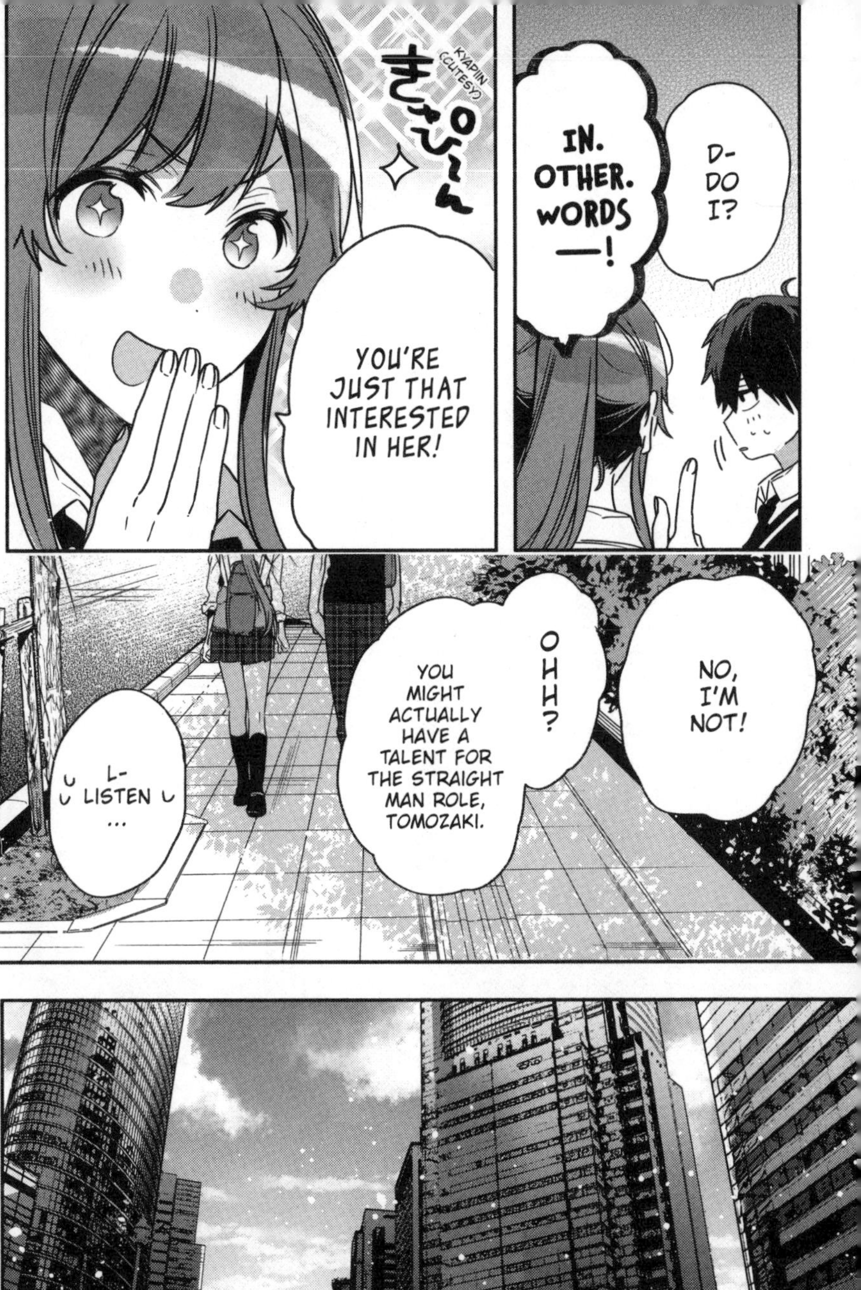
D-DO I?
IN. OTHER. WORDS—!
KYAPIIN (CUTESY)
YOU'RE JUST THAT INTERESTED IN HER!
NO, I'M NOT!
OHH?
YOU MIGHT ACTUALLY HAVE A TALENT FOR THE STRAIGHT MAN ROLE, TOMOZAKI.
L-LISTEN...

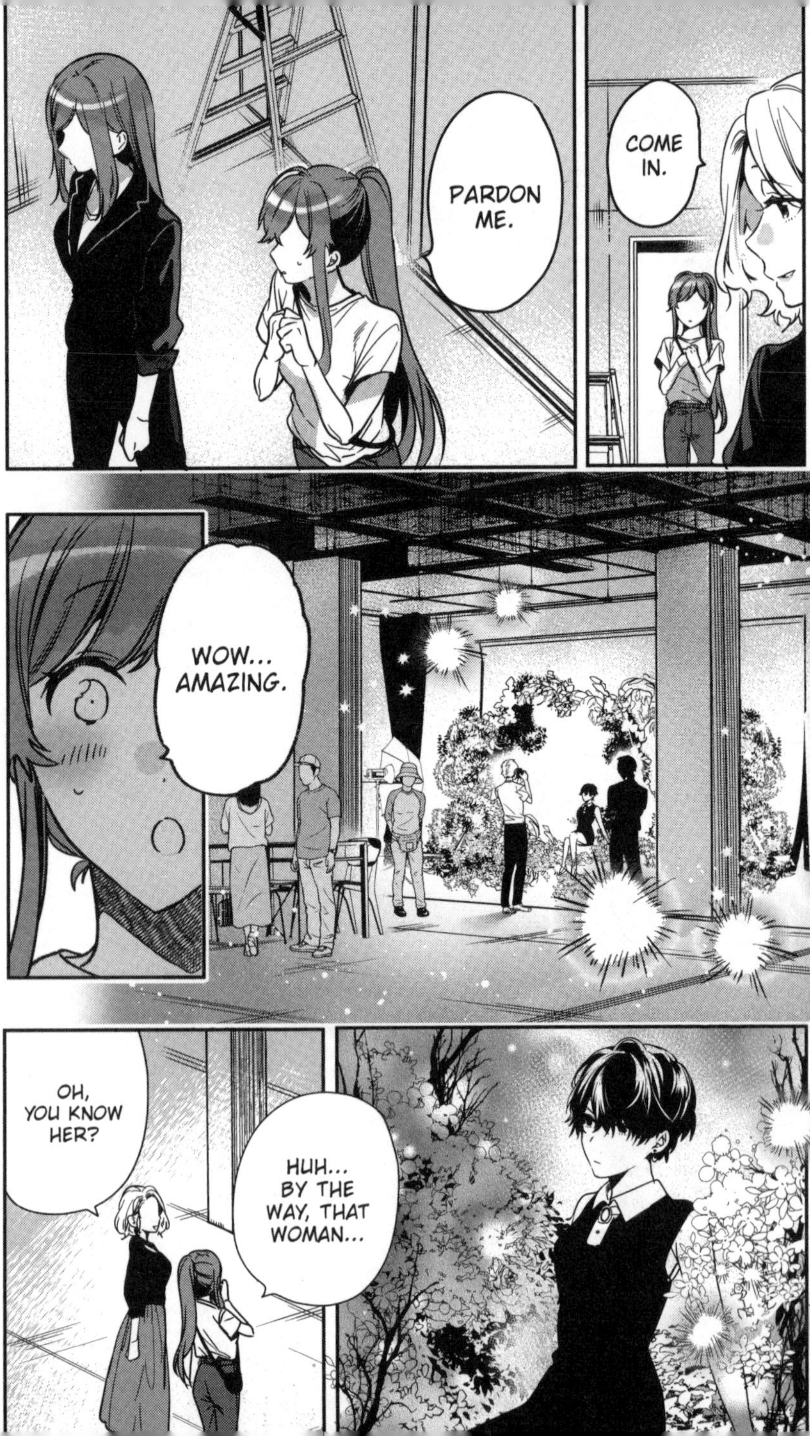
COME IN.
PARDON ME.
WOW... AMAZING.
HUH... BY THE WAY, THAT WOMAN...
OH, YOU KNOW HER?

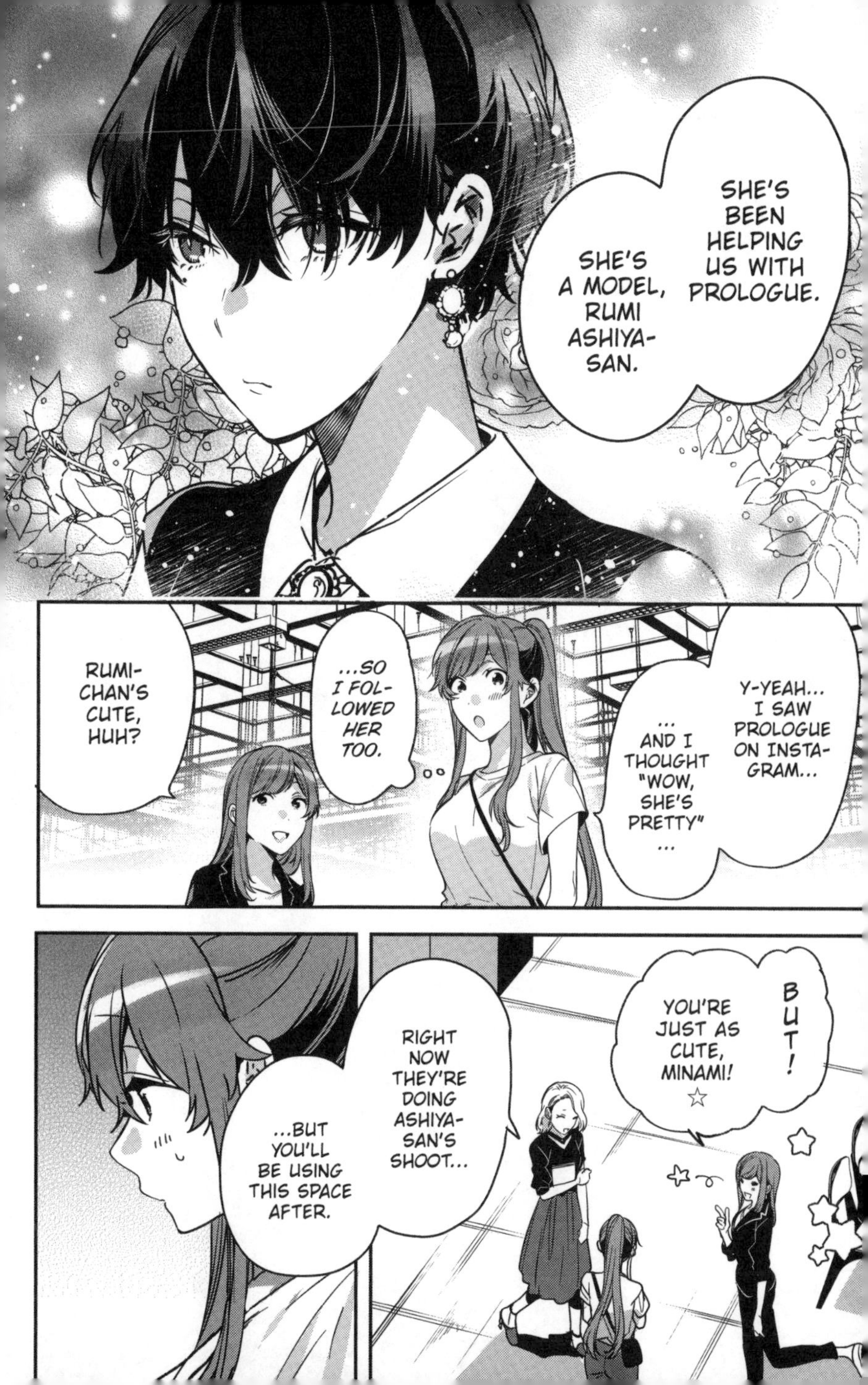
SHE'S BEEN HELPING US WITH PROLOGUE.
SHE'S A MODEL, RUMI ASHIYA-SAN.
Y-YEAH... I SAW PROLOGUE ON INSTAGRAM...
... AND I THOUGHT "WOW, SHE'S PRETTY" ...
...SO I FOLLOWED HER TOO.
RUMI-CHAN'S CUTE, HUH?
BUT!
YOU'RE JUST AS CUTE, MINAMI! ☆
RIGHT NOW THEY'RE DOING ASHIYA-SAN'S SHOOT...
...BUT YOU'LL BE USING THIS SPACE AFTER.

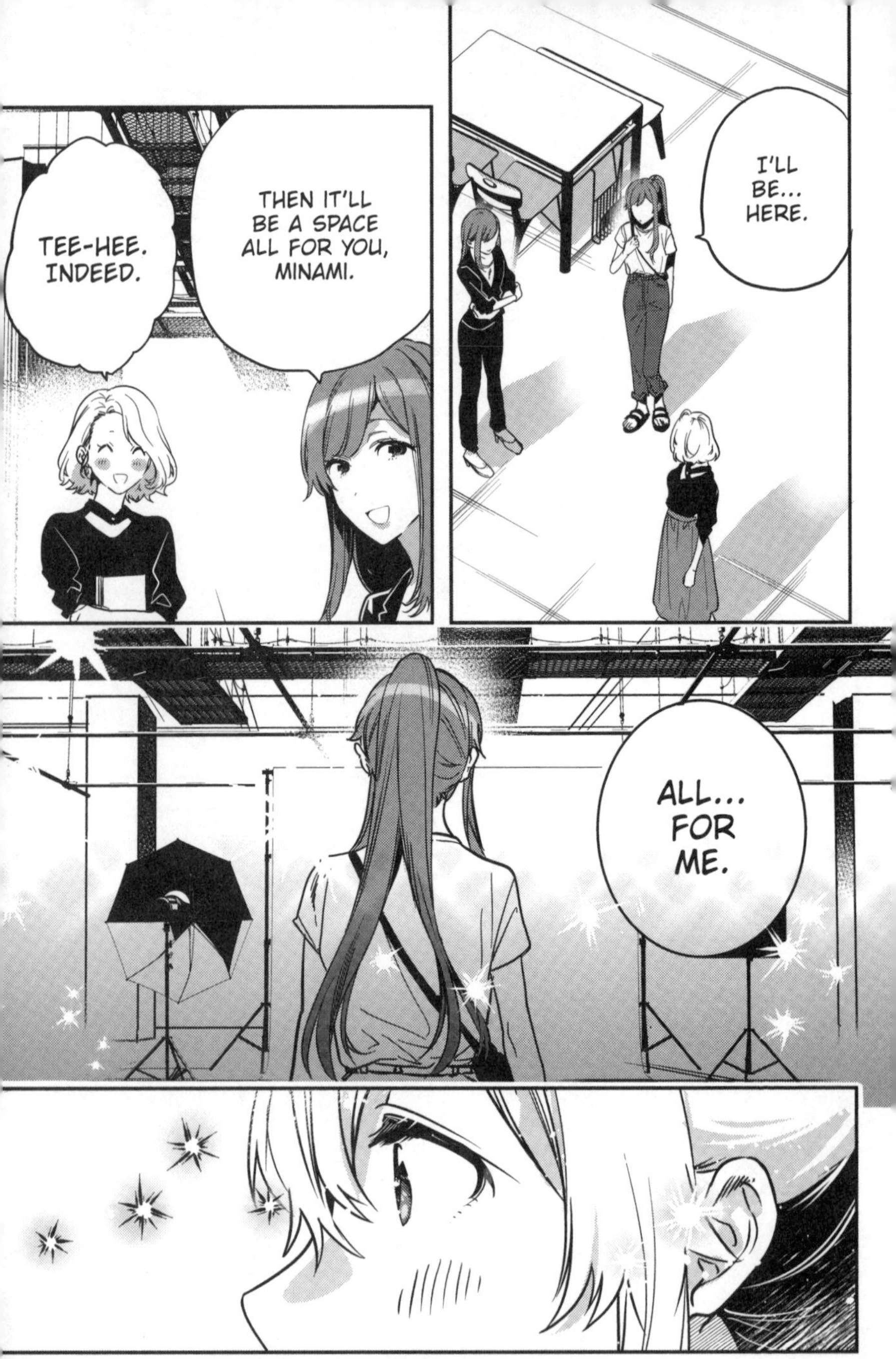
I'LL BE... HERE.
THEN IT'LL BE A SPACE ALL FOR YOU, MINAMI.
TEE-HEE. INDEED.
ALL... FOR ME.

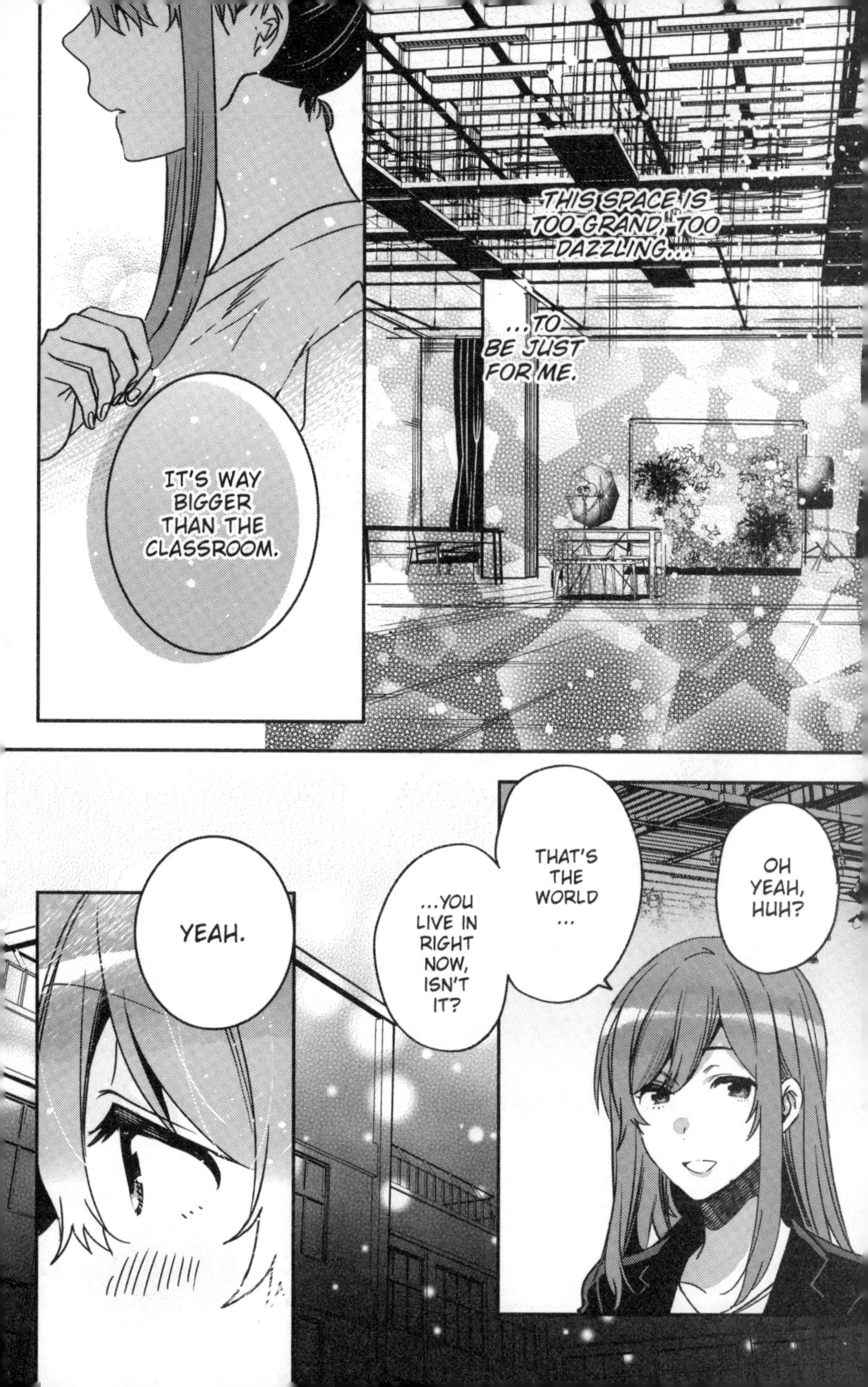
THIS SPACE IS TOO GRAND, TOO DAZZLING...
...TO BE JUST FOR ME.
IT'S WAY BIGGER THAN THE CLASSROOM.
OH YEAH, HUH?
THAT'S THE WORLD...
...YOU LIVE IN RIGHT NOW, ISN'T IT?
YEAH.

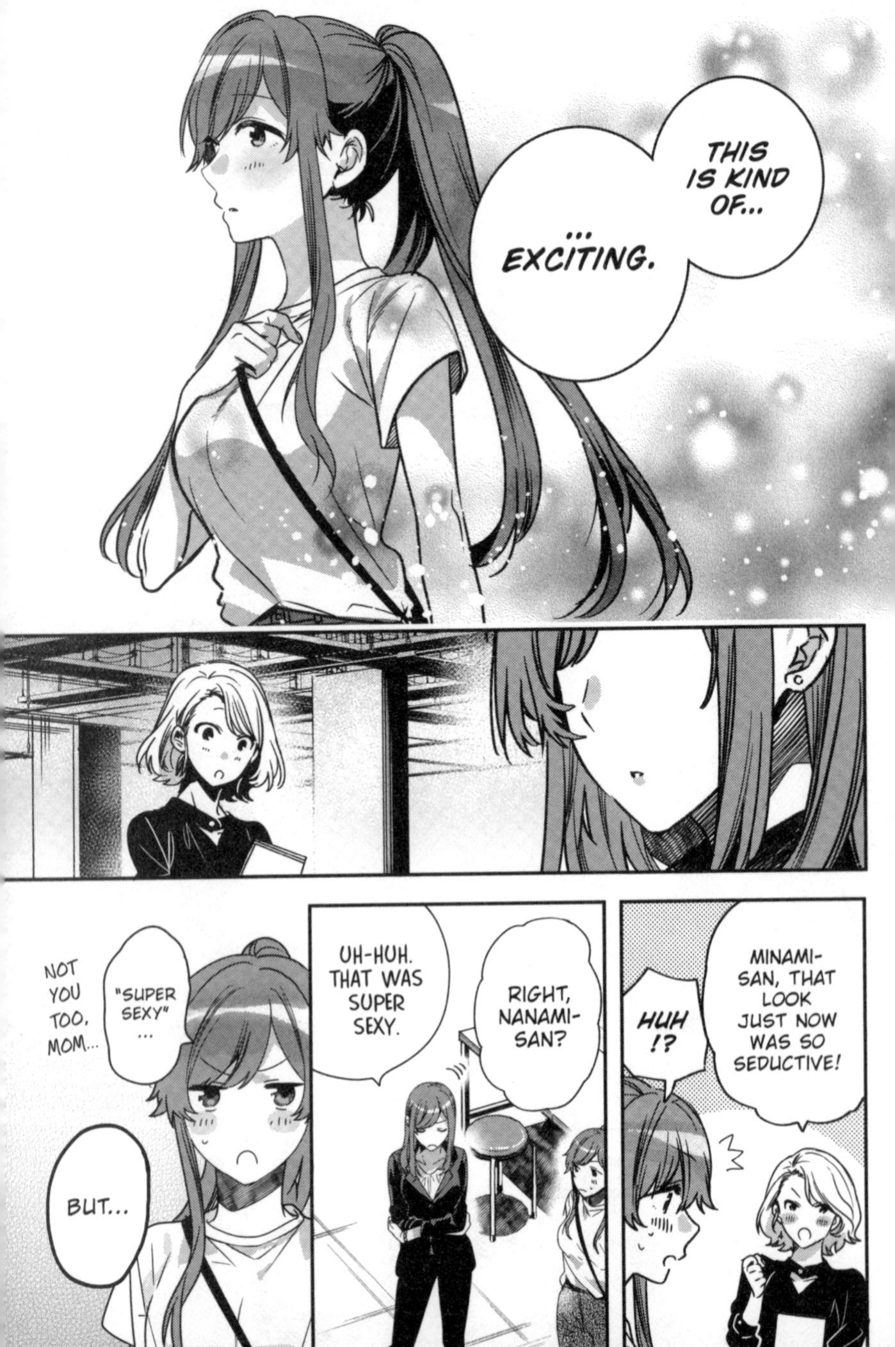
THIS IS KIND OF...
...EXCITING.
MINAMI-SAN, THAT LOOK JUST NOW WAS SO SEDUCTIVE!
HUH!?
RIGHT, NANAMI-SAN?
UH-HUH. THAT WAS SUPER SEXY.
"SUPER SEXY"...
NOT YOU TOO, MOM...
BUT...

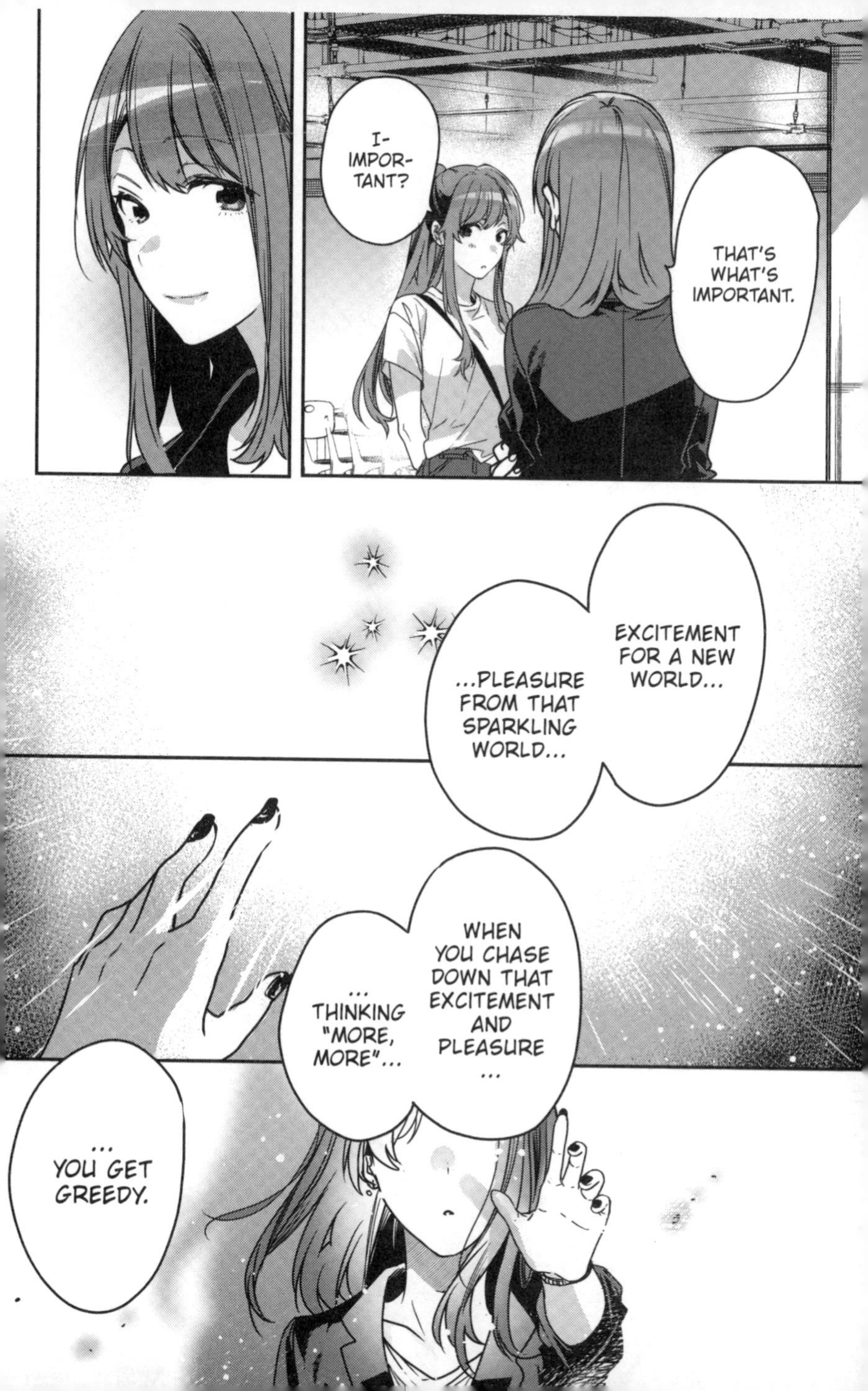
THAT'S WHAT'S IMPORTANT.
I-IMPORTANT?
EXCITEMENT FOR A NEW WORLD...
...PLEASURE FROM THAT SPARKLING WORLD...
WHEN YOU CHASE DOWN THAT EXCITEMENT AND PLEASURE...
...THINKING "MORE, MORE"...
...YOU GET GREEDY.

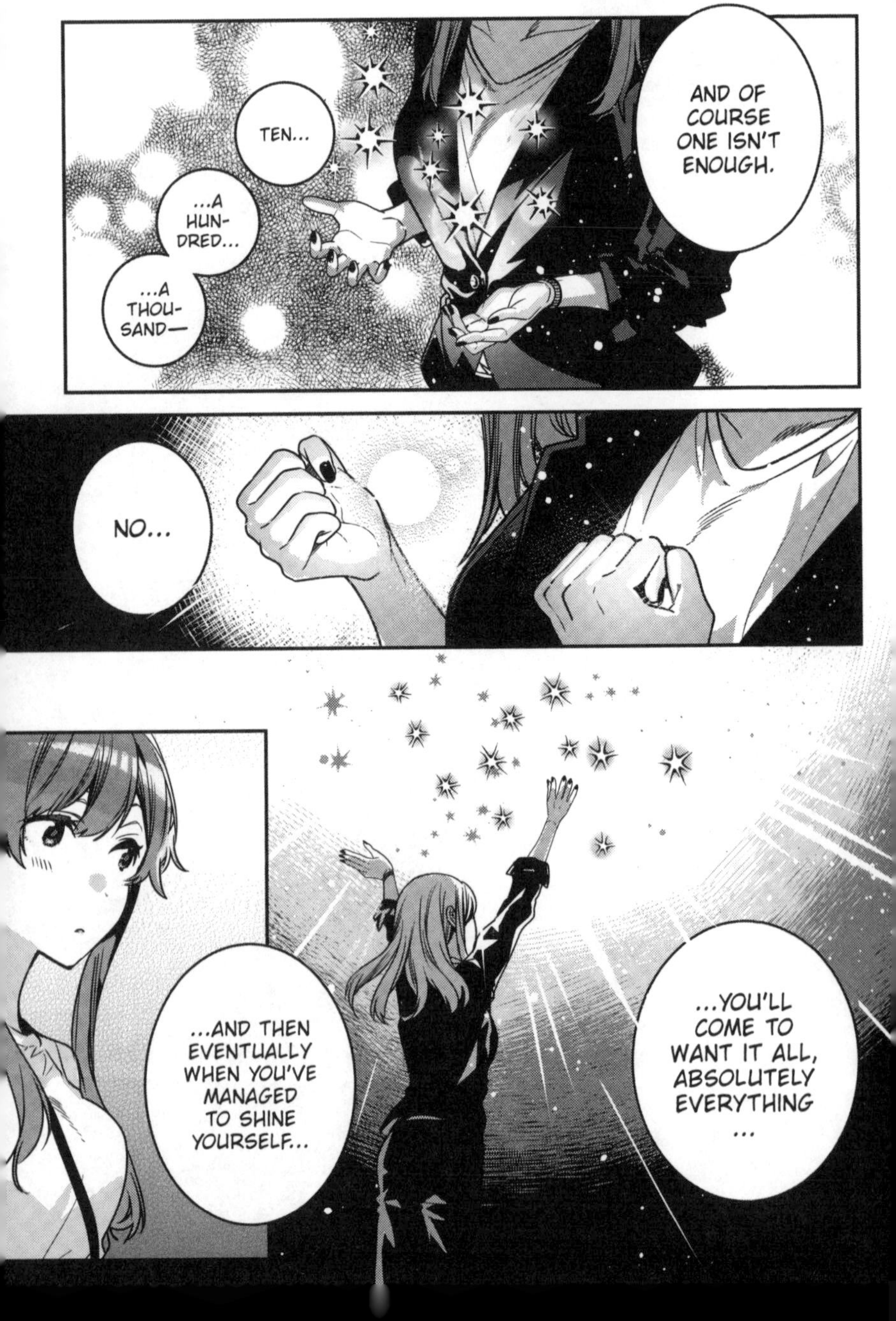
AND OF COURSE ONE ISN'T ENOUGH.
TEN...
...A HUNDRED...
...A THOUSAND—
NO...
...YOU'LL COME TO WANT IT ALL, ABSOLUTELY EVERYTHING ...
...AND THEN EVENTUALLY WHEN YOU'VE MANAGED TO SHINE YOURSELF...

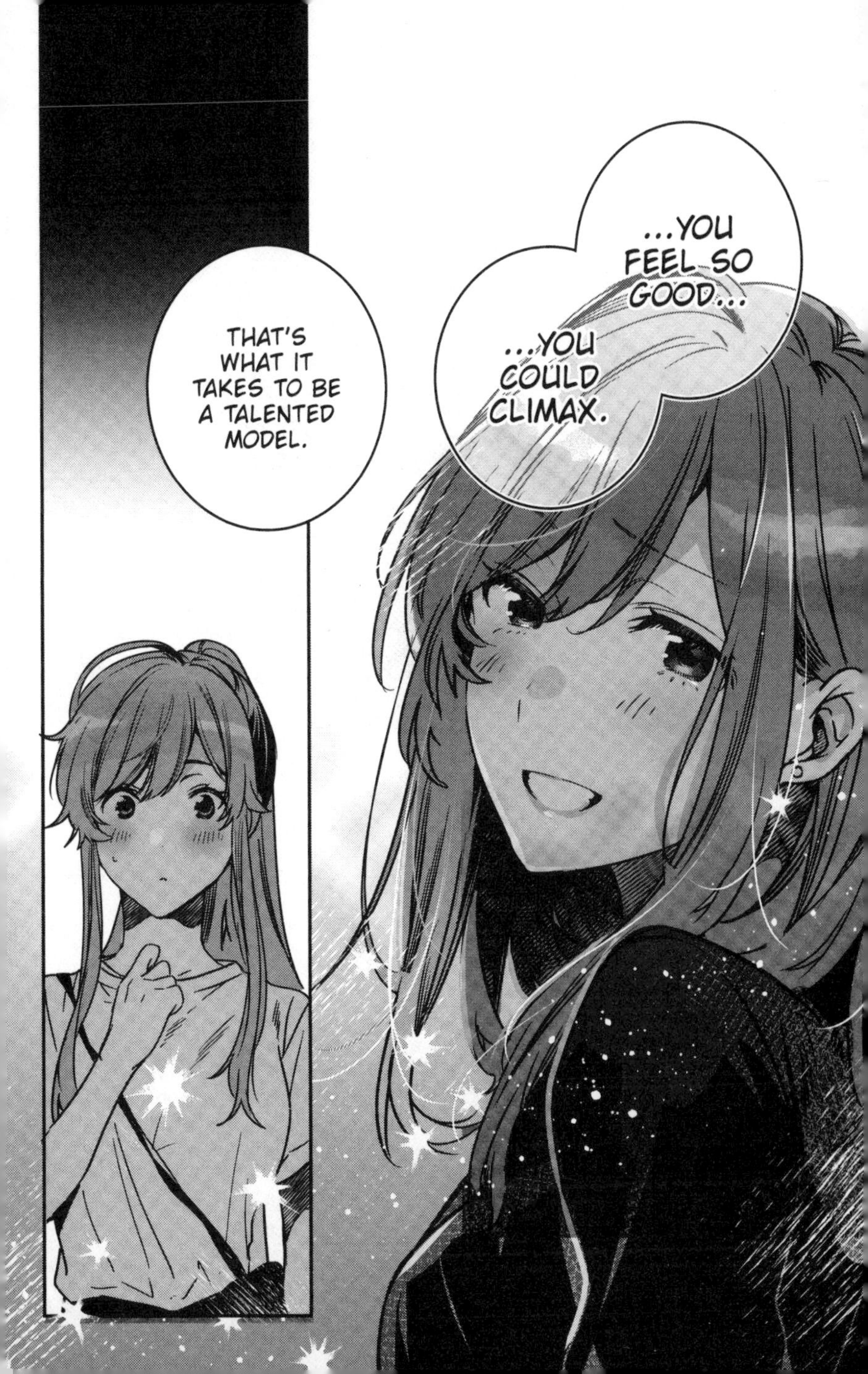
...YOU FEEL SO GOOD...
...YOU COULD CLIMAX.
THAT'S WHAT IT TAKES TO BE A TALENTED MODEL.

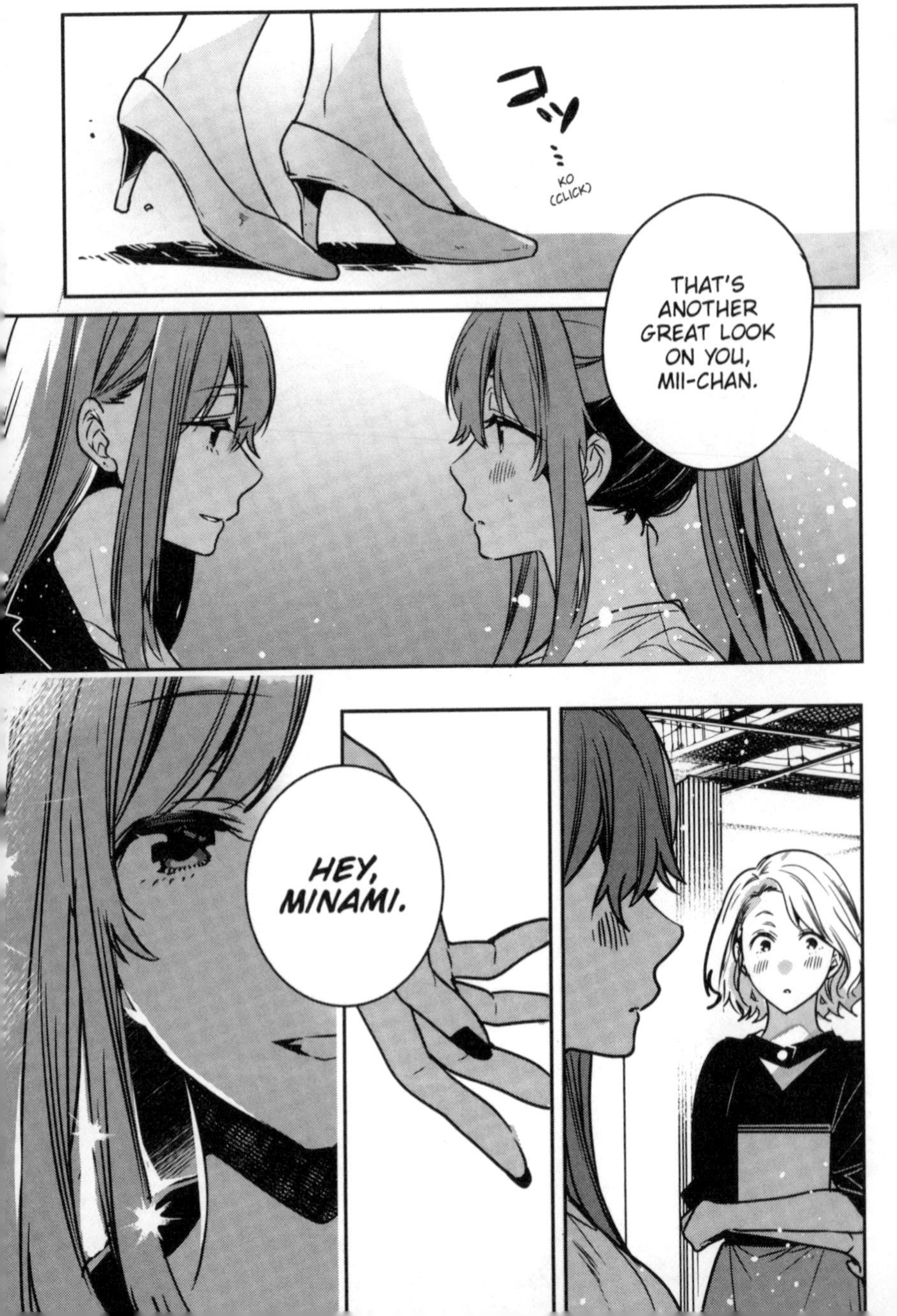
KO
(CLICK)
THAT'S ANOTHER GREAT LOOK ON YOU, MII-CHAN.
HEY, MINAMI.

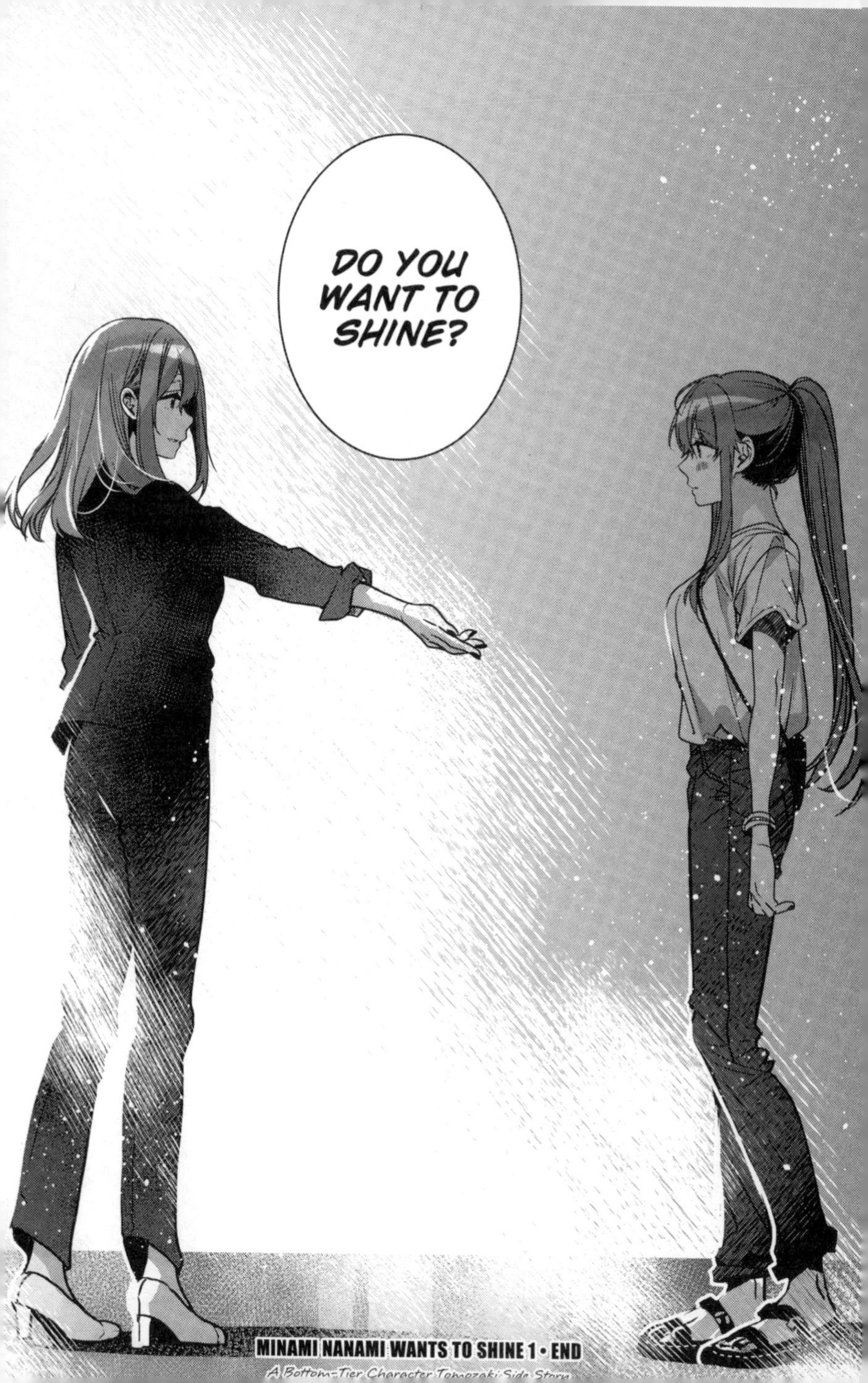
DO YOU WANT TO SHINE?
MINAMI NANAMI WANTS TO SHINE 1 • END
A Bottom-Tier Character Tomozaki Side Story

Bana Yoshida

Manga artist ✦ Illustrator
Important Works:
✦ *Kekkon ga Zentei no Love Comedy* (Shogakukan)
✦ *Yano-kun ni Oshi-hen wa Dekinai!* (Kodansha)
✦ *Chuuko (?) no Mimori-san to Tsukiatte Mitara, Yakeni Ore ni Kamatte Kuru* (Kodansha)

Yuki Yaku

Winner of the 10th Shogakukan Light Novel Grand Prize
Important Works:
✦ *Bottom-Tier Character Tomozaki* (Shogakukan)

Fly

Manga artist ✦ Illustrator
Important Works:
✦ *Chasing After Aoi Koshiba* (Story: Hazuki Takeoka / Ichijinsha)
✦ *Bottom-Tier Character Tomozaki* (Shogakukan)

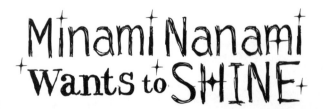

Minami Nanami Wants to SHINE

Minami Nanami wants to SHINE

1

Story by **Yuki Yaku**

Art by **Bana Yoshida** ✦ Character design by **Fly**

Translation: JENNIFER WARD ✦ Lettering: BIANCA PISTILLO

This book is a work of fiction. Names, characters, places, and incidents are the product of the author's imagination or are used fictitiously. Any resemblance to actual events, locales, or persons, living or dead, is coincidental.

NANAMI MINAMI WA KAGAYAKITAI JAKU CHARA TOMOZAKI-KUN GAIDEN Vol. 1
by Yuki YAKU, Bana YOSHIDA, Fly
© 2020 Yuki YAKU, Bana YOSHIDA, Fly
All rights reserved.
Original Japanese edition published by SHOGAKUKAN.
English translation rights in the United States of America, Canada, the United Kingdom, Ireland, Australia and New Zealand arranged with SHOGAKUKAN through Tuttle-Mori Agency, Inc., Tokyo.

Original cover design: Yuko Mucadeya+Caiko Monma[musicagographics]

Yen Press
150 West 30th Street, 19th Floor
New York, NY 10001
Visit us at yenpress.com ✦ facebook.com/yenpress ✦ twitter.com/yenpress
yenpress.tumblr.com ✦ instagram.com/yenpress

First Yen Press Edition: March 2022

Yen Press is an imprint of Yen Press, LLC.
The Yen Press name and logo are trademarks of Yen Press, LLC.

The publisher is not responsible for websites (or their con

Library of Congress Control Nu

ISBNs: 978-1-9753-3898-5 (
978-1-9753-3899-2 (eb

D1207735

10 9 8 7 6 5 4 3 -

LSC-C

Printed in the United States of America